MORE THAN AN
ASPIRIN

MORE THAN AN
ASPIRIN

M. GAY HUBBARD

DISCOVERY HOUSE
PUBLISHERS®

Feeding the Soul with the Word of God

Discovery House Publishers is affiliated with RBC Ministries,
Grand Rapids, Michigan.

Discovery House books are distributed to the trade exclusively by
Barbour Publishing, Inc., Uhrichsville, Ohio.

Requests for permission to quote from this book should be directed to:
Permissions Department, Discovery House Publishers, P.O. Box 3566,
Grand Rapids, MI 49501.

Scripture quotations marked NLT are taken from the Holy Bible, New
Living Translation, copyright 1996, 2004. Used by permission of Tyndale
House Publishers, Inc., Wheaton, Illinois 60189. All rights reserved.
Scripture quotations marked NIV are taken from the HOLY BIBLE,
NEW INTERNATIONAL VERSION®. Copyright © 1973, 1978, 1984
International Bible Society. Used by permission of Zondervan.
All rights reserved.

Interior design by Sherri L. Hoffman

Library of Congress Cataloging-in-Publication Data
Hubbard, M. Gay, 1931-
   More than an aspirin : a christian perspective on pain and suffering /
Gay Hubbard.
     p. cm
   ISBN 978-1-57293-257-9
1. Pain—Religious aspects—Christianity. 2. Suffering—Religious
aspects—Christianity. 3. Concolation. I. Title
   BV4909.H74 2009
   248.8'6—dc22   2009032335

Printed in the United States of America

09 10 11 12 / CHG / 10 9 8 7 6 5 4 3 2 1

CONTENTS

ACKNOWLEDGMENTS

In writing this book I have spent many hours alone with my computer. I am aware, however, that the thinking, living, and learning from which this writing has emerged are rooted in a lifetime of relationships. Some of these relationships have extended over many years and remain a foundational part of my life. Some have been less permanent, but all have taught me much about the human journey. I am both grateful and indebted to those who have been my companions on the way.

The following individuals have contributed in specific ways to the writing of this book.

Alice Mathews. Throughout our professional affiliation and friendship, you have believed in the worth of my work. You have opened doors of opportunity when I had little vision to see and even less courage to knock. In many ways, through your faith and your life, you have contributed richly to this book. Thank you.

My clients. It is not appropriate to write your names here, but I acknowledge with gratitude the contribution you have made to this book and to my life. In sharing your journey you have shaped and enriched my own. Your patience with my writing process and belief in its value has been a sustaining grace.

The present caring community in which I live and work has provided the support and the challenge that have made it possible for me to hear my own story and to learn from it and to write the stories that others have shared with me: Laura Zach; Cheryl Arnold; Tim and Christine Dea; Dom and Julie Garino; Claire Gosnell; Alice Mathews; Paul and Ginger Reinert; Wayne and

Carla Wilcoxson; Kay Herder; Melissa Luzzi and Wolf Thompson; Mike Childers; Julie Kjack; Judith Waldo; Jim and Barbara Singleton. You have been the support system and the friends who have taught me two things: one, we cannot, any of us, do it alone; and two, once having experienced life in the context of community no one would want to do so. I trust that what I have written here about community reflects the rich reality of what I have learned in relationship with all of you.

Miriam Dixon; Deborah Rillos, Margaret Sewell. Thankfully, you have often permitted me to lean against your faith and to profit from your journeys. My own pilgrim's progress has been sustained by your prayers and shaped by the steadfast example of your lives. What I have written here about hope and endurance and new life in the context of loss has been influenced by your steady encouragement and your loving, listening, patient support of my faith journey over the years.

Anita Leyden; Janet Angelico; Molly Ross; Diane Kyncl; Karen Blackman; and Ellie Allyn, who form the remarkable Saturday Garden Club of Growing Saints. You have applied in difficult life circumstances many of the pain management principles I have written about here. With grace and generosity you have shared your stories with me so that I could then learn. I am grateful for the way in which you have steadily supported the writing process by prayer, practical assistance, and care packages. Elwyn Allen, thank you too. Because of your kind thoughtfulness, good food from your kitchen often ended up on my dinner plate on days when my cupboard was bare.

My family. Even at those times when you do not quite understand what I am doing, you have believed in me and the value of my work anyway. Your love and loyalty have supported me through many dark places on my journey. There is no sufficient way to tell you—each of you—thank you for that.

It is not possible to list all of you who, through your prayers, have sought God's blessing on this work. I am deeply aware that it could not have been finished without you and the Spirit's enabling response to your prayers. I am grateful that God has kept a careful record of your prayers and will reward your contribution to this work.

The following people committed to persistent prayer in special ways. Ginger Reinert—Thank you for your daily petitions, regular as the dawn, with which you have supported this work. Laura Zach—Thank you for your daily prayers, and for those dentist-encouraged extra hours of concentrated prayers. Lori Clark—Thank you for the praying miles you've walked, helping to bring this book about. Laura Barnett—Thank you for the faithfulness with which you have made work on this book a regular petition on your Monday day of prayer. Sue Gablinske—I am grateful for your faithful reminders to God that this book needed more than human energy to complete. And thank you, Father Scott Anderson, St. James Episcopal Church. Your dedication prayer committing the manuscript to fruitful use in God's kingdom was an important step in bringing this project to completion.

Many of you have served patient hours as listeners and readers of the manuscript in process. Laura Zach, Cheryl Arnold, Tim Dea, Anita Leyden, members of the Saturday Garden Club, Russ Kyncl, Lori Clark, Melissa Luzzi, Dom and Julie Garino, Sue Gablinske, Jim and Barbara Singleton—all listened and read portions of work in process and provided valuable feedback. Susan Spear gave skill and time to editing first drafts of early chapters and provided a needed word of encouragement into the bargain. Cynthia Thomas read portions of the manuscript at a time of great pain in her life. Her response made effort to complete the work worthwhile. Kay Herder provided valuable assistance in the task of proofreading. Tim and Shannon Jenkins, together with Haley and Morgan, provided the best cheering section ever; additionally, they provided prayer, proofreading help, and, bless you Shannon, hours of patient listening.

Carol Holquist, Judith Markham, Annette Gysen, and staff of Discovery House Publishers. In our work together you have demonstrated a rare commitment both to the well-being of the writer and to excellence in bookmaking. I appreciate deeply your unfailing courtesy, your skilled professional assistance, your patience, and your belief in the value of my work.

Walter Brueggemann. Over the years, Dr. Brueggemann's scholarship and pastor's heart have taught me to understand and value the Psalms in new ways as God's gift for his people's use in all cycles of life. I have learned to cherish them particularly as God's gift in times of pain and disorientation. I have formally acknowledged specific aspects of Dr. Brueggemann's studies where I have incorporated them into this work. However, over the years I have consulted Brueggemann's work so frequently in study, prayer, and work that I suspect at times I think Brueggemann's thoughts after him in ways I do not consciously recognize and so cannot formally acknowledge. That does not cancel my debt. Some of this usage is likely marked by a sea change to the original with which Dr. Brueggemann would not agree. Nonetheless, I believe that he would approve my effort here—however awkward—to incorporate into the therapeutic process the Psalms as the voice of God's people in pain. In those places where I have not followed Brueggemann's thinking, I trust that my work carries with fidelity Brueggemann's love for the text and his passionate faith. Errors in understanding and application are solely my own.

Soli Deo Gloria

INTRODUCTION

It was a spectacular ice cream cone—the Giant Special of the day with two large dips—one chocolate, one strawberry—in a sugar cone. The new owner of the Giant Special was, I guessed, about four. His eyes were bright with eager anticipation; he held his ice cream cone carefully with both hands as he walked away from the counter where his mother was paying their bill. But alas, "Four" kept his eyes focused on his ice cream cone as instructed, but while doing so, he accidentally walked into an adult. This adult, unfortunately, had his attention focused on the attractive young cashier. Six feet tall (or more), he was unaware of the four-year-old who, well below his eye level, was navigating cautiously through the crowd carrying a very large ice cream cone in small, unsteady hands. The collision produced catastrophic results. One after the other, first the chocolate dip, and then the strawberry dip slid off the cone and fell on the floor.

Several things happened at once.

Staring at the lost ice cream, Four dropped the cone as well. Then, realizing the full extent of his loss, he wailed, "Oh—on the floor—*all* on the floor," in tones of utter misery. The adult that he had bumped said crossly, "Watch it, buddy." Mother, responding to the puddled mess of ice cream on the floor, said sharply, "I told you to be careful." Four was now faced with the loss of his ice cream and the injustice of not one, but *two,* public scoldings for a catastrophe for which, in his mind, he was not at all responsible. Undone by events, Four simply sat down on the floor by his lost ice cream and began to cry—enormous tears of grief intermixed with wordless wails of complete frustration.

The manager came immediately with paper towels and a damp mop. "Don't cry," she said comfortingly. "I'll clean it all up."

A white-haired, grandfatherly-looking man said, "Son, I've got just the right amount of money here in my pocket to buy another ice cream cone. What do you think about that?"

Mother, belatedly catching her own emotional balance, said, "I'm sorry. I know you were being careful. It was just an accident."

After brief confusion, order was restored. The manager personally delivered a second ice cream cone to Four, sitting safely now at a table by the window. With gentle prompting from his mother, Four said thank you with admirable politeness to the white-haired, grandfather-type person who had purchased his second cone. Business as usual resumed. Four was no longer crying; he was now eating his ice cream with obvious pleasure. However, watching, I was struck by two things.

One was Four's response to his experience. The second cone was a very fine ice cream cone, perhaps even larger than the first, and Four clearly enjoyed ice cream. Nevertheless, things had changed for Four. The excited sparkle in his eyes was gone, at least for the time, and there were still traces of tears on his face. He ate slowly with painful carefulness; clearly he intended that there be no more accidents. His brush with life, with unexpected loss and injustice, had been buffered by the caring temporary community of adults in the ice cream parlor. They had comforted him and compensated for his loss. But things were not the same. Four had learned that while you are getting ready to eat ice cream, bad things can happen even when you are trying hard to be careful. Learning that life is like that changes things—even when you are only four.

And I was struck secondly by the immediate, emotionally focused response of the adults. People had reacted to more than the fact that Four was outstandingly handsome with dark hair and long curling eyelashes and brown eyes that simply blazed with intelligence and energy. They had smiled at Four's ability to be so articulate about his loss. *"All* on the floor," he had said in a tone of such misery that the Sphinx itself, hearing, would have wept. Nevertheless, I suspected that our adult response to Four's experience was in part a response to something inside ourselves. Four's lost ice cream was potentially one of those life-clarifying moments when something we see suddenly becomes a living icon of truth we have learned. At such times a life event provides a moment in which we see the truth we know. Most of us watching understood immediately the despair at unexpected loss, the sting of injustice, and the helpless frustration Four felt. Out of our lives we understood what Four was learning—you can be walking carefully and thinking about how good the ice cream will taste, when—*all on the floor.* All on the floor, for no discernable reason and with no identifiable option to recoup the loss.

The adult response to Four was in part, of course, a response to Four as the charming young person he was. However, it was also an instinctive response out of our own experience with pain. Four was young and so alive with joyous expectation. Some of the adults watching understood well that hard things can happen on a fine summer afternoon, sometimes unfairly, sometimes without warning. Something in us wanted to ease Four's confrontation with life the way we knew it to be and knew that, already, life was becoming for Four as well.

This book is written in that ice cream parlor tradition, and it describes ways of thinking and plans of action for those times when people find themselves faced with pain, the grief of loss, and limited options to alter relationships and circumstances. It is designed for those times when we feel overwhelmed and over-matched by life itself.

In a practical sense, this is a book of good news about bad news. The bad news is no surprise: We know that life inevitably brings times of loss and pain, often unfairly, often without warning. We know, at least in part, the good news as well. We understand that it is possible to live through these times of pain and disorientation in ways that result in wisdom, maturity, and prosperity for our souls. What we are less clear about, however, is how to make this happen. Making life's bad times produce good results requires more than magic or more than a metaphorical aspirin and a good night's sleep. Producing good results requires effort and conscious choice at a time when energy and motivation are in short supply and faith is often under siege by doubt. Good results are, nevertheless, possible. This book describes patterns of thinking and practical skills that people have found helpful in those hard times when they have felt overwhelmed and overmatched by the events of their lives yet wanted to live with integrity and manage life circumstances well.

This book begins by considering our human responses to pain and loss as we commonly experience them. For the most part, we humans respond to suffering first by attempting to understand why our lives have taken such a painful turn. Often in this process, we blame both God and ourselves. Chapters 1, 2, and 3 explore these responses and their limitations and God's challenging alternative to the "why" question: the possibility that, with the "why" question laid aside, we can learn *how* to live through pain and loss and its disorientation in a way that prospers our souls. Those people who make redemptive use of pain and loss think in distinctive patterns that can be described. Chapter 4 describes the ways in which effective pain managers think about pain, loss, and personal autonomy; about the change process itself; and about joy and hope.

Patterns of effective thinking are foundational, but they must be translated into practical activities of daily living and the discipleship of self-care. Chapters 5 and 6 deal with daily living in terms of MEDDSS—mastery, exercise, drugs (medication), diet, sleep, and spiritual growth. These chapters reflect the author's concern that the emphasis of this material focus on ways to do truth rather than simply to describe it. Chapter 7 continues this emphasis on the "how to" management of pain—embracing the biblical concept of endurance, developing the habit of looking for epiphanies, practicing the art of valuing the half loaf, and accepting the lifelong discipline of dealing with failure in a redemptive, life-altering way.

Those who through experience have mastered the skills of effective pain management are quick to acknowledge the value of community. Chapter 8 deals with the community of the walking wounded and the reality that no one can effectively travel life's journey alone.

If we permit it to do so, redemptive management of pain leads us into a deeper relationship with God and new patterns of prayer. Chapter 9 deals at length with learning to pray the Psalms in times of despair and trouble and with our need to keep clear the long perspective that God has a story too. Chapter 10 summarizes the journey and comes back round at the very end to the "why" question from a different perspective.

As it winds its way from *why* through *how* and back to *why* again, this book pivots around stories of people struggling to manage the pain and brokenness in their lives with grace and effectiveness. In one important sense these stories are fiction. When talking about clients and friends, names have been changed and circumstances altered. Events and outcomes have been reconstructed deliberately and carefully so that the original reality no longer exists in the story as it is told. In the form in which these stories appear here, the disclaimer often used in novels factually applies: Any resemblance to people living or dead is purely coincidental.

But in another important sense every story included here is true. In dealing with human suffering, the author strongly believes that it is emotional malfeasance to traffic in unlived truth. In this context, each story embodies in a fictionalized form a real journey through pain that clients and I have shared or others have lived and shared with me. Every story is fiction. Every story is true.

My own stories are my own, and I trust much more truth than fiction, although I acknowledge that time and my unconscious will have altered memory and understanding of events in ways I do not recognize. I have attempted, however, to keep the ratio of truth to fiction as high as my conscious mind and memory permit.

chapter 1

DOES GOD PROMISE A HAPPY ENDING?

Pain has many faces, but these faces often wear a mask.

At first glance, a congregation on Sunday morning appears to be a group of friendly individuals greeting one another, settling into their customary places, preparing for worship. People gathered in an airport terminal lounge appear to be preoccupied travelers, concerned primarily with catching their scheduled flights. But behind the social façade of their everyday lives, most men and women struggle with another reality. With their outer mask securely in place, the majority of people move through life with their emotional pain hidden, at times even from themselves. And for the most part, people carry their burdens in lonely isolation. They have few companions on their painful personal journeys and few skills to ease the downward drag of suffering in their lives.

Most of us become quite skillful in masking emotional pain. Few people around us guess its presence from the appearance of our lives. And in turn we rarely gauge accurately the size of the burden our neighbor is carrying.

Picture people moving through the hurry and confusion of the departure process at a major airline terminal. Suppose that as the passengers board their flight, one man is pleased to find that his seatmate is an attractive young woman; he has noticed that she is not wearing a wedding band. He likes what he sees and engages her in social small talk. What he does not see behind the mask of her cheerful conversation is the pain that travels with her.

She is a single mother of four, one of whom is a preschooler. She is en route home from a doctor's appointment in a neighboring city. Early this morning a specialist at the clinic confirmed her family physician's diagnosis: the lump in her breast is malignant. Surgery is necessary; the outcome uncertain.

Suppose that as a congregation enters for worship, a cheerful young usher greets members by name and provides a warm smile and nametag for visitors while keeping a watchful eye on the clock and the door to the choir loft. People like what they see—his smile, his skill with people, and his obvious love for his task. What they do not see, or guess, is the pain that he carries. His wife and mother of his four-year-old son recently informed him that she has fallen in love with a man with whom she works and no longer wishes to keep their marriage intact.

Managing the Inevitable

Wherever we go, whatever path we walk, we come into contact with the walking wounded, people whose pain is cleverly masked but brutally present in their lives. There is the pain of justice delayed, of justice denied, the pain of loneliness, of grief and loss, of betrayal, of lost and broken dreams. For untold thousands, there is the grinding pain of poverty and economic fear. For many of us, there is the relentless pull of temptation and the shaming pain of failure when we yield. And while we seek to keep it safely below the radar of conscious awareness, we all live each day with the existential pain of our own limitations and the limitations of others. However we may wish to evade reality, we must live out our lives as flawed and finite creatures in a flawed and finite world. Pain is an inevitable part of this life, and, despite our best efforts, it is a part of life from which we cannot run away.

Given this reality, we are confronted with an important question. If pain is inevitable, is it possible to live with pain in such a way that we alter its negative impact on our lives? Intuitively we expect that the answer to this question is yes. Most of us know at least one individual whom we privately admire, a person whose flawed humanity is marked by the faint scent of developing sainthood. We may know little of that person's life history, but we don't believe that the whiff of saintliness we catch from time to time is the product of easy living. We may not like the implications of what we understand, but if pushed to explain what we see, we would guess that pain has likely had a part in shaping those qualities we respect and admire.

Yet at the same time, we also know individuals whose unyielding anger and bitter despair suggest that, like most life tasks, managing pain may be done poorly with life-altering consequences. We sense that it is possible to influence the impact of pain in our lives. We rightly suspect, however, that this task is likely to be easier to read about than to do.

Confronted with pain, our first impulse, and a sensible one at that, is to attempt to make the pain go away. But if we find that avoiding or removing our pain is not a workable option, what then? Confronted with managing what we cannot avoid or remove, we often find ourselves with limited skills. We do not know how to think clearly about pain, and we do not know how to deal practically with the experience of pain. We alternate angry attacks of *I-just-don't-get-it* with despairing times of *I-just-don't-know-what-to-do*. We find ourselves at the point Barbara

Brown Taylor has described: "[We are] people who do not know how to suffer. We know how to relieve suffering, and we know how to evade it. What is hard for us is to confront it, with no power to make it go away."[1]

Acquiring Management Skills

Finding a remedy for this deficiency in skills is not an easy task. When we undertake to work out good management of our suffering in practical terms, we find ourselves facing difficult questions. Should we deny the pain? Minimize it? Dismiss it? Hide it? Ask God for miraculous deliverance? Accept it as God's discipline? Abandon in anger or despair a God who has failed to keep us from harm's way? What can—and should—we do?

Our problem does not usually lie in motivation. We want to deal well with the hard things in life. We want to come through the dark times triumphantly, faith intact. But often we have no clear biblically buttressed understanding of ways in which we can deal effectively with disappointment, loss, and the destructive life circumstances in which we may find ourselves. Despite our best intentions, we are often unable to manage grief and suffering in a way that permits *us* to be all right when everything around us seems to be all wrong.[2]

And we don't always find God's instructions at this difficult point to be of great help, at least at the moment of crisis. For example, James speaks clearly to us regarding our behavior when trouble comes: "Dear brothers and sisters, when troubles come your way, consider it an opportunity for great joy. For you know that when your faith is tested, your endurance has a chance to grow. So let it grow, for when your endurance is fully developed, you will be perfect and complete, needing nothing" (James 1:2–4 NLT).

We hear the text. We nod our heads in public agreement. We may not speak our doubts aloud, but nonetheless they rise in silent private objection. How, we wonder, can trouble become a window opening into joy? And how is it that we can be changed through suffering into a person of strength with increased ability to meet the challenges of life? At times of crisis, these verses can appear almost nonsensical. Experience teaches us that loss and grief lead more often to bitterness than to joy; we know that pain and suffering lead more often to exhaustion than to strength and energy. What the text *says* is plain enough, but faced with pain and suffering we are none too certain what the text *means* in practical terms of everyday living.

Redemptive Management

A client whose daughter had been murdered came to me for help in the early weeks of her grief and struggle. In her first appointment she noticed a Bible lying open on my desk and burst out in angry tears.

"Don't read me Bible verses about praising God or verses that say God took Lindy because He wanted her with Him. I don't want a therapist who will read me verses like that."

"No. I won't read you verses like that," I told her gently. "I understand this is not the time for that."

Our first hour together was clearly not the time for that. Nevertheless, rightly understood, and in the right time, James's characteristic bluntness expresses a radically wonderful truth. God means for us through His grace to *redeem* our pain—to use it as a journey into joy and maturity. He means for us to be more than survivors; He means for us to be conquerors in every circumstance of life, however difficult that circumstance may be.

No matter how terrible the events through which we must live, it is God's intention for us to be transformed, not destroyed. Now *that* is good news.

However, we have a part in bringing about God's remarkable intended outcome. Transformation is not a matter of heavenly magic. Neither is it solely the result of human will power. It is a mysterious joint project in which God invites us to participate. And invite is precisely what God does. While God desires our participation, He does not coerce. We discover that at the core of participation lies something far different from a blind obedience to rules. Participation is relational; it is a call to know God [3] and the fellowship of His suffering (Philippians 3:10). And it is this participation through relationship with Him that changes our hearts, alters our view of the world, and transforms the outcome of our pain.

Wise Management

It is not coincidental that James's instructions about dealing with trouble were followed by the often-quoted promise of God's gift of wisdom to those who ask in faith.

> If you need wisdom—ask our generous God, and he will give it to you. He will not rebuke you for asking. But when you ask him, be sure that your faith is in God alone. Do not waver, for a person with divided loyalty is as unsettled as a wave of the sea that is blown and tossed by the wind. Such people should not expect to receive anything from the Lord. Their loyalty is divided between God and the world, and they are unstable in everything they do. (James 1:5–8 NLT)

It takes more than human wisdom to implement good stewardship of life's painful experiences. Only God's wisdom can enable us to grasp and hold a God's-eye view of circumstances in the chaos and suffering that life can bring. In the joint project of transformation, human knowledge and common sense are necessary, although at times in the thick of things we sometimes find them in short supply. However, in themselves knowledge and common sense are not enough; we need the wisdom that comes from God. Gaining this wisdom, James explains, is a matter of steady faith. None of this wind-tossed-wave behavior for James, or for us, if we are serious about a plan for pain management that prescribes more than an aspirin and a good night's sleep.

Effective stewardship of pain includes many practical matters. It includes commonsense things like paying attention to rest, exercise, and sleep.[4] These actions may not be easy to take when we are feeling overwhelmed and disoriented, but they are for the most part straightforward and easy to understand. Other steps, such as facing and dealing with the pain of failure, are less easy to describe and more difficult to translate into concrete life skills.[5] But simple or complex, the development of these skills begins with an initial faith-based choice that has at its core an agreement with God.

An Agreement with God

The idea of an agreement with God may appear at the outset to be a very bad idea. There is a good reason for thinking this. We are often faced with taking this initial step when we are personally uneasy with the whole idea of faith and more than a little angry with God. We may feel that God is absent and unresponsive and has failed to keep His word. In this case, we are likely to raise a good question: *Why should I make an agreement of any kind with this God who has, from my point of view, failed to keep me from harm's way?*

This initial agreement does not ask that we pretend that these issues do not exist. It does not require us to tell God that we think our pain is a good idea. Neither does it require us to tell God we approve of the way our lives are going nor the way (from our perspective) He is managing things. This agreement assumes that the questions and feelings about God that initially come with suffering will be changed through the process of our experience.[6] We cannot expect to feel and think at the beginning in ways that will come only after we have lived into new answers and ways of thinking. While faith based, this initial agreement with God does not require skills or wisdom that we can acquire only through the process of the journey itself.

The terms of this initial agreement are quite simple. We elect to agree with God's radical, countercultural message: Good can potentially come from pain, and we agree to seek that good. We first agree with God that out of pain and loss, new life and good things *can* come; we then commit to managing our pain in ways that help to bring this about. While these terms are easy to understand, it is admittedly no easy agreement. If in our lives we are already caught in the pain and disorientation of a Good Friday experience, when death prevails and it seems all hope is lost, it is no small thing to agree to live as though Easter, a day of rebirth and new life, were coming. We sense that there may be more of this agonizing Good Friday yet to endure; there may be that terrible silent Saturday yet to come. From this place we cannot see the empty tomb; there is no evidence that Easter is coming.

What our agreement calls us to do is *to agree that Easter can come and then live as though it were going to do so.* What we agree with God about is *the potential good outcome* of pain, and we commit to do our part to bring this good about. We say, in effect, "God, this pain and loss make no sense to me. But you can see a potential I cannot see, and I agree to take your word for it. And more—I agree to cooperate to bring this outcome about."

In essence, we agree to agree with God and to keep on agreeing with God even when circumstances around us and our responses to those circumstances point to a vastly different bottom line.

This is not a program of passive acceptance. A client working on her agreement with God made this important distinction one day in a way that made me smile. She said seriously, "Well, I can agree with God and still argue with Him. I mean I think I can be with God like I am sometimes when I'm out hiking with Jim [her husband]. My sense of direction isn't very good, so sometimes I say things like 'I know you think this is north, but it sure seems like south to me. I'll go this direction with you but *I* don't think we're going in the right direction. And do we have to walk so fast? And you should have brought more water.' I think I can agree with God and criticize and argue with Him too."

I laughed and then assured her, "You've got it right. The Psalms are full of God's people telling God that they don't think that He's doing it right and arguing with God while at the same time they are walking along with the God with whom they're arguing."

This agreement rests on the logic of faith: It is the character of God, not the content of our circumstances, which makes our choice to agree with God a logical one. It is reasonable to assume that God, because He is the God of the Exodus and the God of Easter, knows what He is talking about, that suffering *can* be a window into joy, part of the journey into a new place. We assume that we *can,* by God's grace, both survive *and* thrive whatever the circumstances of life. And, hearing James's caution about the futility of a doubtful mind, we commit to holding this God's-eye point of view no matter how contrary it may feel to our experience at a given moment.

At the same time, we hold fast to our understanding that this agreement exists within a relationship that allows for protest. Unlike responses in some of our human relationships, expression of criticism, doubts, and disagreements does not alter God's acceptance and love. Indeed, with God, the dialogue of protest can serve as a faithful expression of covenant, as we shall see.[7]

The agreement is straightforward. We agree with God about the potential good outcome and to cooperate in bringing this about. We then begin to express this agreement through action, to take the practical steps that turn our faith into experiential reality. The process of linking faith and work that was so dear to James's heart lies at the core of good stewardship of our pain. We assume God's point of view by faith, and then we undertake the work of learning, sometimes in the grinding grip of despair, new ways of thinking, new choices; we take whatever small step we *can* take by God's enabling grace. At the beginning hope is often only an inaudible whisper, but, cliché or not, the journey of a thousand miles *does* begin with a first step, no matter how tentative. And the journey's joyful end pivots ultimately upon the succession of steps—some small and many weary—that follow that first step no matter how uncertain it may have been.

Good stewardship of our pain entails affirming by faith *God's radical and counterintuitive goal*—joy through the pain—strength and wholeness through suffering and loss—the new thing springing up from the rubble of destruction. Then, having agreed with God about the end of the journey, we *act,* taking the practical steps by which this transformation comes about.

The Journey

The journey is neither quick nor easy; it is often long and marked by many dark nights. Nearly a year after her daughter's death, Barbara came for her appointment. She sat silently for a time and then said, "I didn't cry this morning while I drank my coffee. And I felt glad about that good coffee taste." She paused. "Do you think God counts this for joy in the morning (Psalm 30:5)? I cried again by nine." It counts. Indeed, it counts. While this is not the end of Barbara's story, it provides a realistic if unwelcome picture of the process by which transformation comes. In this regard stewardship of pain is much like good stewardship of money. There are no reliable get-rich-quick schemes in management of money. There are no sainthood shortcuts in effective management of pain.

Survivors report consistently that the journey through grief and loss and the disorientation that pain brings is not marked by magic or by instant healing. It is better described as a long obedience in the same direction, to borrow Eugene Peterson's apt use of Friedrich Nietzsche's phrase.[8] But at the same time the journey through pain is filled with epiphanies in which—often in sheer astonishment—we find that while weeping has indeed endured through the night *again,* joy *has* come in the morning, no matter how brief its initial stay may be.

It is not easy to agree with God's view regarding the human experience of pain, particularly in the midst of the chaos and suffering. We can view rain as a blessing much more easily when we are sitting by the fire eating toasted muffins. It is much more difficult to do so while watching our house float away in the flood. Learning to think and act in ways that lead to spiritual competence and emotional mastery is an ongoing challenge. When our lives are filled with pain and disorientation, the task becomes much like learning to put up a tent in a tornado at a time when all we want to do is run from the storm. There should be no misleading expectations at this point. Discipleship is a joyous experience, but, practically speaking, discipleship is not built on easy automatic responses. God calls us to an effective stewardship of pain in the face of the worst that life can bring. Carrying out this stewardship is a challenging task, but it is possible by God's enabling grace. "Work hard to show the results of your salvation, obeying God with deep reverence and fear," Paul exhorted the Philippians. "For God is working in you, giving you the desire and the power to do what pleases him" (Philippians 2:12–13 NLT). Since effective stewardship of our pain is a joint project with God, it remains a reasonable, doable goal despite the difficulties we may experience in the process.

Getting Stuck on "Why"

But the beginning point itself can cause considerable confusion. In dealing with pain, people are far more likely to begin by asking "*Why* is this happening to me?" than by asking "*How* can I manage this constructively?"

The problem does not lie in our desire for meaning. In fact, good stewardship requires that we must eventually grapple with the meaning of pain. *Theodicy* is a specific field in theology that seeks to explain human suffering in a way that does not compromise the loving character of God or His power and sovereignty.

But grappling with the theological problem of pain does not necessarily produce good skills in managing our pain. It is dangerously easy to get stuck at the "why" question and never move on. But there is a second reason to be cautious about the "why" question. Interestingly enough, it is possible to develop a theologically sound answer to the problem of pain, as C. S. Lewis phrased it, but fail to develop the joy and maturity of which James writes. Perhaps for this reason God appears less interested in dealing with the "why" question than we sometimes think He should be. Somewhat to our surprise, God appears to think that coming through pain into a place of joy and maturity depends far more on our relationship with Him than on any answer to the "why" question that we may work out.

Job: Moving from "Why" to "How"

That is not to say that the way in which we think about God's character and His power in relationship to His suffering world is irrelevant to our journey—far from it. But Job's story gives an interesting God's-eye view of the "why" question. And in the context of good stewardship of our pain, Job's story makes clear that it was *not* God's response to his "why" question that moved Job through his pain and loss into a place of joy and peace, significant as God's conversation with Job proved to be.

The materials in the following chapters emphasize skills that increase effective management of pain rather than theologically sound explanations of it. But because Job's story provides a powerful insight into God's point of view, Job's struggle with the "why" question can be helpful in moving us from "why" to a "how" that results in a deepened relationship with God.

The text of Job's story opens with a cosmic confrontation between God and His adversary, the great fallen archangel, Satan. In the text, Satan was no small player in precipitating the confrontation between God and Job, but God too played a decisive role. We must consider the motivation and behavior of both God and Satan when we raise the "why" question in regard to Job's suffering. But the central dialogue of the drama plays out not between God and Satan, as we might expect from the opening scene, but between God and Job around the issue of Job's understanding and management of his pain.

In the text, Job's suffering, the agony of his body and his soul, is a matter of commanding concern to God. But the conversation between God and Job is challenging and confrontational—God feels no need to "make nice"—in deference to Job's terrible, inscrutable losses and his physical pain. At times, God appears to act more as Job's adversary than his friend. But when we pay close attention to the text, we see that God dramatically moves the conversation away from the "why" question to something beyond comfort or explanation. God's goal was relational.

In the text it is clear that God meant to change the relationship between Him and Job and to change Job's understanding of God and of himself. Since Job's friends had also assigned themselves a large role in the drama (although apparently uninvited), God dealt with them as well. Before matters were settled, God clearly expressed His view of the opinions of Job's friends in a fashion that must have altered Job's relationship with them forever as well. After Job's meeting with God, nothing—his family, his friends, his faith, or himself—remained the same.

The text, even at the cursory level considered here, is utterly absorbing. Here is God—He who made the great leviathan and cast the stars into the boundless void of unmarked space, the creator and sustainer of the universe—in face-to-face controversy with the great dark angel, Satan himself. The stakes in this vast cosmic conflict?

The relationship between God and Job.

Job is being required to live through catastrophic loss, the grief that accompanies these devastating losses, the injustice and inscrutability of an apparently hostile providence, physical pain and suffering, and the utter angst of his questioning soul: *Where are you, God? And where am I with you? What is the sense of what is happening here?*

It is difficult to overemphasize the relational risk for God and Job. Can pain and the inscrutable malignancy of what appears to be a blind, uncaring providence sever the connection between God and Job? Is Satan correct? Does the relationship between God and His people require a "good life" as the *sine qua non* for its existence? And are Job's friends correct? Is suffering the inevitable consequence of sin and personal culpability? And can God legitimately be held to account for His acts?

There are few finer summaries of the dialogue between God and Job than that provided by Frederick Buechner. Buechner writes:

> [Job] asks some unpleasant questions...
>
> God doesn't explain. He explodes. He asks Job who he thinks he is anyway. He says that to try to explain the kinds of things Job wants explained would be like trying to explain Einstein to a little-neck clam...
>
> Maybe the reason God doesn't explain to Job why terrible things happen is that he knows what Job needs isn't an explanation. Suppose that God did explain. Suppose that God were to say to Job that the reason the cattle were

stolen, the crops ruined, and the children killed was thus and so, spelling everything out right down to and including the case of boils. Job would have his explanation.

And then what?

Understanding in terms of the divine economy why his children had to die, Job would still have to face their empty chairs at breakfast every morning. Carrying in his pocket... a complete theological justification of his boils, he would still have to scratch and burn.

God doesn't reveal his grand design. He reveals himself. He doesn't show why things are as they are. He shows his face. And Job says, "I had heard of thee by the hearing of the ear, but now my eyes see thee." Even covered with sores and ashes, he looks oddly like a man who had asked for a crust and been given the whole loaf.

At least for the moment.[9]

A redemptive stewardship of pain does not depend upon the answer to the "why" question that we may ultimately work out. Our part in bringing about a good outcome is not simply a matter of thinking differently *about* pain, although that too happens on the journey. Redemptive stewardship is faith-based living—head *and* heart—into and through the pain. It is living the questions in such a way that we live our way into a new relationship with God and with ourselves. It is living into a new kinship and community with each other and into a new understanding of the world and the journey by which we have come into a new place.

And the joy to which James encourages us does not lie in an explanation of pain as such. It lies in the relational consequences of living through the process. Listen again to Job.

"I have heard of thee by the hearing of the ear: but now mine eye seeth thee" (Job 42:5 KJV). "I have seen him," Job says. "I have seen him. And that is enough."[10]

The patterns of thinking and behaviors suggested in the chapters that follow are intended, by God's grace, to aid those on the journey to move into and through their trauma and pain in a way that permits them, like Job, to say, "I have seen him. I have seen him and that is enough."

Happy Endings—Guaranteed?

Job's story can pose a serious problem, however. It has a happy ending.

At the end, God makes a spectacular entrance—riding in on a whirlwind, no less—and talks with Job directly, face to face. In the conversation God does not explain Job's suffering or address Job's questions regarding divine justice. However, at the close of his encounter with God, Job's new understanding of God's goodness and his own limitations leaves Job at peace with these unanswered questions. But talking to Job is not all that God did. God confronted (and scolded) Job's friends and publicly affirmed Job's relationship with Him. Then, to wrap things up, God made Job prosperous again, giving him twice as much as he had before. What an ending—a face-to-face encounter with God that made Job's unanswered questions immaterial, a confrontation with Job's doubting friends that produced public vindication of Job's integrity, and then double restoration of Job's lost wealth and family, crowned by a long life of honor and respect.

Immersed in our own struggle, this happy ending can tempt us to a sour-grapes attitude. We may think that we too could demonstrate heroic faith if we knew that the end of the story included a face-to-face talk with God, public vindication, and the joy of losses restored. The text, however, does not support such grumbling.

God's choice to supply a happy ending for Job's story does not lessen the severity of Job's suffering or the significance of Job's integrity. Job did *not* anticipate a triumphant resolution to his ordeal—to the contrary. In the presence of his friends, we hear Job wishing for death to come quickly and bring an end to his pain. The text describes Job's faithful perseverance *without* assurance of a happy ending and in the face of God's inscrutable silence. Indeed, the silence of the hidden God was one of the things Job found most difficult to bear. Job's greatest joy at the end of his experience was not centered in God's vindication of his point of view or in the restoration of his wealth and family. Job's joy lay in his new relationship with God, in his experience of seeing God face to face. Job's story did indeed have a happy ending, but Job lived through his ordeal without any expectation that he would be vindicated and his losses restored.

But there is another point at which Job's happy ending can provide a problem. If we regard the happy ending of Job's story as a promise that if we too are faithful, our story will have a similar spectacular ending, we open ourselves up to a major crisis of faith. Some stories, like Job's, do have happy endings in this life. But that is not always the case; it is not even frequently the case.

In this life, the end of the story for many people is nothing at all like Job's. These stories are marked by losses that are not restored and unanswered questions that continue to spin endlessly in the dark of sleepless nights. In many of these stories, at the end as at the beginning, faith continues to be challenged by God's apparent hiddenness and silence. What then? How then are we to understand the stories that do *not* have a happy ending? Does God have anything to say about stories like these?

He does, indeed. A famous chapter in the letter to the Hebrews, chapter 11, deals with this hard reality with straightforward honesty. The chapter begins with a roster of the great heroes of faith; the writer begins with the stories of those who, like Job, came by faith into a happy ending of their story. There is Enoch, who escaped death; Noah, who saved his family and the human race from extinction; Abraham, who after years of being childless became the father of descendants as numberless as the stars; Sarah, who mothered the child of promise after years of barrenness; Moses, Joshua, the prostitute Rahab, David— the writer continues a long list of those who, "gained what was promised; who shut the mouths of lions, quenched the fury of the flames, and escaped the edge of the sword; whose weakness was turned to strength; and who became powerful in battle and routed foreign armies. Women received back their dead, raised to life again" (Hebrews 11:33–35 NIV).

Then—taking a long breath, so to speak—the writer launches into the rest of the story, the story of those who in faith were tortured and *not* released, who were flogged, chained, imprisoned, stoned, sawed in two, put to death by the sword, who went about destitute, persecuted, mistreated— wanderers whose homes were in caves and holes in the ground. God makes it very clear that, humanly speaking, there was no happy ending in this world for these folk. Yet these people, the writer points out, also belong in the roster of the heroes of faith, commended by God. If we find our life story marked by trouble and pain, the writer encourages us to remember those who have also suffered, and, so that we do not become weary or lose heart, to consider the experience of Jesus himself, who endured the cross (Hebrews 12:1–3).

The point of the writer of Hebrews was not that some of God's people do not have happy endings; the point was rather that not all stories end happily *in this life*. In God's loving embrace at death, in the great eternal company of the redeemed saints— the ending of the story for all of God's people encompasses life and joy beyond our imagining, but that ending comes in a world far different from the one in which we live through our struggle to manage pain well. However, the goal of living though pain without becoming weary or losing heart in this world is not what most of us have in mind. Humanly, if we cannot avoid pain, what we want is a formula that at least insures a happy ending. We want a story like Job's in which in this present world God puts in a visible appearance, vindication of faith is publicly established, and all losses restored. But good stewardship of pain cannot rest on such a hope. We have no promise of that.

Profitable management of our pain—good stewardship—is not a matter of following a process that predictably produces a happy ending. Good stewardship, in contrast, entails living with suffering in ways that we become people whose joy and distinctive strength does not lie in the power to make life turn out wonderfully but in the ability to live triumphantly when it doesn't.

chapter 2

WHOSE FAULT IS
THIS ANYWAY?

At times it is very difficult to agree with God. In most instances, we recognize that agreeing with God increases significantly our odds of getting it right. And schooled to be politically correct, we disguise discreetly, particularly from ourselves, any differences of opinion with God that we privately entertain. But however illogical or theologically incorrect disagreement with God may be, there are times when we simply do not, or cannot, see things from God's point of view. Our disagreement with God is often strongest when, confronted with pain and trouble, we discover that, as Barbara Brown Taylor phrased it, we have no power to make it go away.[1] At such times, if we are fortunate and our understanding of God has been shaped by the Psalms, we may take our courage in hand and tell God plainly what we think. In that event, our complaint usually works out something like this.

We point out to God that His divine job description makes the events and people in His created world *His* responsibility. We may seek to deliver our complaint in a respectful manner, but the issue is a simple one from our human point of view. We experience loss and grief, injustice and betrayal, the persistent presence of pain; we observe the soul-wrenching events in a bent and broken world, and we report them to God as *prima facie* evidence of problems in His divine management. We may conclude—in a dangerous leap of illogic—that the presence of such things in God's world is evidence of His approval of them. Or we may assume—frighteningly—that God does not like these things but lacks the power to make them different. Either way, we conclude, "God, *you* have a problem."

The possibility that God has a plan already in operation that will make all come right in the end—the idea that God can and will bless the mess, so to speak—is rejected out of hand. We dismiss *that* prospect as a theology of rose-colored glasses, a theory of pie-in-the-sky that is a silly denial of common sense. As for the possibility that we ourselves might have played some part in hurting one another and trashing the place up—well, that, of course, is irrelevant, an absurdity that we consider immaterial to our complaint against God.

We reduce the whole complex matter into a simple bottom line. Pain and suffering are bad. A powerful, loving God should not permit pain and suffering to happen—particularly to *us*. We conclude virtuously that since we are not God we cannot logically be held responsible for the problem or the solution. God did it—or He permitted it to happen—so it is His problem and He gets to clean it up. We get to criticize and complain.

But sooner or later we become tired of hitting our heads against the unyielding stone wall of existential reality. With or without our permission or understanding, the world is what it is: full of suffering—some merited, most undeserved, and shaped by randomness and chance. But, in a paradoxical other-side-of-the-coin, the world is what it is: full of joy and goodness and love—some merited, most undeserved, and shaped by order and comforting predictability. Through necessity, if for no other reason, we eventually abandon protest for pragmatism. Life—and the paradoxical world in which we must live our lives—*is what it is*, the best *and* the worst. We acknowledge, in effect, that truth may lie beyond the facts at our disposal and that God may know things we cannot explain. We stop—temporarily, at least—charging God with divine malpractice and table our attempt to construct a unifying theory of blame that accounts for all the problems of the universe. We make a working agreement with God and set out to live productively with our pain, our pain we do not approve of, and our pain that we cannot fully explain.

It's All My Fault

At this point we describe our goal in fairly simple terms. If asked, we say something like this: "I am *not* trying to work out a rational explanation for the presence of pain in the universe. I am *not* even trying to explain *why* there is suffering and trouble in *my* life. I am attempting to live productively with the pain I experience. I am trying to deal with things as they are in a way that makes good things happen."

But just as we are set to get on with things, we find to our surprise that we are tangled yet again with a "why" question. It isn't the original "Why-did-God..." form of the question—we have attempted at least to place that question on the shelf. What has emerged is a mutation. This "why" question does not raise the issue of theodicy (God's responsibility). Instead, it raises the matter of, to manufacture a term, *ego-odicy*—responsibility viewed in terms of the self. We have moved in fine pendulum fashion from "It's all *God*'s fault," to "It's all *my* fault." Without our conscious awareness, the "Why-did-God..." question has evolved into a "Why-did-I…" question with its own set of entangling tentacles that slow or stop our progress.

This re-emergence of the "why" question is disconcerting, but it is easy to understand. In truth, we did not actually abandon the "why" question. We kept the question, but we moved our search for an answer to a new arena. We put ourselves—rather than God—in the dock, to borrow C. S. Lewis's phrase.[2] We morphed the original process of questioning and blaming God into a program of questioning and blaming ourselves. We soon find, however, that this approach has not solved any problems. Indeed, the "why" question, when focused on ourselves, produces its own equally hard stone wall. In this form the "why" question produces self-blame that can quickly immobilize us and become a habit that is hard to lay aside.

Understanding the process and the seductive appeal of self-blame requires careful thought. Self-blame is tricky. Some forms of it could well be used to illustrate Paul's observation that evil sometimes masquerades as an angel of light.[3] Practical understanding of self-blame requires clear thinking; it often requires some painful honesty as well. Relinquishing self-blame entails taking responsibility for those things that *are* our responsibility while, at the same time, we reject blame for those things for which we are not accountable and over which we have had no control. Refusing self-blame is a demanding lifelong discipline in which, by God's grace, we choose to live honestly with ourselves as we are, not as we wish—or fear—ourselves to be.

We deeply flawed mortals are paradoxical. While we do not easily come to honest acknowledgment of our sins, we are at the same time quite fond of self-blame. We slyly entertain the heretical notion that self-blame—particularly when it is unjust—earns

God's favor. We think that when we blame ourselves—especially when we demean our worth and distort the charges against us—we earn God's approval through self-condemnation. Such a process both insults the character of God and demeans the work of the cross. Additionally, it erects a barrier against the kind of honest accountability that can lead to true repentance. In tricky ways, self-blame also encourages self-deception. At times, self-blame serves cleverly as part of a moral rabbit-in-the-hat trick. Loudly blaming ourselves for the rain on the picnic distracts everyone so that no one—including ourselves, we hope—notices when we take the biggest piece of pie.

Job's Friends and the Problem with Personal Blame

Self-blame is one of the major themes in Job's story; it provides an interesting picture of God's view of this matter. Job's friends are notoriously remembered for their failure to comfort. However, at the end of Job's story, the issue of self-blame, not comfort, became the crux of their issue with Job and God.

When Job's friends learned of the catastrophe that had befallen him, they set out to visit Job to comfort and sympathize with him. They were rightly concerned; Job was in a terrible situation. At the end of their journey when Eliphaz, Bildad, and Zophar actually saw Job, the text tells us they were so appalled at his condition that for a week they were utterly silent. They simply sat on the ground beside Job and said nothing.

Up to this point, Job had maintained his integrity. He had not blamed God for the events in his life and had steadfastly refused to take his wife's advice to curse God. Frederick Buechner notes, however (tongue in cheek), that Job may have come close to cursing God when after seven days he found that his friends planned to extend their visit for a second week!

Impoverished as Job now was, the social requirements of feeding and housing his friends did not appear to concern him. The problem erupted when his long-staying guests abandoned their silence. They undertook, with the best of intentions, to explain Job's fate to him and to instruct him, at considerable length, regarding his proper response. Job was not pleased or blessed by either their explanations or their instructions. Nor, for that matter, was God, as we will see.

Given the circumstances, one might be inclined to consider Job's rather fierce response to his friends to be an understandable case of frayed nerves if it were not for the fact that God was severely displeased as well. Whatever Job's human limitations, the text makes it clear that neither God nor Job were responding unreasonably. This was no trivial matter; a serious issue was at stake. At this point, we may well wonder: What on earth did Job's concerned friends do that caused such trouble? How did they manage to upset both God and Job to this degree?

Job, the good man, had lost everything—wealth, family, and health. He had steadfastly refused to blame God. But when his friends arrived, Job openly acknowledged his mental and emotional turmoil. In his suffering, he wished that he had never been born and desired that death would come soon. What could his friends say in the face of such terrible loss and pain?

Once they had regained their breath, what Job's friends said was *very* long—thirty-four chapters of closely argued theodicy! Their bottom line, however, was quite short. The source of the problem, they argued, lay in Job himself. It was Job's own attitudes and behavior that had moved a just God to act against him. Acknowledging his personal culpability was the way out of his dilemma and back into the favor of God.

Job was not perfect, and said so. He had a lot to learn, as his later conversation with God made plain. Nevertheless, to his friends' increasing annoyance, Job stubbornly refused to blame himself for the catastrophe that had occurred in his life. While there was some truth in what Job's friends said, their well-intended lectures seriously misrepresented God, mistakenly blamed the victim, and, further, insisted that the victim blame himself. It was this misrepresentation of both God's actions and Job's character that landed Job's friends in deep trouble.

Job was correct in his refusal to blame God. He was also correct in his refusal to accept the personal blame-based explanations of events advocated by his friends. We know this because at the end, God vindicated Job's defense of himself and appeared personally on the scene to set both Job and his friends straight about a number of matters.

It is great drama. After days of debate between Job and his friends, God blew onto the scene out of a great whirlwind. He abruptly initiated a life-altering conversation with Job, and then, when He had finished His conversation with Job, God confronted Job's friends. He pointed out indignantly that it was Job, not they, who had spoken rightly of Him. To make His point even clearer, God made restoration of His relationship with Job's friends dependent upon a substantial sacrifice on their part— seven bulls and seven rams! He then publicly reaffirmed His relationship with Job. He informed Job's friends that He would fully restore His relationship with them only after Job had personally interceded on their behalf. "Listen," God said, in effect, to Eliphaz, Bildad, and Zophar, "First, you apologize directly to me *big time* [the sacrifice], and then, after my friend Job—yes, that same man you insisted was in truth a terrible person— has asked me to forgive you, I will do so."

Why They Were Wrong

Reduced from the complex issues of theodicy in which their presupposition was shaped, Job's friends started with one of the common forms of self-blame. They assumed that there was an inevitable, direct, causal, punitive linkage between *all* suffering and sin. Job's pain and loss was terrible—that was evident. Therefore, they reasoned, it was also self-evident that Job's sin must be equally terrible in order to have evoked this response from a just and holy God. And despite Job's protests of innocence, they continued to insist on attributing the catastrophe in Job's life to his sinfulness. They were wrong.

First, they were wrong about Job.

Of course, as readers, we have the advantage of having looked in on the opening scene of the drama. We know that God, in an in-your-face moment with Satan, had said, "Have you noticed my servant Job? He is the finest man in all the earth. He is blameless—*a man of complete integrity.* He fears God and stays away from evil" (Job 1:8 NLT, emphasis added).

But to understand God's point of view, we need to bracket that opening assessment of Job with Job's own testimony from the last scene of the drama. There, altered forever by his encounter with God, Job acknowledges that in those former days he spoke glibly of things he now knows he did not understand. And having now seen God in His glory, Job thinks much less highly of himself; he repents "in dust and ashes" (Job 42:3, 6).

Job was wise, although he came to realize that he knew less than he thought he did. He was a good man, although in the face of God's glory, he came to see himself with a dramatically reduced sense of pride. In surviving his ordeal Job gained a new sense of self-knowledge and a sharply adjusted sense of self-worth. But God's affirmation of Job came at the beginning, *before* the ordeal, *before* Job came to know God and himself in new and deeper ways. It was *that* beginning Job, with all his limitations, with whom God challenged the dark angel Satan, presenting Job as God's good man. And it was *that* Job, with all his limited understanding but with all his integrity, who got it right: While less than perfect and with much to learn, the suffering he experienced was, nevertheless, *not his fault.*

Patterns of Self-Blame

When we examine some of the common patterns of self-blame, we can see how the process sabotages redemptive management of pain. In some instances, we do indeed carry some portion of responsibility for what has happened. However, self-blame rarely points to this truth. The problem emerges from the way in which the charges levied in self-blame wrap themselves around faulty beliefs. These faulty beliefs usually consist of small portions of truth mixed with large amounts of error. This misleading mix is then coated with religious-sounding language that gives a high moral tone to the process. In this deceptive form, self-blame can appear to be a virtuous effort to assume responsibility for oneself when in plain fact the process is self-condemnation based on distortion and denial of the truth. While patterns of self-blame are as unique as a given individual, they incorporate four basic belief systems that sound plausible but sabotage redemptive management of pain. These faulty beliefs include these ideas:

- My pain and suffering have happened because I am a bad person and/or have done a bad thing. I'm getting what I deserved.
- My pain and suffering have happened because I am incompetent. I didn't plan well. I didn't choose wisely. If I had been smarter, I would have prevented this from happening.
- My pain and suffering have happened because I am unlovable. Because no one cares about me, pain and suffering happen to me. If I were loveable, this wouldn't have happened. The loved and beautiful people escape things like this.
- My pain and suffering have happened because in the universe of people, *my* life has no purpose or value. I am an appropriate (logical) target for suffering since my life has no value or meaning. My pain and suffering have happened because, in the final analysis, nothing of value is lost if I suffer or if I am destroyed.

Each of these patterns of self-blame immobilizes the individual and blocks effective management of pain.

Does Suffering Come Because I Am Bad?

The foundation of self-blame is often the belief that my pain means that I am bad and I have done it wrong, however *bad* may be defined and whatever *it*, the alleged cause, may be. The tricky part at this point, of course, is the awkward fact that, with rare exception, there is *some* truth in this charge. Avoiding the potential sabotage of self-blame requires both clear thinking and courage. We must sort out and face the truth about ourselves; we must reject those charges that are not true.

It is true that we are often the authors of our own misery. In such instances something of great value happens to us inwardly and to our pain when we take responsibility for our behavior. Most of us know from personal experience that, however uncomfortable the process, something profoundly healing occurs when we acknowledge that we are at fault and then do what we can to mend the brokenness that we have caused. However, the pattern of self-blame that says, "This pain is *my* fault," rarely reflects this kind of honest assumption of specific responsibility.

In contrast, this pattern of self-blame pivots around a global generalization of blame—*everything*, at all times and in all places, is *all my* fault. Blame is focused around an endless litany of self-assessed, self-assigned personal faults. This pattern of self-blame results, paradoxically, in avoidance of responsibility rather than acceptance of truth in a way that brings about change and lessens pain.

We experience this at the simplest level in conflicted relationships. When in the heat of disagreement a friend or spouse says, "Oh, it's *all* my fault. I'm the one who is *always* wrong," we know that meaningful dialogue has ended, and, for the time at least, the door to productive change has been closed. The individual has effectively used self-blame ("This is *all* my fault.") both to avoid specific responsibility ("*This* was my part of the problem") and to evade specific change ("*This* is what I can now do to change things."). The individual has rejected productive accountability ("I can see that this was my part of the problem.") in favor of global blame ("It's *all* my fault."). True repentance

("This is what I can—and now will—do to change things.") was rejected in favor of global self-condemnation ("I'm always wrong."). In a parallel sense, self-blame tangles our relationship with God. When in the face of suffering we engage in self-blame and self-condemnation, we shut the door to the personal transformation that God desires and intends.

A client whose daughter had committed suicide said, "It's all my fault. If I had been a better mother, this would not have happened." This woman faced the incredible pain of losing a much-loved child and the resulting challenge of living through her loss into a place of self-knowledge and forgiving grace for both herself and her daughter. However, at the beginning of her work, ruminating on her self-assigned guilt and revisiting her self-assigned faults kept her imprisoned in her pain and chronically focused on herself, which resulted in intensifying her pain. This woman, whom I will call Sue, certainly had not been a perfect mother. But self-blame, simultaneously reporting *and* distorting this fact, obscured the truth that there was more to Sue's life and to her loss than her limitations as a mother. There was more to her daughter's choice to die than her mother's parenting. The emotional myopia that resulted from this global self-blame prevented Sue from recognizing the possibility that, imperfect through she was, she could live *through* the experience into a transforming place of forgiving grace, new self-knowledge, and peace that eased her pain. Self-blame about things she could *not* change effectively blocked Sue from looking at her present choices and the changes that she *could* make. Sue used her chronic litanies of self-condemnation, for example, to avoid considering the option of forgiveness. Despair came with Sue's self-condemnation. However, for a long period of time, living with this despair was preferable to Sue than entering into the struggle to forgive both herself and the daughter who had chosen to die.

The way in which self-blame can appear deceptively "spiritual" makes it possible for us to assume the role of Job's friends with ourselves without becoming fully aware of what we have done. We look at the circumstances and the suffering of our lives and say to ourselves, as Job's friends said to him, "This suffering is *my* fault. *My* sinfulness and *my* faults and limitations have caused God to bring this loss and suffering into my life." But at this point we, like Job's friends, can be wrong about both God and ourselves. Sue was wrong. So was another client, whom I will call Lois.

Lois came for help with the grief and depression she was experiencing after the death at birth of a child she had desperately desired. "I just want to know what I did wrong. I know it's my fault," she said tearfully, "but God won't tell me what I did wrong. The doctor isn't any help. She says things like this happen sometimes, but I'm not sure she's a Christian. I can't get past this until God tells me what I did wrong."

Seeing herself at fault was emotionally preferable to Lois than seeing herself in a world in which things beyond her control could happen in her life. Without conscious awareness, Lois was insisting on a personal exemption to the truth that bad things do at times happen to good people. On the surface, however, her self-blame appeared to be an effort to understand the "spiritual" components of her suffering and to "do it right." And, in the tradition of Job's friends, she insisted that God agreed with her—that her pain and loss and her personal culpability could not be separated. She was using self-blame to place a "spiritual" spin on her pain and at the same time to avoid an issue with God that she did not wish to face. Clearly, the problem did not lie in Lois's pain as such. That was real and appropriate. Her deep desire to conceive a child, her hopelessness through her long years of barrenness, the wild joy of an unexpected pregnancy, then the inexplicable death of her child at birth—truly, this is the stuff of suffering that cannot be made to go away. This is the pain that can only be lived through. Saying desperately, "This is all my fault" is not, however, a constructive first step on that difficult journey.

In a world of bent and broken people, none of us is perfect. Like Job, most of us acquire considerable insight into that imperfection as we live through our pain. This increased self-knowledge comes, however, when we lay self-blame aside and enter into the transformation process that God desires. This transformation process rests upon integrity rather than self-blame, as Job's story makes clear. Integrity requires that we deal with our human brokenness with straightforward honesty, acknowledging specific faults and then doing what we can to remedy the consequences of our actions. But integrity requires as well that we take responsibility *only* for that which is ours and resist steadfastly the error of Job's friends. All pain is not a matter of personal culpability. Effective pain management requires that we make—and maintain—a clear distinction between self-blame and honest accountability.

Does Suffering Come Because
I Am Incompetent?

Thinking clearly about the relationship between pain and incompetence is also complicated. Avoiding faulty patterns of self-blame requires us to think through two different questions—one easy, one difficult, each with a different answer.

Integrity requires clear thinking and honest accountability, and these become impossible when we muddle these two questions together and then confuse their answers.

The first question is relatively straightforward. Can we, by incompetent thinking and behavior, bring about circumstances that result in pain? While difficult to live with, the answer to this question is easy. Experience teaches us early that we can, and often do, act as our own nemesis. Through years—or an instant—of faulty thinking; by an unskilled, lazy, or fear-filled response; or by chronic, careless, immature, undisciplined choices, we can make for ourselves pain that will last a lifetime, at least in its ripple effects. But it is important to pay careful attention to the limits of this question.

Stated simply, we have asked: Can incompetent behavior produce painful results? The answer we have given to this question in this form is yes. But, in anticipation of question 2, we need to keep clearly in mind that this first question regarding incompetence is limited to consideration of behavior and its consequences. We need to keep in mind as well that human behavior and the consequences that follow it are neither simple nor linear in real life. However, in order to clarify the tricky way a faulty form of self-blame creeps into the competence issue, the yes response in this simple form serves well as a beginning point.

The second question grows out of the first. It is commonly shaped something like this. If my incompetent behavior has produced pain, does this incompetent behavior stem from something wrong with me as a person? Is my pain the result of my incompetent behavior, or is my incompetent behavior the inevitable side-effect of my being an incompetent person?

It is easy to see that the second question in effect asks a "why" question in a "where" form: Where is the root of the pain—in the behavior or in the person? Where does the pain originate—in choices, attitudes, and actions or in the essence of the person, in the essential parameters of the self? Why do I hurt? Is it because of what I do or who I am? Are the things I do and the pain that results from the things I do evidence of who I am? Does my pain mean I have defective skills or that there is something essentially deficient about myself? Should I blame my pain on my deficient incompetent self?

Once we see clearly the direction this question can take us, we see the risks for a faulty pattern of self-blame. Did I lose the game because I have not developed a competent backhand, or did I lose the game because I am a loser—a born loser? If so, no amount of tennis lessons can correct my inherent lack of coordination, limited visual skills, and physical ineptness. Or, in a different context, did this marriage relationship founder because I lack skills to negotiate conflict and have neglected to develop them, or has this pain come because I am a loner unable to connect with people and, therefore, I am a born loser in the marriage game?

If I cannot perform because I am faulty at the core of who I am, I cannot be held accountable. Initially, for some individuals that may appear to be good news. But it is never, in fact, unqualified good news. If I cannot perform and am not accountable, then my inept, ineffectual, deficient self is my permanent barrier to hope and to new things. If my present pain is the consequence of my incompetent self, then tomorrow will produce only more pain since my defective self lies essentially beyond the possibility of significant change. This thinking, growing out of the second question, leads to a self-blame focused on incompetence that blocks redemptive management of pain.

It is important to keep our questions and answers straight. Can my incompetence cause my own pain, and, not incidentally, pain for others? Unfortunately, yes. When my incompetence causes pain, is this pain evidence of an incompetent self? Thankfully, no. However, keeping this distinction clear in managing pain requires careful thinking and the courage to act with integrity.

Faulty patterns of self-blame in relation to competence stem from confusion of the person with the behavior. It is easier to see these faulty patterns if we first look at a productive use of pain related to incompetence. What does good pain management look like at this point?

The first step requires us to acknowledge honestly our specific lack of skills and knowledge, our undisciplined attitudes, and our poor choices that have led to our present dilemma and its accompanying pain. But this step requires some caution. With Job-style integrity we need to take responsibility for our deficiencies—but take responsibility only for those things for which we are, in fact, accountable. The next step requires us to identify and accept the consequences that have resulted from our behavior and choices and then take action to remedy the consequences of our incompetence in ways that are realistically possible. This eases pain and encourages the development of new skills and new patterns of thinking that lead to new levels of competence.

Talking with me about this process one day, a client described it in this fashion: "You mean, figure out what I did that made the mess and say so. Then clean up the mess the best I can. Then learn things that will keep me from making any more messes like this. And if I do this I won't feel so bad about the mess I made in the first place." I smiled, but I thought to myself that although I might have put the essentials more elegantly, I could not have stated them more clearly if I had invested a month of effort in doing so. But as I remembered Carl, another client, I thought too that living out these steps in some instances entails a lifelong process of redeeming pain.

Carl, driving while intoxicated, had hit a bridge abutment in the rain. Carl's wife Ginny, who was not wearing her seatbelt, was killed. Carl survived relatively uninjured but suffered some mild but permanent closed-head injuries. Andrea, their daughter, was staying overnight with grandparents and thankfully was not involved in the accident.

Carl became my client some time after the accident occurred. He had already taken good steps to manage his pain and the consequences of his choices. He was actively participating in a recovery program in which he had faced and acknowledged the true extent of his misuse of alcohol. In his recovery program, Carl was working hard to correct the characteristic patterns of distorted thinking and poor choices that had marked his life prior to the accident. He had vigorously pursued an intense program of rehabilitation and was now able to perform adequately cognitively and physically, although not at the level he remembered himself being able to function before the accident occurred. But Carl was snagged at two different points.

The first snag lay with the lifelong nature of the consequences of Carl's choices. Carl expected that his efforts toward recovery, when coupled with God's forgiveness, would enable him to "clean up the mess." At some levels this had indeed happened and was continuing to happen. But Carl was struggling with the reality that, despite his success, some of his pain was hooked to consequences that were lifelong and brought pain that would not go away. This was pain that could be eased and managed, but it could not be eliminated. Nothing could change the fact that Ginny would not be present as mother of the bride on Andrea's wedding day. In the concrete context of his life, Carl was learning to live with the truth the Teacher pointed to when he said: "What is wrong cannot be made right. What is missing cannot be recovered" (Ecclesiastes 1:15 NLT).

Carl and I talked at length about the fact that God's forgiveness does not erase all human consequences. We talked about the things that could not be changed, the consequences with which Carl would have to cope his entire life. We talked too about the new things, the good consequences that were coming into his life. We discussed the fact that while the consequences were lifelong, this did not mean that Carl would experience the same pain he was experiencing now for the rest of his life. We worked out the distinction that good management of pain rarely erases it completely, but that good management of consequences changes not only the way the pain impacts us but the intensity of the pain as well. We made some progress.

Carl said one day, "I chose to drink and drive, and now I pay the penalty. No matter what I do, I can't get Ginny back. No matter what I do, I can't undo the pain and loss I've caused Andrea and Ginny's folks and mine and me too. But for everybody's sake, including my own, I've got to move on."

I was, of course, pleased. But I soon noticed something. Carl did not move on. Instead, he sat down. He continued his recovery program. He continued to work at the recreational center in his neighborhood where he was employee of the month. He continued to spend time with Andrea and to care for her. He did the "right" things. He attended church regularly, where he was an active part of an older co-ed singles group. He played handball regularly at the local gym. He participated cooperatively in our work, but my sense of Carl's inner world told me that Carl wasn't going anywhere. He was stuck. Somehow Carl was hooked.

One day I put out a cautious feeler. "What are your plans for school?" I inquired.

"Don't have any," Carl replied abruptly with an uncharacteristic edge to his voice.

"Why not?" I asked, pushing the issue.

"Why would a loser like me make plans like that?" Carl said, suddenly savagely angry, peppering his conversation with uncharacteristic profanity. "I'm a drunk who killed his wife and messed up his head. Why would a loser like that plan anything but staying out of trouble and out of people's way? There's no tomorrow for me. There's nothing I can do."

Carl had initially done well with the consequences of his self-produced life tragedy. He had agreed that his alcohol-related incompetent behavior had produced enormous pain and terrible consequences and had set about dealing with the consequences in productive ways. However, Carl had given the wrong answer to question 2. He had concluded that his reckless behavior, which had resulted in pain, was solid evidence that he was—or had become—an inherently defective person with no present worth and no future worth pursuing.

Mastery in difficult life circumstances consists of doing what we can do with what is at hand, a skill that is essential to management of pain as we will see.[4] But when we conclude, as Carl had, that what we have at hand to work with is a defective self, we logically then assume that there is little or nothing that we can do. When self-blame holds the self as essentially incompetent, we close the door on mastery, and, in some ways, distort both time and choice.

In a later conversation, Carl and I talked about the impact of the distorted way in which he was thinking about himself on both his sense of hope and the choices he now had. Carl had opened the issue by insisting again that there was nothing more that he could do with his life or himself.

"Not true," I countered. You can go to school *now*. Maybe you can't go to the graduate school of engineering that was your first choice, but you can go to school. You cannot have life with Ginny. But you can build, step-by-step, a good life filled with good things for you and Andrea. Your choice *then* led to loss of some things that cannot be recovered. But it did not make you an inadequate self. You have another choice *now*. The life you have *now* comes from the choices that you make *now*. It is not determined solely by the choices you made *then*."

Good stewardship of pain requires that we accept with rigorous honesty both past choices and their consequences and present reality in dealing with those consequences. The present reality includes God's generous grace that comes to us precisely at the place of failure. When self-blame is focused on the alleged incompetent self, the reality of grace and God's gift of hope are distorted and often lost.

A client recently illustrated this thinking in a memorable conversation.

"What do you think you can do to make things better [that is, less painful]?" I asked.

"Nothing," replied the client in a depressed tone. "You know I just can't do anything that works out."

"Maybe God could do something," I suggested.

"Not with me," answered the client. "Even God has to have something to work with."

Self-blame that pivots around the beliefs that I am bad and inherently deficient as well are dangerous. The believer in personal culpability becomes the victim of the bad self, and the believer in personal incompetence becomes the victim of the inadequate self. Options for change are severely limited for those who see themselves as hopeless victims of the self. This form of self-blame leads to despair that is, for most people, a much more serious problem than pride, as Barbara Brown Taylor has pointed out.[5] This despair tempts us to limit God himself and to act in ways that give our "badness" greater importance than God's goodness, as Taylor rightly observes. In contrast, the kind of accountability and repentance that heals pain "has more faith in God's power to make new than in our own power to mess up."[6]

Does Suffering Come Because I Am Unlovable?

The belief that suffering is linked somehow to issues of love leads to particularly painful forms of self-blame. The reasoning, often without words, runs something like this. *Love prevents pain. Therefore, if I feel pain, I am unloved. The person who injured me does not love me. God, who permits these circumstances that cause my suffering, does not love me. The meaning of my pain is simple: I am not loved.* This form of self-blame is shaped around a complex reality. It also incorporates an equally complex pattern of faulty thinking that is difficult to dislodge.

It is true that being unloved is one of the most intensely painful experiences that humans can suffer. Dealing with this painful reality requires us to consider an option that God offers, but it is an offer that we may be initially inclined to reject.

Grace makes God's love an available option even when human love has been lost or is absent. When we feel utterly alone, we can refuse to drown in the waves of our own despair. Like Peter in the storm, we can take hold of God's hand. But it must be admitted that for a person who is just beginning to work through this struggle, God's option does not always appear to be an attractive one when the pain and aloneness feel overwhelming. It's one of the situations where it's particularly difficult to agree with God.

"Don't tell me God loves me," a tearful client said angrily. "I want somebody real to hold me and touch me and kiss me goodnight."

But this form of self-blame does not really pivot around the painful experience of being unloved. Instead, this form of self-blame implies that suffering is evidence that an individual is not simply unloved, but is unloved because he or she is intrinsically unlovable. Pain (the lack or loss of love) is then the logical consequence of being inherently unlovable.

In a way that parallels the previously described patterns of blame-based pain, when an individual views personal suffering as the consequence of being inherently unlovable, the result is the assumption of a victim role. A person may be a "forever victim" of an assumed bad self, the "forever victim" of an assumed incompetent self, or, similarly, the "forever victim" of an unlovable self. Assuming a victim role becomes a powerful force, sabotaging good stewardship of pain and management of difficult life circumstances.

A client came for help with the grief and loss she was experiencing following the break-up of her thirty-year marriage. "He shouldn't have left," she said bitterly. "But in a way I don't blame him. Who could love somebody like me?"

The history of the marriage confirmed that this woman had contributed in major ways to the conflict and alienation that led to the disintegration of the marital relationship. But I suspected as well that her long-term belief that she was unlovable had led her to act in ways that had encouraged her partner to leave.

In any event, it was clear from the beginning that her deeply rooted sense of being inherently unlovable posed potential long-term problems. She would remain anchored in a life of bitter loneliness unless she learned to place her suffering in a context other than self-blame. She did indeed need to deal with integrity with those acts and attitudes for which she was responsible. But in order to do that, it was first necessary for her to recognize the prison of self-blame into which she had locked herself. In her blame-based logic she believed, "Since I am inherently unlovable I inevitably act in ways that make people want to go—and stay—away from me."

She could not appropriately repent her unloving acts (or move on to new patterns of relationship) if she believed her unloving acts were simply the logical and inevitable product of her essentially unlovable self. Regret?—yes. Repent?—no. After all, she had simply done "what came naturally." With her intrinsically unlovable self, she believed that she had had no real choice. And while she was theologically orthodox—she believed that the unlimited grace of God was present in Christ—she did not believe that theological truth had personal significance for her. In the emotional reality of her pain, her unlovable self placed her beyond the reach of God's grace and realistic hope of change.

Does Suffering Come Because My Life Has No Inherent Worth?

This is the most complex form of self-blame and (perhaps arguably) the most difficult to see clearly and to change. For this reason, beginning with a real-life account may be helpful.

One late autumn day I met a friend for lunch whose mother had recently died. My friend had had a particularly close relationship with her mother and continued to struggle with deep unyielding grief. We chatted briefly, and then when the waiter had left to place our order, I asked her how she was.

"How are you doing?" I asked. "Pretty sad, I'm thinking when I look at your face."

"Yes," she acknowledged, and then added, "But in the grand scheme of the universe I doubt that that matters much."

Had I asked my friend directly at that moment if her life had value, she would have responded positively. However, this truth that she knew well in sunnier times, and still believed at some levels, had begun to erode away in her grief. Somehow, in ways she herself had not consciously identified, the pain and loss she was enduring had produced a sense of decreased personal value. Her suffering, she thought, was not important "in the grand scheme." She was closer than she realized to the second step in a dark downward spiral: If her suffering were not important "in the grand scheme," then it was likely that she herself lacked importance "in the grand scheme." And for those who continue down that road, the end of that bitter logic often emerges without words but in a form much like this: "Since neither my suffering nor I matter in the grand scheme of things, then perhaps in the grand scheme of things I was elected to suffer simply because I do not matter, because I have no worth. I am a victim of my worthless self.

Christians who seek to deal with their suffering in terms of their faith often retain at this point "head knowledge" of their God-given worth. However, if they are in a safe place, they too will sometimes acknowledge a painful uncertainty. "It feels like I don't matter much and what is happening to me doesn't matter much to anyone," a friend once said privately. "And perhaps that's as it should be. I know God notices sparrows—the Word says He does—but the Word doesn't make it clear that whether those sparrows live or die makes much difference in the end to God's plans or the fate of the world."

Ann Weems, whose beloved son Todd was murdered on his twenty-first birthday, catches the power of grief to erode a sense of being and significance in "Lament Psalm Thirty-five."[7]

> The sky has fallen
> and no one seems to notice...
> Everywhere I look
>   there is nothing
>   but devastation,
>   and yet,
> everyone goes about
> their business as usual.
>   O God, my life
>   is destroyed,
> but people go to the bank
>   and to the store.
> They eat and they drink,
>   and I crumple
> under the weight of my heart...

In *Psalms of Lament*, Weems brings the great gift of her persevering faith to her grief process and sheds light in the darkness of her loss. For this reason, we will revisit her work in more detail later. Here, however, we follow her into her world of pain at the point where, devastated and destroyed, she feels unseen, unheard, and unvalued in a world busily going to the store and to the bank and eating and drinking, while she crumples under the weight of her broken heart.

The first steps forward out of this dark place are neither easy nor self-evident. Issues of self-worth are never simple in the intricate world of the inner self. And, as a further complication, the culture itself sends a mixed message regarding personal worth that makes it a confusing subject.

Theoretically, the present culture places great value on every human life. Practically, however, the culture assigns highest value to those individuals who are powerful and wealthy and who are high consumers, those who have the most toys. The culture also values highly those who have physical beauty and high levels of sexual attraction, the "beautiful" people whose lives are characterized by social excitement and public admiration. Individuals who are most valuable are those who hold membership in the culturally exclusive group of the elite "haves," those who possess those attributes prized by the culture.

The culture values differently those whose lives are marked by economic struggle and whose work consists of common, unglamorous tasks. The farmers, the truckers, the teachers, the maids that clean motels, the short-order cooks, the weary clerks and waitresses, the maintenance people, the mechanics, the child-care staff, the assembly line workers—these are not commonly characterized among the "haves." It is ironic that vital services such as production of food and the education and care of children do not take high positions in the cultural hierarchy.

And the culture does not echo Jesus' opinion that the poor are blessed (Luke 6:20). Although those who function at the margins of the world of work—often standing in the unemployment line, looking for work, and hoping at best for a job that will let them "make ends meet"—are also among God's chosen, they are among the culturally ignored. Those who are caught in the grinding reality of poverty and who have no work at all, these too are God's people, but for the most part the culture keeps them unseen and unrecognized.

But pain is nondiscriminatory. "Have" or "have not," sooner or later most of us experience suffering in a form that raises the question of the value of who we are and what the worth of our lives is.

Suffering as a "have"

A client whom I will call Janet was referred by her physician. Janet was an exquisitely beautiful woman whose family trust provided lifetime economic safety, an affluent lifestyle, and social significance. Janet had a lifetime membership in the "haves," but that membership did not protect her from a personal crisis any more than Job's wealth had protected him.

Janet had been seriously injured in a skiing accident, but at the time she was referred to me her physical recovery was proceeding satisfactorily. She was, however, increasingly depressed and complained of chronic pain that both she and her doctor believed to be unrelated to her injuries.

"What do think your body is trying to tell you through this pain?" I asked one day.

"How do I know?" she responded irritably. I waited. Then, in a very different tone, she said, "I think my body says that there's no reason for me to get well. The world would go right on without me. Terry would remarry—likely in less than a year. My sister would love to have my kids. Frank (the trust officer who administered her family estate) would look after the kids' stuff. The Spring Gala would make a half-million dollars, and Jane (the society editor of the local paper) would describe everyone who was there, but no one would notice—or care—that I was gone."

She paused and then added, "There's a kind of justice in this. When bad things happen they ought to happen to people who can pay for treatment and whose lives don't count for much if they don't get well. I guess I'm a logical candidate for this."

Suffering as a "have not"

From the cultural viewpoint, Richard, in contrast, began life as a "have not," the son of a migrant farm worker. School was difficult because of the family's frequent moves and because Richard perceived much of what he was required to study as having little relevance to life as he knew it. He dropped out of school at fifteen. In Richard's life, money was significant mainly because of its absence. In his adolescent years acquiring things was more likely a matter of stealing them than of purchasing them.

By a rather remarkable series of events, however, Richard became a successful over-the-road driver for a large trucking firm. He married and had two sons of his own, both of whom graduated from high school and found steady blue-collar jobs. Life became better than Richard had ever hoped it could be. But then Linda, Richard's wife, died suddenly, a victim of breast cancer.

The grief and disorientation Richard experienced were overwhelming. He was immobilized, paralyzed by his loss, bewildered and confused by the flood of emotions he experienced. His patterns of eating and sleeping were severely disrupted; his ability to drive safely was at risk. His sons and his supervisor eventually intervened, insisting that Richard see a counselor as a condition of his continuing employment.

Resistant at first, Richard came to look forward to talking with me. One stormy winter evening, Richard missed an appointment without first calling to cancel. When eventually a call from Richard was forwarded to me, he had left a number asking that I call back.

"Sorry I couldn't call earlier," Richard said when my call reached him, "but I was stuck at the tunnel. I had to chain up, and then there was an accident. Nothing moved for about three hours."

"It's fine," I reassured him. "With this weather, I guessed you were stranded. Are you okay?"

"Yep." There was a long silence. Richard could not yet talk much about his pain. Nevertheless, it filtered wordlessly through the static of the storm as it crackled over the landline connecting us.

"Richard," I asked again, "Are you all right?"

"Yep, I'm good," he said. But then he added, "But if somebody has to go, better be me. Wouldn't matter much in the end."

Alone in the dark, treacherous icy miles between his truck-stop shelter and home where an empty bed awaited him, Richard was dangerously at risk from more than bad weather and mountain roads. In his pain he had moved to a place where his own lack of personal worth made his physical survival of questionable value to him.

Jesus spoke bluntly to the point about the "have" or "have not" issue and the value of life.[8] Life, Jesus said in Luke 12:15, is not about having. However, Jesus never romanticized poverty. In the context of the point Jesus was making, life is not about *not* having either. But when we are faced with the "pain that cannot be budged," we often find ourselves in serious argument with both ourselves and with Jesus about that point.

The culture presents a dangerous counterpoint to the truth Jesus taught. In the culture, "haves" are not only of greater value than "have nots," the fact that they are "haves" is assumed to be evidence that they are good as well. In the logic of the consumer culture, prosperity ("having" those things the culture values) is evidence of providential blessing and good character. Scarcity ("not having") is evidence of questionable character and personal failure to strive. When we adopt this cultural view of the matter, our suffering then becomes simultaneously both cause and consequence of our "have-not" status and the appropriate focus of justified self-blame.

By the culture's mythology, to be a "have not" is to be at serious fault since, presumably, having is the result of good character and hard work (with perhaps a small sliver of luck thrown in), factors that for the most part lie under the individual's control. The truth, of course, is much more complex than this, and, in at least one aspect, provides a sharp surprise. Whether a person is a "have" or "have not," suffering raises issues of worth that rapidly make the cultural formula of value and goodness irrelevant.

How a "have" can be a "have not"

Janet was suffering from an existential sense of meaninglessness that her affluent world was powerless to relieve. Her grandfather sent the family's private jet to take her to the family "cottage" estate for a month of rest and recovery.

"Did you have a good time?" I asked her when she returned.

"Yes. The beach was nice. And Maria always spoils me and the kids. But the trip was not enough to solve my problems, if that's what you were asking."

What, indeed, is enough? What we discover, to our surprise, is that the "not enough" litany reflects a chosen point of view. It rests upon a constructed virtual reality, so to speak, rather than a demonstrable fact. The fact that our scarcity is often self-assigned comes as a profound shock to most of us.

And it is an even greater shock when we discover that we can find nearly limitless reasons to assign ourselves to the "have not" category and incorporate our "have not" status as reason for self-blame (and blame for God as well). The consumer society encourages us to view ourselves through a lens of scarcity. "I don't have enough," we say privately, if not publicly. "I don't have enough—enough faith, enough money, enough love, enough sex, enough friends, enough intelligence, enough opportunity, enough education, enough passion and purpose in my life, enough health and energy, or enough of anything, actually," since the ways in which we can imagine scarcity are nearly limitless. Culturally approved reasoning leads us then to infer from this supposed scarcity a consequent lack of personal value (and evidence of lack of God's love). And then self-assigned to the "have not" category with its built-in component of self-blame, we grapple with our suffering and loss in that context of depleted personal worth. It is our lack of worth, we think, that makes us the recipients of pain. Pain means that we are the victim of our worthless selves. Without clear awareness, we see pain as the unyielding direct consequence of a self without value.

But being economic "haves" does not automatically prevent us from holding membership in the "have not" world, as Janet's life demonstrates. What Janet discovered was that while she was the recipient of enormous personal wealth, in her inner world she was a "have not"—not enough peace, not enough fun, not enough love, not enough faith in herself (or God), not enough hope about tomorrow, not enough joy, not enough safety.

Although they had begun life in contrasting "have" and "have not" economic worlds, pain brought both Janet and Richard alike to the issue of their intrinsic self-worth. Each was saying, in effect, "I have little worth or meaning. In the big picture I don't even show up on the radar screen. Maybe my pain has occurred because in the end my life doesn't matter much. It's no big deal if bad things happen to people who don't matter in the end."

"You are not a bug."

The issue of justice poses great difficulty in dealing with the meaning of pain. Why, indeed, do bad things happen to good people? And, equally troublesome, why do good things happen to bad people? But the issue with which Janet and Richard were struggling presents a different but no less significant question. Do bad things happen to some people simply because they lack value?

I sensed that Richard was stuck in his grief in part because he believed that it was his connection with Linda that gave him value and that when he lost Linda, he not only lost the woman he loved, he lost his self-of-value as well. Without Linda he had reverted inwardly to the old place where he had begun adult life as a marginal male with little or no value, no purpose in life, no intrinsic significance. However, after his comment on the telephone that his death wouldn't matter much in the end, Richard refused to discuss the purpose and value of *his* life without Linda. One day I decided to tackle the issue head on.

"Richard," I began, "do you think bad things happen to people sometimes because they're bad?"

Richard considered the question, eyeing me cautiously. We knew each other fairly well by this point in his work, and he suspected that I was heading for territory he didn't want to explore.

"Well, yes, sometimes," he conceded, and we discussed a couple of examples he could think of.

"Richard," I moved on, "do you think bad things happen to people sometimes because they're flat-out incompetent—just don't have their act together?"

"Of course," and the professional driver in Richard immediately provided a number of graphically clear examples of disaster related to incompetence.

"Well," I said a bit more cautiously, "do you think bad things happen to people sometimes because they're just so awful—I don't mean just that they do bad things, I mean that they are just so awful *as people*?"

This was more difficult. Richard hesitated, then said tentatively, "Well, maybe. But that's hard to know."

We discussed the issue briefly and agreed it was hard to think and talk about. I then raised the issue toward which I had been moving.

"Richard," I said, "do you think bad things happen to people sometimes because they are the kind of people that just don't matter—that it just doesn't make any difference what happens to those people?"

"What do you mean?" Richard asked, in part I suspected to buy some time, but it was a fair response nonetheless. I needed a graphic simple way to make the issue plain.

"Well," I said, "it's hard to explain. But think about this. Suppose there was a bug here on the floor."

At this point, Richard's face showed clear distaste for my story. Richard had a low opinion of bugs, in part because of the way bugs persistently interfered with his effort to maintain a clean windshield.

I persevered. "And suppose Josh [Richard's new grandson] were here on the floor too," I continued. "Then suppose this book fell off my desk. Would it be the same if it fell on Josh and if it fell on the bug?"

"Of course not," Richard said and added, "but I wouldn't put Josh down there on the floor. That's a dumb example."

"Probably," I conceded, "but come on, Richard. Try to talk about it. Losing Linda is the most awful thing that has ever happened to you. I know that because you tell me that, and I can see it in your life. But losing Linda is a big thing not just because you lost her but because losing her hurt a person who has value. *You are not a bug.* Losing Linda didn't make you a nobody. And losing Linda didn't happen because you're a nobody who doesn't matter to God or anybody else."

I stopped, feeling a little surprised and embarrassed by my intensity. Richard's face looked as blank as though I had spoken in Swahili. Belatedly wise, I chose not to dig my hole any deeper and to stop talking. Richard and I had built a good working relationship, so I waited for him to figure out what to do next. Then, after what seemed a long while, Richard spoke reassuringly into the silence and my discomfort with a hint of a smile in his voice.

"Well," he said, "at least I'm glad to know now I'm not a bug."

It was not a comfortable beginning, but our exchange opened the door eventually to new steps in the healing process for Richard, new ways of handling his grief.

Richard, for all his protests, had in this complex way blamed himself, his presumed lack of value, his assumed lack of worth. If he had had more value, been more powerful, been more important, he reasoned, then his "being more" would have made Linda less open to risk. And his presumed lack of value and assumed lack of worth made recovery from his grief immaterial. But, as Richard came to concede, the management of the grief and loss experienced by a person with intrinsic value is a quite different process from sweeping up the remains of a hapless insect whose chance demise resulted from a randomly dropped book.

One day, near the end of his work with me, Richard stated the issue with admirable brevity.

"Well," he said, "I suppose I'd better get my act together since I'm not a bug." Indeed.

Embracing the rock-bottom foundational value of our lives is the essential first step in management of pain. God calls His people out of suffering into a new thing of incredible value—a new life, a new relationship with Him. But the process of entering into that life and relationship requires far more than taking steps to increase our comfort. It is a process that requires hard choices that stretch our souls. But entering into that transformational process makes sense when we remember that, despite the pain and chaos, we continue to carry the indelible inerasable *imago dei*, the image of God.

This is the point that, in the end, both Richard and Job got right. For those who share a life form far different from bugs, getting our lives together in the face of loss and suffering is more than possibility, it is responsibility. And when we learn to walk through suffering, at the end, as James said, we learn to count it all joy, but it is joy that lies centered in the person we have become on the journey and the God whom we, like Job, have learned to see with new eyes.

Learning from the Teacher

In managing pain, charging God with failure to supervise His world properly is not particularly helpful. Patterns of self-blame that make us victims immobilize us and lead us away from the transformational process of turning to God, again and again, for His grace and promise of new life in the face of pain and failure. What helps is an agreement with God in which we agree about the potential good that can come through our loss and suffering and commit ourselves to manage our pain in ways that increase the possibility for this potential to become real in our experience. In a practical sense, we decide to get on with things. And in this context the conclusion of the Teacher, writing in the book we now know as Ecclesiastes, is comforting.

Pleasure is not the answer to the riddle of life, the Teacher wrote. I tried that—everything—and found no answers there. I examined wisdom and learning, and while I learned that being wise was better than acting foolishly, I found that death ultimately takes both the wise and foolish man, and both are soon forgotten. It is true that work can provide great satisfaction, but here too is frustration. When all the work and weariness and worry are done, death comes, and all the wealth and knowledge that have been accumulated are left behind for someone who has not worked for it. And all too often righteous men get what the wicked deserve, and wicked men get what the righteous deserve.

It is clear that God has a pattern, the old Teacher continues. There is a time for everything, for loss *and* suffering and for laughter *and* joy. But God's pattern is riddled with enigma:

> The race is not to the swift
>   or the battle to the strong.
> nor does food come to the wise
>   or wealth to the brilliant
>   or favor to the learned;
> but time and chance happen to them all.
>
> (Ecclesiastes 9:11 NIV)

The dimensions and the ultimate meaning of God's pattern lie outside human comprehension even for the wise, the Teacher concluded, no matter how hard they may try to understand.

In my search for wisdom and in my observation of people's burdens here on earth, I discovered that there is ceaseless activity, day and night. I realized that no one can discover everything God is doing under the sun. Not even the wisest people discover everything, no matter what they claim. (Ecclesiastes 8:16–17 NLT)

What, then, is the Teacher's advice?

Live life fully. "I commend the enjoyment of life, because nothing is better for a man under the sun than to eat and drink and be glad. Then joy will accompany him in his work all the days of the life God has given him under the sun" (Ecclesiastes 8:15 NIV). But do this carefully, the old Teacher cautioned, remembering this:

> Here is the conclusion of the matter:
> Fear God and keep his commandments,
> for this is the whole duty of man.
> For God will bring every deed into judgment,
> including every hidden thing,
> whether it is good or evil. (Ecclesiastes 12:13–14 NIV)

The Teacher was remarkably to the point. "Life is like it is," he concluded bluntly, "and nobody can figure it out no matter what they say. So here's my advice. Get on with it, and leave the bottom line up to God."

But what does it look like in everyday behaviors to leave the bottom line to God? What do we need to do to get on with managing our pain redemptively?

chapter 3

HOW CAN I DISCOVER
WHERE I AM?

Because pain makes us feel confused and uncertain about ourselves and our changing life circumstances, it is important to begin by orienting ourselves. The orientation process itself is not easy when we are frightened and confused, but it is a necessary first step. It is helpful to begin simply by asking, "Where am I?" then follow by asking two additional questions: "Am I alone?" and "Am I lost?"

Because pain narrows our vision and distorts our perspective, these questions are difficult to answer. Nevertheless, focusing on what we *do* know helps us to keep oriented even when we cannot describe fully our inner turmoil or the outer circumstances in which we find ourselves. It is comforting to remember that a clear vision of the beginning place comes only, paradoxically, at the end of the journey. With good stewardship of our pain we will know many things at the end that we cannot initially understand. T. S. Eliot wrote, "And the end of our exploring will be to arrive where we started and know the place for the first time."[1]

Where Am I?

Whether we like it or not, at the point of beginning we see through a glass darkly, to borrow Paul's apt phrase (1 Corinthians

13:12). We are able to identify in a general sense what has happened, of course. A person can identify the event that has led to suffering and might say, "I am experiencing bankruptcy and loss of resources"; "I am grieving, suffering the loss of a child"; "I am dealing with shame and failure"; "I am confronted by a broken marriage... a broken friendship... a forced retirement and loss of job... lost health... approaching death... lost opportunity." But even as we name the source of our pain, we are aware that we understand the circumstances of our lives only in part ourselves —we sense that we do indeed see darkly. We feel bewildered about people, events, and, at times, confused about choices we have made. We do not fully understand the journey that brought us to this place. We know with certainty only that we are not where we intended to be. We did not expect to arrive at this place of pain and suffering. We did not set out to reach this place of loss, injustice, and defeat. And we are not at all sure how to get from this place to another place where life can be better.

A sense of disorientation appears logical when we consider the facts that we face. We have arrived at a place we do not want to be. We are unsure about this unwelcome place and anxious about what it may hold. We are not sure how we arrived at this place and are even less sure how to move to a better place. Additionally, we have severe misgivings about the road that lies ahead. We know it is a road we have not traveled before, and we sense the journey may contain new dangers and bring new fears. And the effort to understand brings distress and uneasiness. To say where we are, no matter how imprecisely, and to acknowledge the unknown road ahead requires us to face the reality of the pain we are experiencing and the altered circumstances of our lives.

At this point, it helps immeasurably to take God's promise to heart and pray for wisdom (James 1:5). It may seem like a daunting project, but it is far safer and far more profitable for us to take our initial orienting steps in God's presence, seeking there for insight and understanding, coming with whatever small measure of faith and common sense we can gather up. It helps to begin by saying to God something like this:

> *As you know, God, I've thought about things over and over. The best I know, here is where I think I am.*

At this point it is important to be as honest and detailed with God and ourselves as we are able. It is likely that the account will not be pretty, but, thankfully, pretty is not necessary. Writing out a rough outline that lists crucial events and decisions is helpful preparation for this time of orienting prayer. An outline encourages us to bring directly to God each important point, however painful or humiliating, and to begin to face ourselves and our lives as they are honestly:

> *And as best I know, God, I've thought about things, and here is how I think I got here.*

At this second point it again helps to be as detailed and honest with God and ourselves as we are able. An outline here too helps keep prayer on track and encourages us to avoid the temptation to skip the messy parts.

> *But God, you know I cannot see clearly where I am or the road ahead of me, and you know I cannot know for certain where this journey will end. I need wisdom from you.*
> *Help me understand where I am, particularly if it's a different place from where I think I am. And help me see where I am, even though it's where I don't want to be. And help me know where I am, even if I resist knowing where I am.*

Sit quietly and listen. You may not become consciously aware of new wisdom, but God is faithful to keep His promise to provide wisdom when we ask. Don't hurry. Just sit with yourself and wait.

And God, show me the next step I need to take.

Then again sit quietly and wait. You are not likely to hear an audible voice, but after a while you will sense some beginning awareness of new self-knowledge and wisdom and some sense of peace. Keep your outlines (and journal entries, if you journal). Remember, this is a place of beginning, and you may need to revisit this prayer a number of times. Don't be concerned about the form or formality of your prayer—God is more interested in honesty than format. Good stewardship of pain often produces excellent but rather odd-sounding prayers. Also, keep in mind that gaining wisdom requires patience as well as faith. Seeking God's wisdom is a quite different process from "surfing the 'Net" for instant information.

Naming and describing our pain lead to clearer orientation, particularly when we carry out this process while at the same time seeking God's wisdom about our affairs. But whatever the specific findings that come from this spiritual geography session with ourselves and God, when it is finished we frequently hear ourselves saying something like, "I can't believe I'm *this* depressed," or "I can't believe my life has turned out like *this*." We are surprised and bewildered to discover our place.

Risks in the Place of Surprise

At its worst, pain has the power to loose the anchors of the soul. Such pain changes us and alters forever the contours of life as we have known it, but we often arrive poorly prepared and astonished to discover ourselves in such a place. We find ourselves in the storm before we've had opportunity to set our course, and we are threatened by drowning before we've had time to alter the set of our sails. We feel unfairly blindsided in part because of the eerie unexpectedness with which trauma sometimes walks casually into our everyday lives. We are not ambushed by surprise simply because we are foolish or lack information. We know that life brings unexpected turns in the road. We remember that James cautioned us about our tomorrows and warned us about being overly confident that our plans will play out according to schedule (James 4:13–15).

Nevertheless, knowing life's uncertainty, we go about our everyday lives—both by necessity and habit—thinking, "I need to stop by the grocery store tonight on the way home, and tomorrow I must remember to mail my sister's birthday card." Then into this cluttered but relatively cloudless space of everyday living, a bolt of cosmic lightning strikes—a routine doctor's appointment, a letter, a telephone call, a policeman at the door, a farewell note left on the kitchen table—and we find ourselves catapulted into suffering and change, our lives irreversibly altered.

In December 2003, Joan Didion and her husband, John Dunne, had just returned from visiting their hospitalized daughter Quintana, who was comatose, on life support, and suffering from septic shock. As Joan and John sat down to dinner, John suffered a massive fatal coronary. In *The Year of Magical Thinking*, Didion's memoir of this terrible time, she writes,

> Life changes fast.
> Life changes in the instant.
> You sit down to dinner and life as you
> know it ends.[2]

But this sudden catastrophic splintering of life is not the only road by which we come to a place where suffering and grief become overwhelming. Sometimes, to our surprise, we come dangerously close to drowning while wading through the brackish slow-moving backwater of broken dreams.

Those of us who grew up playing in prairie rivers remember the sensation of wading in knee-deep water, then stepping into an unexpected hole and finding ourselves suddenly in water up to our chins. The Missouri River, for example, is infamous for this characteristic. The river meanders more than two thousand miles from its headwaters in Montana to its confluence with the Mississippi at St. Louis, collecting tons of silt along the way. Big Muddy, they call it, a mile wide and an inch deep. But the river is deceptive. Under its surface there are deep holes and unsuspected currents that can trap the unwary and inexperienced. In the ballad "Waist Deep in the Big Muddy," folksinger Pete Seeger tells the story of the captain who drowned while moving his troops across the Missouri in a shallow, "safe" place. The pain that overtakes us as we are wading waist-deep in the big muddy of life is certainly as difficult to manage as life's clear catastrophes, and, arguably, perhaps more dangerous in the end.

Jane's journey began in a routine visit to her doctor, shortly after her twenty-fourth birthday. Several years later, sometime after her thirtieth birthday, Jane sat in my office, her face emptied of all expression, filling out required paperwork. "Reason for consultation?" read the form. "Infertility issues," she wrote stoically.

While her response was factually accurate, it did not reflect the emotional emergency that Jane now faced. Jane's crisis did not emerge from a sudden catastrophe, however. She was caught in emotional deep water into which, unsuspecting, she had stumbled in her long, painful effort to conceive a child.

On that first visit to her gynecologist, Jane's physician had been emotionally supportive and cautiously optimistic. However, that visit had been followed by years of complex medical procedures often marked by unrecognized, unintended humiliation for the woman patient. There had been years of questions, comments, and advice from family and friends that, while well intended, had wounded nonetheless. Sharp, private pain sneaked into joyful life events: the birthday parties with her exuberant twin nieces; the expectant celebration of baby showers for friends and family; her mother's joy in her grandmother's ring with its four representative stones (her sister's birthday gift to her mother).

And there was the pain of the struggle with her faith. Does prayer make a difference? And what was Jane to do with the anger she eventually felt when she was given one more earnestly inane explanation of God's will? And how could she best respond to the emotionally myopic practice of Mother's Day celebrations at the church she attended? And what were faith-consistent answers to the complex unexpected ethical dilemmas presented by medical choices? And there was the unavoidable continuing pressure that the fertility issue exerted on the emotional and financial well-being of the marriage.

Eventually, without her conscious awareness, as Jane worked through her struggle, day by day, year by year, her hope and her will to life eroded away. Jane was scheduled late one summer afternoon for a routine doctor's appointment. ("We just need a blood sample, dear. Won't take long.") Returning home, Jane sat in her car in the garage for a long time. She found herself thinking how easy it would be to make an end to the struggle and to the pain and, in releasing herself, to release her husband as well. Realizing the danger into which she had moved, Jane made an appointment to seek some professional help.

"How did I get to this place?" Jane asked me one day shortly after we had begun to work together. "I wasn't raised to be a quitter."

The problem did not lie, of course, in a character defect in Jane. Her emergency surfaced suddenly out of her undramatic but dangerous gradual journey into life in a broken dream, enduring day through dateless day, her hope denied. It was then, unexpectedly, on one common unremarkable day in that long, stretched-out journey that Jane drifted down—unsuspecting— into an unmarked hole of deep despair.

The words (and tears) that we use to describe the ways in which suffering alters our inner selves and our lives reflect the experience of being flooded with feelings that seem too intense and too painful to endure. Our words reflect too our sense of powerful change, of finding ourselves, whether by sudden or gradual journey, now facing life in a new and frightening place where the landmarks for daily living have been irreversibly altered. This sense of surprise, linked with the experience of feeling overwhelmed by emotions and circumstances we cannot control, evokes a number of responses. We are often angry. We often experience a strong impulse to "take charge" of everything within our reach and more.

Anger

Anger is one of the early responses to this sense of surprise. It is important to differentiate this response from the deep, thoughtful anger that the Psalms encourage us to recognize and express to God. In contrast, this initial anger is a flash-in-the-pan kind of thing, a quick flare of intense irritation, parallel to the intense automatic anger we feel when in the dark we accidentally stub our toe on a chair or bump our head on a cabinet door left open. We are hurt—unexpectedly hurt—and (we feel) undeservedly hurt. At this point it is all too easy to strike out at others simply because they are within striking distance.

Charles Schulz, the great cartoonist who gave us Charlie Brown and the Peanuts gang, understood this well. One sunny winter day, Lucy, on her way home from school, walked under the eaves of a roof loaded with snow. Just as Lucy walked by, the snow, warmed by the sun, unexpectedly slid off the eaves, burying Lucy, book bag and all. Lucy dug herself out, shook off the snow, and started for home with a very grim look on her face. As she came around the corner she met—who else—Charlie Brown, walking peacefully down the street. Lucy marched up to Charlie Brown and, without a word, hit him—POW!—knocking Charlie Brown head over heels into a nearby snowdrift.

"Why did you do that?" asked a confused Charlie Brown, struggling to extricate himself from the snow.

"Well," said Lucy with her impeccable logic, "somebody's got to pay."

At the surprise stage of pain we are often more like Lucy than we care to admit. However, if we recognize the impulse to strike out, we can exert some conscious control of it. Recognizing this about ourselves, we can often structure the amount of time we spend in potentially difficult situations and with difficult people. Knowing that our controls, like Lucy's, are apt to be thin at this time, we are wise to plan carefully and to seek the help of friends who have the skills and understanding to buffer us from situations and individuals who may easily trigger our "Lucy" responses. We are more likely to deal constructively with our pain if we understand that initially we must manage the quick anger that frequently accompanies the surprise factor.

Impulse to control

Surprise triggers an unhelpful impulse to control as well. Just as we respond intuitively to our hurt with anger, we often respond to our sense of changing circumstances with the impulse to control. Whether we arrive at the place of pain and change by gradual journey or by sudden event, we find ourselves determined to "take charge" of things and make the circumstances better. Our intuitive sense is that the pain and the change can be altered by the human solution of power—we just need to "power up" and take charge of events and people and make things better. This is, of course, the very thing we cannot do. In the cycle of life, when we find ourselves in those times of grief, of loss and the scattering of stones, we do not have the option of saying, "Stop this process. I have decided to have my life go differently from this point on."

Paradoxically, however, there is an important element of power in pain management, as we will see, but it lies in the power to cope rather than to control. "For God has not given us a spirit of fear and timidity, but of power, love and self-discipline" (2 Timothy 1:7 NLT), Paul reminded Timothy at a time when Timothy was facing difficult circumstances. By God's empowering grace, we may cope triumphantly with change, but we cannot by sheer human effort prevent its occurrence. God's grace provides more than sufficient power to cope, but it does not permit us to control life so that it reflects our choices and serves our comfort. And if in our initial surprise we focus on exerting power over events and people, this misplaced emphasis can interfere seriously with our progress in learning to control ourselves (something by the Spirit's empowering that we *can* do) in the midst of those life circumstances that we cannot change or control.

Revisiting self-blame

Surprise can tempt us to revisit the "why" questions and re-enter the miserable process of self-blame. Neither of these responses is helpful, as we have discussed earlier. Surprise can, however, tempt us to do both, even though we know that these patterns of thinking do not aid us in making good things happen in the midst of our pain. Self-blame can dangerously increase our sense that events have reduced us to victim status and can immobilize our efforts to undertake productive management of pain.

Dealing with Bad Advice

In the early surprise stages of pain, we are often flooded with advice, some of which is unhelpful and can unintentionally intensify our pain and confuse the choices available to us.

Inevitably, some of our friends, hearing and seeing the devastating impact of our suffering, respond much like Job's friends. They don't know what to say, and while our friends don't often sit down on the ground with us like Job's friends, they are appalled at our pain and wait, hoping that somehow things will get better. But when, as in Job's case, things do not become better, they too can be tempted into well-meaning but unwise speech. While we are in this initial stage of surprise, still learning to chart our course, it is easy to be confused by two fine-sounding but unhelpful pieces of advice.

These pieces of advice can be summarized simply. The first has a fine religious ring to it: "Just take your burdens to God. God will help you." The second is a good specimen of bootstrap philosophy: "Just hang on. You can make it. Just hang on."

Obviously, there is some valuable truth here. God is indeed our source of refuge in trouble. Equally clearly, from the human standpoint, the choice to persevere through difficulty is central to the process of bringing about good things from trouble. The problem is that both of these pieces of advice recommend two things that we are unable to do, at least in the form of action the advice recommends.

Take It to God? Where? How?

On first glance, the advice to take our burdens to God seems an indisputably good idea. This advice has a deceptive appearance, however. It can multiply problems rather than solve them. The problem is apparent, once we look logically at the proposed solution: In order to take our burdens to God, we have to know where God is. At this point, the advice to take our burdens to God can be dangerous because, unwittingly, it can lead away from a biblical answer to the important question of God's whereabouts in time of trouble.

"My pastor just doesn't get it," a client said one day in angry anguish. "He says just take my burdens to Jesus and leave them there. It's good advice, and I'd be glad to take it if I could just figure out how to do it. God knows how glad I'd be to dump this stuff on Jesus if I could. But that's the problem: I can't find God—*I can't find Him.* How can I take my burdens to somebody I can't find, talk to somebody who isn't there anymore?"

When we are feeling overwhelmed and disoriented in our pain, the first dangerous presupposition implied in the take-it-to-God approach is that God is in a place somewhere else—removed from the dilemma of our suffering, detached from our experience of agony, perhaps, at minimal best, watching as an interested celestial on-looker as we struggle to deal with our earthly pain. The take-it-to-God idea implies at least indirectly the dangerous idea that if we want God to become involved actively in the solution to our problem, God must first be found. When we attempt seriously the take-it-to-God approach, we soon find ourselves thinking, "I *want* to take this to God. I *need* to take this to God. Somehow I've *got* to take this to God. It's too much for me alone. Somehow I must go to Him wherever He is. But how do I do this, dragging this unbearably heavy burden of loss and pain? To find the relief only He can give, I must go to Him where He is. But how do I know where God is?"

Whether dealing with our own pain or that of others, the idea that we need connection with God in order to survive is correct. One of the great gains we can make from having to deal with pain is the practical understanding of our limitations that we soon acquire. We can't do it alone, and that reality, if no other, leads us (once we permit it to do so) into a new and deeper relationship with God. The problem does not lie in the idea of the need for connection with God. The problem lies in the idea that we have to find God, that we must somehow hunt God up in some cherubim-guarded heavenly dwelling place and take ourselves and our burden to Him there. This idea tempts us to think that *wherever it is that we are* in our pain, *God is somewhere else.*

Logically, "carrying burdens to God" requires at a minimal bottom line that the burden bearer know where God is or at least has some idea where God can be found. It requires also that the burden bearer have the strength to drag an aching heart into God's presence. It requires too the faith to believe that this God who has not voluntarily come to our place of suffering will receive us, wounded as we are, and help—providing that God can be found.

For this reason, making God a destination problem to be solved by some super-spiritual guidance system becomes mockery for people in pain. For the most part, we are already grappling with the "where" question. Telling us to go to God simply intensifies the terrifying aloneness we already feel. It is our sense that our pain has loosed the very anchors of life, and we are now adrift, if not already lost.

I once had a client who, after years of service in her company, had been fired legally but unjustly only months before she became eligible for retirement. She had been advised that she had no legal basis for appeal. She came for help because she was depressed. She was indeed depressed, but she was also suffering from the pain of injustice, from justice denied, and from an exhausted fear of her future. She had faith issues as well.

"How are you doing?" I asked her one day at the beginning of an hour together.

"I don't honestly know how to answer that," she said. "I just keep going over it—how could they do that to me after all these years? But they did it, and there's nothing I can do. Well, I don't know how I'm doing or where I am, to tell the truth. One of the scariest things about this is that I feel like I've lost God. I don't know where God was when this was happening, and I don't know where God is now that it's over. I can't take my troubles to Him even if I wanted to because I don't know where He is. Maybe God fired me too—feels like He transferred me to Permanent Misery with no vacation and no benefits."

We smiled. Then she added sadly, "I wish I knew where God is."

The second dangerous aspect of the take-it-to-God advice is its potential to confuse us about the human necessity to live through the experience of pain. The take-it-to-God approach indirectly implies that God runs a celestial emergency room somewhere in which (if we can only find Him) our pain can be instantly erased. It is wishful thinking, but with a spiritual twist. Clearly God didn't keep me from having this pain, we think, but if I find Him surely He'll fix it so I won't have to live through it.

Contrary to such thinking, God refuses to play the magician's role, nor is God in the business of providing free placebos or heavenly strength aspirin. The idea that if we can only get our burdens to God He will make us instantly feel better is bitterly unfair misdirection to people in pain. It forms a serious barrier to a grace-based process of bringing good things out of our pain.

God did not promise pain-free living to His people or instant alleviation of the pain that occurs on our life journey. To suggest that God grants His people a permanent exemption to pain opens the door by way of simple logic to the possibility that our pain indicates we are not members of the family of God. Or, equally alarming, it suggests the possibility that while we may be members of the family of God, we are members to whom God chooses to break His promise.

Additionally, this kind of focus on God as the great pain reliever leads us away from the biblical answer to the "where" question. By simple logic, this "fix-it" approach makes pain a measure of our distance from God. Indirectly, this idea encourages us to think, "If I hurt, I'm a long way from God. If I were close to Him, He would make the hurt go away. Where am I? My pain tells me that I am a long way from God."

In dealing with suffering, our own or that of others, it simply cannot be said too often or too plainly: Pain cannot be used either as a measure of God's absence or as evidence of His lack of love. God is, as Paul pointed out to the Corinthians, the father of compassion and the God of all comfort (2 Corinthians 1:3–7). That is an identity quite different, however, from the idea of God as the "Great Pain Reliever."

When we focus on finding God as the "Great Pain Reliever," it becomes tragically easy to walk past the God of all comfort and to miss entirely His compassionate presence. He is the suffering God who understands suffering, Alfred North Whitehead once observed. When life has cut our hearts to shivering ribbons, God knows our pain and cares as only He can care. But in God's comforting presence, pain can still feel overwhelming, and the necessity to live through it can still seem more than we can bear.

Stewardship is a matter of making our pain count for good. In order to do this, we must be absolutely clear about what pain does *not* mean. The presence of pain does not mean God is not present, nor does the presence of pain mean that God does not care. However, in the process of living through the experience of pain, we learn—often to our initial dismay—that God declines to be reduced to a spiritual pain pill. He is, blessedly, the God of all comfort, but He refuses to make removal of pain (His own or ours) His first priority.

In our suffering, God is interested in far more than administering anesthesia or stitching us up skillfully so that the scar tissue will not show. Our loving parent-God takes no pleasure in His children's suffering, nor is He the source of our pain. Indeed, He cares about us and for us in our pain; that is the unchanging expression of His character, the truth of who He is. And He remains the ultimate compassionate source of all comfort. But in God's economy, good stewardship of pain is inextricably linked to the transformation of our character. He cares about our pain. However, He cares even more about the person we are becoming as we make our painful way through a broken world. A fallen creation and the wrenching reality of human limitations make pain inevitable, though not by His design. Thinking of the unavoidable, Jesus said gently to His followers, "Here on earth you will have many trials and sorrows" (John 16:33 NLT). But if in this world pain is inevitable, the impact of pain on the state of our souls is not. We get to choose about that. That is what stewardship is all about.

The Hang-On Approach

The first time that I saw it I instantly formed an intense dislike for a poster that was popular some years back. On the poster a kitten with an anguished expression was hanging on a rope, clinging desperately to a large knot at the end of the rope. "Hang on," ran the heading across the bottom of the poster, in what looked like 48-point type. Had it been economically possible for me to do so, I would have purchased every one of those miserable posters on the spot and taken them home and burned them.

Hang on, indeed. And what was the alternative?

I assume that the poster was intended to evoke the viewer's smile. In life, as in buildings, we can indeed climb into places from which an exit is difficult, if not impossible, without help. Hanging on in those conditions is a necessity, not an option, and few of us need to be instructed to do so. Having attempted to rescue my share of kittens as a child, I know with what frantic strength those little claws hold that rope. The terrified kitten could not *not* hang on. I know from experience the rescuer has great difficulty in getting a kitten to release its hold in order for it to be lifted to safety. In rescue, letting go, not hanging on, is the difficult issue.

It is quite likely that I misunderstood the original point of the poster. Perhaps there is something humorous in stating the obvious—telling the kitten to hang on is certainly the epitome of unnecessary advice, close kin to the irritatingly unnecessary advice we commonly receive in daily life. Perhaps there is another point I missed entirely. But nothing about that poster ever seemed funny or clever or insightful to me, no matter how many times over the years I saw it. In real life, being at the end of the rope is a dreadful experience for kittens or for humans.

Presumably, since the poster was human-only communication, its message had no impact in the feline world. In contrast, the hang-on message has enormous impact in the world of suffering people. And, like the take-it-to-God message, the hang-on advice is a difficult mixture of helpful and unhelpful ideas.

For the most part, people who send the hang-on message mean for it to be encouraging and reassuring. They mean to communicate their faith in our strength to survive the circumstances and the pain. In some instances, they wish to communicate as well their understanding (often gained through their own suffering) that changes will come. No matter how long the night may seem, the morning does eventually dawn. And the hang-on message reflects too the enormous importance that our personal choice can make in the midst of pain and destructive life circumstances. As we will see in greater detail later, the recognition of strength in the context of pain, the anticipation of the positive impact of time, and the acceptance of the basic bottom-line significance of choice are all essential factors in pain management. But for all its good implications, the hang-on message often has some unintended negative consequences when we are caught in pain and its surrounding life circumstances and find ourselves unable to extricate ourselves from them.

In the first place, the message unintentionally communicates a serious misunderstanding of what we are experiencing. When we are caught up in pain, emotional or physical, intuitively we *do* hang on—to someone's hand, to the sound of a voice, to a memory, and sometimes, grimly, to the edge of a bed if that's all we can reach in the dark. We *do* hang on, at times with frantic intensity. To be told to do what we are already doing with all our remaining strength is not helpful and deepens the sense of alienation that comes with suffering. We hear the message and think that those around us simply don't understand, that they have no real connection with us in the pain-filled world through which we are making our way. Do they not see or understand that we are doing all that we can do? We wish for the energy to say, "Hang on, indeed! And what exactly is it you think I am doing if this isn't hanging on? And what else besides hanging on is there for me to do?"

But there are terrible times when pain has indeed loosed the anchors. Overwhelmed, at these times we sometimes abandon all conscious effort to hold on to life as it has been and cling only lightly to life itself. In this context the hang-on message has a grimly ludicrous incongruity. Our strength is gone—and desire too. We are aware only of the exhausted emptiness that tempts us to a final abandonment to the dark.

"My mom says 'hang on,'" a client said one day. "I can't 'hang on,' however that looks. And I don't want to even if I could. I don't want to be connected to anything or anyone anymore."

At such a time the hang-on message does nothing to stop the dark downward drift. In the face of the overwhelming pain, it does nothing to strengthen our choice to live either. Instead it carries the mocking incongruity and added pain of an exhortation to eat when the house is utterly empty of all food.

The "Hang on! You can do it!" message is sometimes expanded by an additional idea that is phrased this way: "Hang on! God will not give you more than you can bear." The problem at this point is, again, the confusing mix of truth and error this idea contains.

It is true, thankfully, that God knows our limitations and acts tenderly, gently, in response to these limitations. He tempers the wind to the shorn lamb; the dimly burning flax he does not quench (Isaiah 42:3 NIV). He knows how weak and fragile we are. That, thankfully, is a truth on which we can stake our lives.

Unfortunately, when we are feeling overwhelmed, when life seems to have delivered trouble far beyond our limited strength to cope, at these times we are not at all convinced that God is as cautious as He should be in regard to the load we are carrying. Under these circumstances it is not easy to view God as a concerned parent. It is far easier to think of God as a celestial quality-control expert who, without our permission, enrolled us in a life endurance contest. On our worst days we suspect that God may be adding straw after intolerable straw in some finely calibrated test designed to determine precisely the number of straws that can be added before we break. To be reassured that God will not add the last proverbial straw that will break our backs is cold comfort indeed.

Further, it begs our more fundamental question. Where is the God who promised that His yoke is easy and His burden light? Where is He? It is this God whom we long to find. It is to Him that we long to run and there lay down our heavy load. We do not want to hang on. We do not want to demonstrate strength and endurance. We want only to lay our burdens down. We long to find the God who lifts burdens—not gives them—so that there, free from our pain, we can lie safely down to sleep.

Reorientation

Pain inevitably produces a myopic view and a narrow focus on the circumstances themselves. But if we are to survive and thrive, then hopefully sooner rather than later we find that we need to stop, take a look at the big picture, and consider some reorientation.

At this place, if we choose to do so, it is possible to take stock of where we have been. At this point we are usually able to see that:

- pursuit of the "why" question does not bring either comfort or increased skills in managing the pain and its surrounding life circumstances
- self-blame neither eases the pain or gives clear direction for its management
- emotional surprise often triggers misplaced anger and unsuccessful attempts to control circumstances and people
- emotional self-effort (increased effort to hang on) does not decrease the pain or make it easier to handle
- spiritual self-effort (taking things to God), while better than other options, does not produce an appreciable increase in emotional strength and spiritual maturity

But past understanding these things, we do not feel certain about much of anything except the pain—and our awareness of that is all too constant and real. And with that we have a deeply unsettling sense of disorientation. We know that life will not be the same again. We have no promise of a sure terminal point for our pain, and we have no assurance of an earthly Promised Land for our journey's end. We feel adrift and overwhelmed.

But at this point we can reshape our sense of our experience if we follow, "Where am I?" with two other questions. It helps to ask "Am I alone?" and "Am I lost?" Both questions stretch our faith. But considering these questions can help us place boundaries around our pain and increase our sense of safety despite the uncertainty of the journey ahead.

Am I Alone?

This question presents a classic example of an instance in which the way we form the question determines the answer. If we ask, in effect, "Do I *feel* alone?" then the answer is certainly yes. Despite the fact that we may know differently intellectually, we feel alone—walled into our grief, our anger, our loss—alone in our pain-filled world where the very foundations shake beneath our feet.

My client whose daughter had been murdered attended a support group for parents of children who had died by violent means.

"I was horrified at the number of people there," she told me. "The room was filled. I don't think there were more than a half-dozen empty chairs." She paused and then added, "But I don't think I have ever felt so utterly alone in my life. Everybody had their story, but their stories didn't change the horror of my own. Their pain didn't make my loss any less." While we cannot eliminate it entirely, surprisingly, there is something we can do about this sense of aloneness.

If you've ever taken a basic psychology class you probably remember a figure consisting of two lines running down the center of a page. Depending on the way in which you looked at the figure, the lines formed two faces looking directly at each other or the outline of a vase. While the lines did not move or change, the reality you saw (faces or vase) was the result of your choice. You saw what you chose to see.

We face a choice much like the face/vase option in orienting ourselves in the midst of our pain and confusion. If we shape our sense of reality exclusively on the basis of our emotional sense of our world (our felt aloneness), this choice becomes a self-fulfilling prophecy that turns our world into a dangerously empty place. We do feel alone. And in deeply felt ways, we are alone. That is real. But in the tradition of the face/vase dualism, it is not the only truth on which we can focus. We have a choice.

The biblical text is blessedly unambiguous at this point. Whatever our human sense of our experience, we are not alone. The reality of the context in which we can choose to work out the pain and loss includes God's continuing intimate presence with us in Christ. His name is Immanuel, "God with us," the one who promised never to leave or forsake us (Hebrews 13:5b). "Bidden or not bidden, God is present," was carved over the door of the home of Carl Jung, the great Swiss psychologist. Sensed or not sensed, God walks with us on the journey. We are not alone. Solving the aloneness problem is *not* about persuading God to come be present with us. Actually, the astonishing truth of the matter is that God's presence is one of the things about which we do *not* have a choice. To our utter surprise—and out of His unmerited grace—God has chosen to be with us and *steadfastly refuses to unmake that choice.*

However, as time goes by, we discover (to our dismay) that God's presence and our sense of His presence are not synonymous. He is with us always, but we are not always able to sense His presence. At times the way can seem lonely indeed, the rooms empty and dark, with no sense of His presence anywhere. We may *feel* utterly alone. At that point our choice is not about His presence. He is there. But in the face of our felt aloneness, we must choose to act in terms of His presence, felt or unfelt, and the knowledge of His presence must be the framework for our experience of suffering. His presence, sensed or unsensed, provides the great safe holding place in which all things can be lived through—our anger, our shame, our loss, our empty sense of abandonment, and our bitter experience of betrayal, our unyielding pain.

In the preface of *Psalms of Lament*,[3] Ann Weems writes,

In the quiet times this image comes to me: Jesus weeping.
Jesus wept,
    and in his weeping
    he joined himself forever
    to those who mourn.
He stands now throughout all time,
    this Jesus weeping,
    with his arms about the weeping ones:
"Blessed are those who mourn,
    for they shall be comforted."
He stands with the mourners,
    for his name is God-with-us...

Good stewardship of our pain requires us to choose to act upon His presence, sensed or unsensed, as the framework for our lives. He stands with us by His sovereign loving choice, but we must choose in faith to count His presence as the safe holding place into which we can bring our pain.

Am I Lost?

When we ask "Where am I?" another question lurks just beneath the surface. If I am not sure where I am, am I lost? If we count on God's commitment to be with us, we will understand that we are not alone. But knowing we are not alone is not the same as knowing where we are or where we are going. One of the most difficult aspects of pain is the sense of uncertainty and disorientation that accompanies it. What will our lives—we and our relationships—look like at the end of this journey, we wonder. We are unsure about where we are and unclear about where we are going. We feel unsure about almost everything except our pain—it is with us always—and our sense of change. Nothing, we suspect, will be the same. In the context of this uncertainty and our powerlessness to control our changing world, it is no surprise that we find ourselves wondering, "Am I lost?"

One woman client had a deep faith and a wickedly clever sense of humor. The year her husband was sentenced to prison for embezzlement, she told me that she had considered giving God an atlas as a Christmas gift. She explained that she thought giving God a set of earthly maps might send His heavenly self a hint that she would like some indication that He knew where He was leading in the chaos of her life.

"I know I'm lost," she said, "but on some days I'm beginning to think God may be lost too." Her laughter did not quite cover her tears.

Settling the issue of our sense of being lost, however, is much like settling the issue of aloneness. This sense of being lost is logical in the context of disorientation and change. Feeling lost is reality; we do not imagine it. It is there. But, again, in the face/ vase context, feeling lost is not the only reality upon which we can choose to focus.

A picture of this alternative reality occurs in one of the psalms written by David. Although he had been anointed by Samuel as Israel's king, David lived for a number of years in exile from the court, fleeing Saul's hatred and determined efforts to kill him. In those terrible years, David fled from camp to camp, often hungry, surrounded by enemies, vulnerable to betrayal and palace intrigue, his kingship a distant dream. David must have felt many times that he was lost. Psalm 139:1–10 (NLT) records what David learned in the course of those pain-filled troubled years.

> O LORD, you have examined my heart
>> and know everything about me.
> You know when I sit down or stand up.
>> You know my thoughts even when I'm far away.
> You see me when I travel
>> and when I rest at home.
>> You know everything I do.
> You know what I am going to say
>> even before I say it, LORD.
> You go before me and follow me.
>> You place your hand of blessing on my head.
> Such knowledge is too wonderful for me,
>> too great for me to understand!
>
> I can never escape from your Spirit!
>> I can never get away from your presence!
> If I go up to heaven, you are there;
>> if I go down to the grave, you are there.
> If I ride the wings of the morning,
>> if I dwell by the farthest oceans,
> even there your hand will guide me,
>> and your strength will support me.

We are not lost. Indeed, we cannot be lost. God charts the path we follow; He both precedes and follows us. If we make our bed in hell, God is there. If we ride on the wings of the morning, God is there. "There is no place I can go away from your Spirit," David sang. "There is no place where you will not guide and support me." When the dark times come, when all the familiar markers of life have vanished, we have a choice. We can focus on our overwhelming sense of being lost. That is a powerful reality. But we have an option. There is no place that we may wander where God has not preceded and followed us. There is no place that is a stranger to His presence, no place His guidance and support do not reach. We cannot be alone. We cannot be lost. We can focus on this reality and rest.

But pain has the power to shake us loose from an awareness of these truths. And at such times it takes all our remaining strength and courage to agree with God. We find ourselves saying like the agonized father who sought healing for his suffering son, "I do believe; help me overcome my unbelief!" (Mark 9:24 NIV). And on the worst of days, we can find ourselves saying, "Oh, God, I do not believe, but I wish I could. Please let that count for something."

And it does, by God's grace. It does. One of the good things that can result from the journey through pain is a whole new awareness of God's mercy and His sustaining grace. When we can no longer hold on, He can—and does. When we can no longer see our way, He knows the path and walks with us there.

chapter 4

HOW CAN I THINK CONSTRUCTIVELY ABOUT PAIN?

God does not waste our pain," we sometimes say. This saying may reflect accurately God's skill in dealing with our human dilemma, but it begs the question that lies closer to home: Can *we* waste our pain? The answer to that question is, of course, yes. But we also know that wasting our pain is not our only option. We understand that lemons can certainly be used to make lemonade; our dilemma stems from the fact that we can be quite clear about the lemon-lemonade connection without understanding the recipe for making it happen. For the most part, we believe that we can make good use of our pain, and we are motivated to do so. The problem lies in our lack of knowledge and skill.

The beliefs and behaviors that characterize effective pain management are no great mystery, however. Individuals who live productively through pain and difficult circumstances act in ways that can be described in common, everyday terms. While the principles of good pain management can be described simply, in practice they are lived out in everyday life through complex patterns of human behavior.

For example, people who are good stewards of their pain characteristically believe that they will survive their pain and are, therefore, less frightened by it. This fact can be expressed as a simple guideline for managing pain: *Concentrate on surviving.*

Life is bigger than pain, and pain does not have the power to take life away. Choose life.

When we think about the application of this guideline in everyday life, however, we are confronted immediately with the complexity of human responses. For example, suppose that Mister-Joke-and-Talk-a-Lot and Miss Privately-Reserved-and-Silent have each managed difficult pain-filled life circumstances very well. Throughout their experience, each held in common the effective pain manager's basic belief: *My life is more than my pain, and I will not die from this pain. I can choose to survive.* However, we would expect Mister-Joke-and-Talk-a-Lot to express this common basic belief in one fashion and Miss-Private-Reserved-and-Silent to express it in quite another way. Stating general principles for managing pain in simple, practical terms is possible and helpful for those interested in learning. Nevertheless, these general principles lead to effective pain management only when individuals work them out in specific behaviors that fit with their real-life circumstances, personality, and lifestyle.

The really good news about pain management skills, however, does not lie in the fact that they can be described. The good news is that once these attitudes and actions are identified, they can be learned. These are skills that can be acquired.

As is frequently the case, however, this good news brings some less-than-good news with it as well. Mastery and application of these skills is, for the most part, on-the-job training, skills learned by necessity while we are living out our life experience of pain. Learning to swim happens while we are in the water, not while we are sitting on the side of the pool. We can certainly strengthen our muscles while on dry land, but learning to swim happens *in* the pool, a regrettably unyielding fact for those who of us who are afraid of water. In a parallel sense, learning to make good use of our pain is a learning-while-living process, one that requires learning in a less-than-comfortable environment. This experience is more like learning to swim upstream against a river's dangerous current than wading in a neighborhood pool. Difficult as it may be, it is possible, however, to learn to make good use of our pain while we live through the experience. This process often tests our faith and stretches our souls. It stretches our minds as well. Consciously tolerating emotionally unwelcome questions while we are learning is an uncomfortable experience, but one that pays rich dividends. Rainer Maria Rilke, the great German poet, attempted to explain this in a letter to a student:

> I beg you… to be patient toward all that is unsolved in your heart and to try to love the questions themselves… Do not now seek the answers which cannot be given you because you would not be able to live them… Live the questions now. Perhaps you will then gradually, without noticing it live along some distant day into the answer.[1]

At times this "lived-into" wisdom comes with little fanfare and in small segments. In a final appointment a client once commented, "One of the hardest things was not being able to see any possible good in this mess. But this morning—and I can't tell you when this happened—I can see a little clearer. There's at least a small good for Lisa in the way this has worked out."

For the practicing Christian, this learning is more than effective life management skills, although at one level it is that. For the faith-focused individual, this learning also occurs in the context of discipleship. Authentic discipleship requires us to live out our faith (and our questions), to work out our salvation in the process of living, including the unwelcome task of living through difficult life circumstances and through the questions that arise.

"Be very careful, then, how you live," Paul encouraged the Christians at Ephesus, "not as unwise but as wise, making the most of every opportunity" (Ephesians 5:15–16 NIV). Stewardship of our pain as a part of our discipleship entails taking advantage of the opportunity pain offers, an opportunity most of us would certainly decline if we could. However, since we cannot decline our ration of life's pain, it is faithful discipleship as well as spiritual and emotional good sense to learn to manage this pain in ways that lead to our good and God's glory.

Managing pain begins with thinking about pain itself and facing the questions pain brings. What we believe about pain and the answers we give these questions determines what we are able to do and shapes the choices we make. Clear thinking—indeed, thinking at all—when we are in pain is not an easy task, but it remains the essential first step toward effective management. What we do with our pain is shaped by the way in which we think about pain and the outcomes of pain that, by God's grace, we believe we can expect.

Initially our thinking may be confused. However, we learn—or re-learn—some empowering truths about ourselves and our journey through the great cycle of life (Ecclesiastes 3:1–8) when we choose to fully experience our pain rather than run away from it. We find ourselves exploring truths we knew in other sunnier days but embracing them in our pain with a startling new level of understanding. We discover along the way that, as Rilke suggested, we have lived into some answers that surprise us. And like Job, we sometimes find that we have arrived at a new place of peace that leaves some unanswered questions in God's hands. While our questions and answers continue to be revisited and revised on the journey, development of pain management skills begins with the answers we give to six basic questions.

Can I Survive This Pain?

In the process of managing pain, we are faced at once with our basic beliefs about pain. Does pain have the power to destroy our lives? Can pain be managed in a way that will result in positive outcomes?

Nothing, Paul wrote, absolutely nothing can separate us from God (Romans 8:38). We also know, however, that it is possible for that portion of Paul's letter to the Romans to rest securely in the memory banks of our heads at the same time that a great deal of uncertainty resides in our hearts. But those who learn to manage pain well believe that life and God are bigger than their pain. They enter into their struggle with their pain and their unanswered questions, clinging to an Easter understanding of life. They place their present story, however difficult, in the context of God's story. They remember that after Saturday's silent dark, God's life-giving sovereignty brought an open tomb and new life on that first Easter morning. They trust that their lives—including their doubts and their pain—continue to be lived out in the presence of this Eastering God who brings new life out of the dark. There is a characteristic pragmatism in this thinking.

My pain is what it is—my pain. I did not choose this pain. I cannot avoid this pain. But life and God are bigger than my pain, and I am more than my suffering. In this pain I can choose life. I can choose to live productively through this pain.[2]

It is what it is: pain. But that is all that it is: my pain. It is not evidence of my inadequacy, my unloveableness, or the absence of my worth. It is neither proof of my personal culpability nor evidence of the absence of God.

The cycle of life is what it is: laughter and tears; gain and loss; joy and pain. In the cycle of my life I have come to this season of pain. I cannot go around it, but I can and will go through it. I can survive. And I choose to do more than survive. I choose to live in a way that permits good things to emerge from this time of pain. I count upon God's promise that I can be more than conqueror in all things (Romans 8:37).

In this pain, I choose life. In the present darkness of my soul and disordered circumstances, I choose life. In wordless faith in an Eastering God, I choose to live.

Those who manage pain well believe with fierce intensity that pain is something that happens to and in them, they can nevertheless choose life and effective living in the midst of their pain. They do not believe that this choice is easy. No one who has endured intense pain, physical or emotional, denies the temptation that comes with pain at its worst. Like Job, we may long for death to end our suffering. But as Job makes clear, managing pain begins with choosing life in the midst of pain.

At times, pain can make us feel as though we are tethered to life by only the thinnest thread and that all our strength is gone. And at that moment, we can be tempted to give pain a power it does not have. Overwhelmed by fear and exhaustion, in that moment we can believe that pain is stronger than life. Caught in that misbelief, we can relinquish life and start the dark, downward spiral toward death. But yielding to pain's impact is a choice, not a necessity. Pain does not have the power to take life away. We can choose life when pain tempts us to relinquish life to regain relief. But the struggle to choose life in this dark time is easier for those who remember that Friday's devastation and Saturday's silence were followed by Sunday's empty tomb. We serve an Eastering God whose death and resurrection make the choice to live a matter of triumphant logic even in the darkest hours.

Choosing life in faithful stewardship of pain does not deny, however, that death too is a part of the cycle of life. It is interesting that individuals who have dealt successfully with pain over a long lifetime often have a deep inner sense of closure when their cycle of life is complete.

My friend's father survived a life filled with trouble and struggle. Pain was no stranger to him. He was orphaned when he was six, separated from his siblings, and sent to a relative to live. In his uncle's house he had a bed under the attic eaves, clothes to keep him decent, and food enough to survive, but life and the people around him were hard. He dropped out of school and moved from place to place seeking employment. He survived military service in World War I, the loss of his farm during the dustbowl years, the death of a daughter, the death of his wife, partial blindness, depression, and the loss of his home again at the end of his life when he was no longer able to live alone. Despite his pain and loss, he was remembered for his wit, his storytelling, and his cheerful acceptance of the ups and downs of life. But one autumn, the year he was ninety-six, while still in apparent good physical health, he began to withdraw from life; he became disinterested in food and the activities around him. Within a short time, he died peacefully in his sleep. Relinquishing life when our journey is finished is a quite different matter from permitting pain to pry us loose from life before our time.

Can I Survive This Loss?

Loss confronts us with the question of what is essential in our lives. When we are struggling with the pain that comes with loss, we must grapple with the significance we have attached to personal characteristics, material things, and human relationships. Individuals who are good stewards of pain believe that life is not determined by those things that can be changed or lost; consequently, they believe that they can survive their loss, however great it may be, whatever the pain their loss may bring.

There is a characteristic pragmatism about survivor thinking that grows out of something like this:

This loss is what it is: loss.

My disbelief insists this loss has not happened. My anger insists this loss must not happen to me. But I know. My pain and my grief say this loss cannot be denied. This loss is real.

In the great cycle of life there is gain and *loss, both the piling up of boundary stones and the scattering of stones. In the cycle of my life I have come now to this place of loss and scattered stones (Ecclesiastes 3:5). Things I deeply valued are lost. Love and relationships are lost. My dreams are shattered. The world I knew has gone away.*

But life is bigger than this loss. This loss does not deplete my essential worth. This loss cannot destroy my capacity for life unless I choose to give it the power to do so.

There is great pain in this loss. I name it for what it is: loss that I cannot undo. But life is not determined by those things that can be lost. In the empty space of this loss I can choose life. I choose to live through this loss, to come through this loss into a place of new beginnings and new things.

Loss comes in the cycle of life, but time shapes and holds the boundaries of its place. Winter is followed by spring. In this time of loss I remember the God I serve is the God of new things who has my well-being at heart.

Loss surprises us. Loss bewilders us as well. And loss entangles us in issues of identity and relationship with ourselves, with others, and, at times, with God.

A cancer patient may think, "I have lost my breast. What does this loss mean? In losing this part of my body have I lost part of my feminine self? And will this body loss mean loss of relationship with the man I love?"

"I have lost my job, my house, and my savings," an individual may mourn. And then wonder, "What does it mean in my relationship with my friends when I have no money to buy a latte at the coffee shop? When I shop for clothes at a thrift store? What will it mean to my place in our family if our daughter has to leave college?"

And sometimes, in times of betrayal and lost relationships, we feel an odd sense of vulnerability in our relationship with God. In a wordless shame we cannot explain, we wonder, *How does God view me now, standing naked in this place of loss?* And then, *Will God too go away when He sees me stripped and broken in this empty place? Will this loss lead to loss in my relationship with God?*

The pain associated with loss inevitably brings us to grips with our beliefs about scarcity. The pain we experience with loss itself becomes intensified by our fear that loss brings with it scarcity that we cannot endure. We fear that loss of love and relationships will lead to an emptiness we cannot survive, that the loss of things, social position, and power will leave us stripped of value and worth and that with loss of health, our productivity will vanish as well. We think fearfully that our loss means that we will not have enough— enough friends, enough money, enough sex, enough love, enough opportunity, or, in a soul-crisis with God, enough faith.

In a consumer culture that believes there is never enough, dealing with the pain of loss requires us to take hold of a radically countercultural belief. The biblical narrative stories of God's people make clear that loss is painful and can result in permanently life-altering circumstances, but *loss is not fatal.* Loss is what it is: loss. We can choose to live through loss and its pain and arrive in a good place by God's enabling grace. Loss and its accompanying pain can be managed in a way that leads to good outcomes and an inner prosperity of the soul.

Our affluent culture sometimes permits individuals to reach adulthood without learning the vital life lesson of going without. In such instances, loss requires the development of new insights and new skills. Loss often requires, too, that we re-work our definition of *enough* in nearly every aspect of our lives. But those who make redemptive use of their pain understand that while the pain of loss can be devastating, loss is not fatal, and the ultimate outcome of loss can sometimes be a surprising good. However, despite our resistance, the way to the good ending is through the loss and not around it.

In the Old Testament biblical narrative of the Jewish people's exile to Babylon, there is great loss and grief. "We have hung our harps on the willow trees," mourned God's ancient people. "How can we sing here in Babylon when we remember Jerusalem and its destruction, when we remember Zion and all that we have lost?" (Psalm 137:1–2, 4, author's paraphrase).

But God's response through the prophet Jeremiah was unambiguous, unsentimental, and painfully to the point.

> This is what the LORD Almighty, the God of Israel, says to all those I carried into exile from Jerusalem to Babylon: "Build houses and settle down; plant gardens and eat what they produce. Marry and have sons and daughters; find wives for your sons and give your daughters in marriage, so that they too may have sons and daughters. Increase in number there; do not decrease... [Then] when seventy years are completed... I will come to you... For I

know the plans I have for you," declares the LORD, "plans to prosper you and not to harm you, plans to give you hope and a future." (Jeremiah 29:4–6, 10–11 NIV)

The loss is horrific and unavoidable, God said in effect to His people, so settle down and live through it. Loss is not my intended end of the story, but living through the loss is necessary to get to the gain I have in mind.

Jesus understood the paradox of loss. In the life of faith, Jesus said, the person who loses his life finds it (Matthew 10:39). The immediate context in which Jesus said this was, of course, the issue of discipleship and the loss and paradoxical gain that comes with choosing to follow Him. But the truth can shape our response to loss at many other levels.

Loss exists in paradoxical tension with gain in ways we find difficult to understand and are reluctant to accept. We prefer our easy black-and-white thinking. Loss is bad. Gain is good. There's no connection between the two, we say, and then, out of a misplaced sense of entitlement, we argue that God owes *us* only good. And yet—somehow, even in the most difficult times, we know it is not that simple. Good stewardship of the pain that comes with loss occurs most often when we become willing to think with less simplicity and greater accuracy.

Reality teaches us that loss *is* real, loss *does* hurt, and loss comes as a part of the cycle of life whether we like it or not. The consequences of loss, however, can ultimately be quite different than our fears permit us to imagine or believe. Loss, while painful and life-altering, is not the entire story. And for those who remember and serve the God of new things, it is reasonable and logical to look for new life when we find ourselves in desolate life spaces that have been emptied by loss.[3]

Can I Ever Be Powerful Again?

Pain challenges our sense of personal sovereignty at the deepest level and raises troubling questions about our knowledge of ourselves. Pain moves us into uncharted waters; we feel overwhelmed and out of control. Indeed, while we may be resistant to the valuable lesson, pain teaches us with brutal reality that there are things—vital, essential things—that we cannot control despite our desperate effort to do so. Those who make good use of their pain learn, however, that this inability to control circumstances and people does not mean that they are powerless. Those who manage pain well exercise personal power through their ability to deal competently with themselves, their life circumstances, and relationships rather than in an ability to power-up and power-over people and life events. They maintain a functional distinction between power and influence and between coercion and persuasion in the process of problem solving. At the same time, they categorically refuse to function out of a victim stance. For some individuals this refusal entails great emotional struggle and can involve physical risk.

Domestic violence and abuse (physical and emotional) remain deeply troublesome realities in our culture. In a scandalously large number of instances, abuse remains the dirty secret of reality in "Christian" homes. Refusing to function as a victim can require a frightening shift in roles and behavior for individuals entangled in an abusive relationship. In such relationships emotional and economic survival seem to make victim behavior the only option possible; the welfare of the family often appears to require the target of abusive behavior to abandon personal needs for safety and well-being. Often the individual who is targeted by abusive behavior has a sense of helplessness that is intensified by self-blame and the powerful self-justifying rhetoric of the abuser.

Nevertheless, despite this sense of helplessness and barrage of misplaced blame, the target of abuse continues to have the power to act in ways that lead to increased safety and well being.

No one suggests that there is an easy solution to dealing with the threat that violence brings or to managing a destructive relationship. The first step out of such an abusive relationship begins, however, when the target of abuse makes an inner choice to embrace personal autonomy and to refuse the victim role. The target of the abuser's behavior (usually, although not always, a woman) cannot control the abuser's behavior. She can, however, control her own and refuse to function from a victim stance. Although initial steps may be small, she can take steps to restructure her life and relationships and to foster her own emotional and physical well-being. She can act to secure her safety and the safety and well-being of her children.[4]

Pragmatic thinking about personal autonomy that leads to good stewardship looks something like this:

My limitations are what they are: limitations. But that is all *that they are: limitations. I am not helpless. I am not a victim. I can choose and act.*

I cannot control people. I can *learn to monitor and manage my own responses. By doing this I can influence change in people's response to me.*

I cannot control life events. I can *act to influence circumstances and outcomes. By doing this I can alter the impact of events in my life.*

I cannot shift responsibility for my well-being to others. I cannot compel caretaking by others. I can *relate to others in ways that strengthen relationships and increase my supportive community.*

Acting responsibly to foster my well-being does not ensure the understanding and approval of others. It may not secure their assistance. But in this experience of pain and limitations, I can nevertheless choose to protect and care for myself when those around me are indifferent to my well-being and act in ways that place my safety and my life at risk.

I can, by God's empowering, act to protect myself and my well-being and the health and well-being of those dependent upon me. I remember that the God I serve has given me the spirit of power and love and self-discipline. In this time of trouble, a part of the continuing gift of the Spirit remains the fruit of self-control.

While effective pain managers reject helplessness, they view personal autonomy in terms of "coping with" rather than "control over." They function out of the understanding that they cannot control life or other people, but they have a God-given power to monitor and manage their own responses. In doing this, they know that they can decisively influence their surrounding circumstances and interact with others in ways that strengthen supportive relationships. Effective pain managers are clear about their limits, but they accept responsibility for what they *can* do. They *can* choose their responses and act to influence outcomes. They can choose to become, in effect, their own bottom line. The gift of the Spirit includes self-control, not control of others or events.

But acting in our own best interest is not as easy as it may sound. In real life the experience frequently feels like swimming against the current. Often we must act when we feel least inclined to do so and feel least capable of making good choices. At times we must act in an environment that is non-supportive and may, in fact, be strongly resistant to our choices and their consequences. At worst, we may find it necessary to take decisive action to ensure safety, growth, and well-being in an environment actively opposed to change or even to our physical and emotional survival.

The story of Abigail plays out in such an environment (1 Samuel 25:1–42). Her churlish alcoholic husband Nabal had insulted David and brought down David's wrath and threatened destruction on the household. Terrified, Abigail's servants fled to her, trusting her to find some way to avoid the approaching disaster. In the immediate crisis there was no one available to help who was powerful enough to confront David—Abigail was on her own with only her own resources. Summoning her servants, she took food for David and his men and set out to meet with David, fully aware of the risk this entailed. Taking her courage in hand, Abigail directly confronted the angry David; her apology and gift saved her and her household. Impressed by Abigail's courage and common sense, David took her to be his wife after Nabal's death. But at the time of crisis, Abigail had no promise of a happy ending to her story. She chose to act when she had knowledge of only the approaching disaster and her own limited resources. The happy ending came *after* she had risked, after she had acted to do what she could.

Intense pain, physical or emotional, makes us feel over-whelmed, defenseless, and vulnerable. We often sense ourselves to be too confused, too weak, and too hopeless to choose or act. When we are despairing and none too sure that life itself is worth the effort required to live, we have little desire and even less energy to influence the outcomes in our struggle. But the choices we make (or fail to make) at this point shape significantly the degree to which we profit from the experience of our pain. It would be emotionally convenient if appropriate self-care prevented loss or eliminated pain. Life, unfortunately, does not play out in that fashion. Nevertheless, acting on our options, limited though they may be, making the choices we *can* make alters the outcome of the struggle in which we find ourselves, sometimes in astonishing and unexpected ways. Doing what we can with what is available, however small, however limited, results in a sense of mastery that is an essential part of effective pain management.

Pain often makes us feel like victims; we are caught in circumstances that are beyond our control. When we cannot control our pain or the surrounding circumstances, we can easily lose our belief in our ability to control ourselves. Despite our sense of helplessness and vulnerability, though, choice remains an option and a responsibility. My grandfather was fond of saying, "You always have a choice. You do not always have a choice over what you have a choice over, but you always have a choice." Acting on this reality is a crucial step in pain management. When consequences of our initial choice prove disappointing or lead to an unanticipated dead end, it is even more important to act on the reality that we always have *another* choice.

The size of the choice is not the only factor that determines its impact and significance. A friend defied medical expectations and survived what her physicians and family expected to be a fatal illness. In recounting her struggle to live, Claire remembers thinking in the first moments of consciousness after surgery, *All I can do is focus my eyes on the door or the window.* She accepted the pain (she could not eliminate that) and the necessity for surgery—removal of her cancerous lung was her only chance for continued life. She accepted the reality of her immediate limitations; in the recovery room, choice was limited to eye focus and her ability to turn her head. But she understood that she could, nonetheless, act to influence the outcomes of her life. She *could* choose to look at the door or the window. She decided that she *would* choose: door or window. Limited, suffering, and utterly alone at the time, she chose still to act in ways that fostered life. *Door or window,* she thought, *I can choose.* And she did.

Later into her recovery, Claire asked her physician one day why he thought she had survived. He thought a moment, and then said, "Well, one of the reasons is that you chose—very stubbornly, I might add—you chose to live."

Acting in ways that incorporated self-care significantly aided Claire's physical and emotional well-being. It did not always earn the approval of those around her, however. She insisted on detailed lists so that she could monitor her daily medications; the hospital staff was at best reluctantly cooperative. She insisted on making the effort to dress in street clothes before she could do so without assistance; those who were assigned to help her were not enthusiastic about her plan. She insisted on long walks before she could walk alone safely; those assigned to walk with her did so less than cheerfully. She insisted on living independently in her own home. Her family labeled this decision selfish because her choice inconvenienced and worried them.

Her daughter said one day in exasperation, "Mother, why can't you just be sick normally like everybody else's mother?"

Quicker than a heartbeat, Claire retorted, "Well, I'm not everybody else's mother. Besides, I'm not being sick—I'm getting well."

When she returned to work, a co-worker said, only half-jokingly, "How come you're back so soon? You're making it hard for the rest of us to get extended sick leave."

Pain, whether physical or emotional, triggers issues of both dependency and independence for the person in pain as well as for his or her support network. As a result, when we are in pain, an odd, unconscious coercion often develops in relationships. The vulnerability that comes with pain at times evokes an expectation that, if we were to verbalize it, would sound something like this: "I'm hurting, and you need to (should) pay attention to me and give me what I want—without reservation." At other times, when our vulnerability causes us to fear that we may be losing our independence, our expectation might be verbalized in this way: "I'm trying to manage my hurt so you need to (should) let me do whatever I choose to do without criticism or opposition."

In those around us who are a part of our support network, there can be similar potentially problematic responses. "You are hurting, and I am (graciously, generously) trying to help you. In view of this, you need to (should) do whatever I ask (tell) you to do—without protest or resistance." Or, "Your pain is *your* problem. If I help you, you are obligated to do whatever I ask (want) in order to even out your account."

Decisions that incorporate our effort to care for ourselves sometimes produce some relational discomfort. When we don't seek the approval of others as the basic guideline for our self-care, those around us sometimes become concerned and annoyed— "they get their feathers ruffled," as my grandfather used to say. Those who believe that they know better than we do what is best for us tend to have the most "ruffled feathers." Nonetheless, if we persist with appropriate self-care, despite this temporary discomfort, we become good stewards of our pain and avoid the addictive habit of passive helplessness as well. By choosing, we can influence circumstances, alter the impact of events, and gain in strength and self-knowledge. Acting out of responsible self-determined choices, however small our available choices, leads to growth and healing and forms in part an essential element in productive management of pain.

Can I Ever Be the Same Again?

For those who mean to practice effective pain management, the answer to this question is *no, yes,* and *it depends*—all at the same time.

Inevitably the experience of pain changes us and challenges our sense of personal identity at a foundational level. We know that in the experience of living in and through our pain we are changed; something about us will never be the same again. Yet, paradoxically, we also know that in a sense that is difficult to describe we survive intact and, as one client described herself, "just more of whom I've always been but with some of the shell cracked, and some edges polished off."

Those who manage pain well accept the tension of two competing truths: pain changes us in irreversible ways; but, conversely, the essential self survives intact. However nonsensical it may sound, good stewardship of pain results from a complex response in which we believe that we can and do *both* change and stay the same.

But good stewardship places this tension solidly in the context of choice. While change is inevitable, effective pain managers understand that within the change process they can still choose options that lead to growth and well-being. People, environment, and resources may remain the same or become different, but choice remains. There is always a choice—and another choice—and still another.

Effective pain managers think about change in a pragmatic way that goes something like this:

Change happens. I cannot prevent change. I can *choose to influence change and shape my responses to it.*

In this time of change I discover again that I am who I am. I find that—for better and *for worse—I remain who I am. In this time of change I can take responsibility to conserve and to value who I am. I can choose to live through this change without loss of my essential self.*

And yet I know that I will not be the same again. My world will not be the same again. I am carried irresistibly away from the old and familiar into new ways of doing, new ways of being. I cannot push back this river. I can choose to enter into change in ways that foster my growth and strengthen my relationship with God.

I grieve the loss of what was, both blessing and struggle. In my grief I set up memory stones. Borrowing from God's ancient people, Israel, I name the past Ebenezer: There the LORD helped me (1 Samuel 7:12).

I move toward the unknown and new with expectation. This place into which I am coming also holds both blessing and struggle. I take as my own God's promise to His ancient people, Israel, as they stood at the river's edge. As with them, He will go with me into this new land (Joshua 1:5, 9).

I recently had lunch with a woman whom I know well. She shared an entry from her journal that catches the ambiguity and ambivalence that comes with change. She had written:

> This has been an odd day.
>
> I had an early appointment, so the alarm rang long before I was happy to get out of bed.
>
> Still half asleep, I looked in the mirror, and there I was, same curly hair with the same obstinate part on the left side. But it's not the same—I'm grayer now—a lot grayer—and I have a new haircut. Still true, however, that "every hair in place" will *never* be said about me!
>
> Had lunch with Jennifer last week. She has colored her hair. It looks nice, but that's not for me. I don't want the aggravation and expense, but that's not the real reason.

I looked at my gray hair this morning, and I wanted to keep it gray like it is. Every one of those gray hairs is earned, something like medals for years of service. That stubborn part is still there, but this new haircut has tamed it a little.

My eyes were tired this morning—too much close work lately in poor light. As I looked at myself in the mirror I thought, same eyes but different, but I wasn't thinking just about the changes age brings. I thought: *Those old eyes have seen a lot of life, the good* and *the bad.*

And then I thought—in the last few years those eyes have cried more tears than I ever thought were in me.

Crying that many tears changes more than eyes.

Still, it's complicated. I know my heart is wiser, yet it is still the same headlong risk-taker it always was. Last week's adventure reminds me of that.

Thought about change off and on all day, and when I got home tonight everything in the house felt like a choreographed dance moving between same/different, old/new, sad/glad, yesterday and tomorrow. Was tired and dropped off to sleep in my chair and woke up with a stiff neck. I had been dreaming that I was driving down empty streets in a place whose name I didn't remember, looking for B. Suppose I dozed off thinking about tomorrows that I long for but will never come.

Good stewardship of pain necessitates our living with the paradoxical tension of change, its simultaneous cross rhythms of loss and gain, of same yet different. But for the faith-committed individual, the context of change remains constant: the loving God who was, and is, and is to come, and who has gifted us with

His presence on the journey home. He shows himself to us in new and changing ways, but His loving heart remains the same.

Can I Ever Be Happy Again?

Like the answer to the question of change, the answer to this question is a frustrating *yes, no,* and *it depends.* While we prefer to think in terms of black and white and either/or, little of what we know about happiness fits well into these patterns. And to further complicate matters, we use two different words to represent a distinction in human experience that we intuitively understand but find difficult to define.

In common usage *happiness* and *joy* function as approximate synonyms. We sometimes say that we are happy; we sometimes say that we are filled with joy. While these human experiences are closely related and often coincide, they are, nevertheless, not precisely the same. Granting the difficulty in definition, it is useful to keep the distinction between *joy* and *happiness.* Keeping this distinction assists us in avoiding the either/or thinking that frames life in terms of *either* happiness and joy *or* pain and grief. It enables us to grasp the paradoxical reality that we may in the most difficult times lose happiness yet experience joy in the midst of our pain.

In the broad sense of common usage, *happiness* is a general emotional response to experiences that evoke pleasure—good food, good fortune, good health, good friends, good progress toward a goal; rest, relaxation; fun, excitement; sexual satisfaction; intellectual and emotional stimulation; beauty. In times of pain and trouble, pleasure that evokes happiness in this sense often appears to be in short supply. In the depths of our pain we echo Job: "My eyes will never see happiness again" (Job 7:7 NIV).

When we use the term *joy,* we're pointing to an aspect of human experience that is different from happiness. Happiness often serves as a precursor to joy and is mixed with it. But joy sinks its roots deeper within the soul and, fortunately, is much less dependent on circumstances to stimulate and sustain it. It is in this sense that James speaks of having joy in trials (1:2).

This distinction occurs in Job's life as well. Job continued to long for death to release him from the terrible circumstances of his life. However, in his ordeal, Job did not deny God. Thinking of his choice to be faithful (one of the few things Job *had* been able to control), Job says, "But it is still my consolation, and I rejoice in unsparing pain, that I have not denied the words of the Holy One" (Job 6:10 NASB). In the *New International Version,* the phrase "rejoicing in unsparing pain" is translated "my joy in unrelenting pain." When we consider Job's words—*rejoicing* in unsparing pain, *joy* in unrelenting pain—we pause. Job is certain that he will never experience happiness again, yet he reports that he rejoices and experiences joy *in* his pain. How can this be possible? While it may be difficult to fully explain Job's experience of joy, we sense that he is talking about something quite different from the pleasure that comes with an unexpected bonus or the fun and excitement that fills a holiday. For Job, life events had destroyed the ordinary human sources of happiness. We understand, intuitively, however, that in some way difficult to define, Job was able to experience something beyond his pain, even when the happiness of a birthday dinner with his children was no longer possible.

Pain pushes us to examine our understanding of joy and its relationship to choice. The notion that people are about as happy as they decide to be has some truth in it. Nevertheless, while pain does not paradoxically preclude joy, experiencing joy in the midst of pain requires more than saying, "I think I'll be happy today." Managing nights of weeping so that joy can come in the morning is a difficult skill to acquire for a number of reasons. Among these reasons is the reality that pain—emotional, physical, or both—can become so intense that choice in any form seems irrelevant and joy seems antithetical, and hopelessly out of reach.

It is ironic that research reports more about depression than about happiness and joy.[5] We know, however, that people can survive disastrous life events without being destroyed by them. We know too that in the midst of such experiences, those who manage pain and disorientation productively mark potential sources of joy in distinctive ways. They laugh a lot—often at themselves. Those who manage pain well understand that on most days, life is absurd enough to provide several laughs, and in each day there are enough of beauty and life's good things for a measure of contentment and joy. Happiness may be carried away with the winds of changing fortune, scattered with shattered dreams. But joy? It is an odd truth that when happiness has gone, joy can still make itself a home in the house of pain.

Thinking about joy in a way that leads to good stewardship of pain goes something like this.

Joy can be present with pain. I can make and hold space for joy in this place of pain and disorientation.

Joy is not about displacing pain or disputing its reality. Joy comes with a message of its own. I recognize joy apart from the reality of my pain and celebrate the truth joy brings—life is more than my pain and exists apart from it.

Joy cannot be compelled to come into this place of pain, but I can invite its presence. Pain cannot prevent me from attending to other things in my life. Joy rides the wings of those things I see and sense when I look away from my pain. I choose to look beyond pain, trusting that joy will come.

I choose to live with the tension of two competing truths. It is true that I cannot control my loss of those relationships and that world in which I was once happy. But it is also true that in this present world I can *act to increase my experience of joy. I can respond to the epiphanies of small things. I can focus on God's thumbprint in the crocus in the snow. I can open my heart to my friend's laughter even when I can only smile myself.*

I hold a space for joy. In each day I make some place where joy can come—a talk with a friend, a walk with the dog, the feel of a soft old shirt, the taste of good coffee in my favorite mug, a book, the sound of music, the smell of a wood fire, pausing to see—again—the familiar beauty of the print that hangs in the entryway. I grant pain its space, but only its space. With these common, familiar things I place boundaries on my pain. My life consists of more than pain and loss. I hold a space for joy.

I remember that joy is God's business, too, and part of the gift of the Spirit (Galatians 5:22). I remember that God is not constrained by my pain and present circumstances, nor does He desire that my pain take all joy away. I take for myself God's promise to His ancient people: after the night of weeping, joy comes in the morning; while we may sow in tears, we may bring home the harvest with singing and with joy (Psalm 30:5; Psalm 126:5–6).

Joy is strong and sturdy. Like flowers that survive and bloom in the alpine tundra, joy can flourish in harsh, demanding environments. But joy will not come where it is not welcomed. The choice to welcome joy requires that we embrace the tension of two competing truths. We must recognize and accept our lost happiness; we must act to increase our joy. In order to welcome joy, we must—with deliberate, focused attention—choose to look beyond our pain, to see other things, other people, the life that is going on around us, juxtaposed with our loss and pain.

To choose in this way requires a willingness to relinquish the tempting sense of entitlement that often creeps in with pain. It also requires us to acknowledge the ways in which we may cling to our pain because we have found ways to make it useful.

A client, whom I will call Kathy, sought help with her grief following her sister's death. Kathy and her sister Kerry, identical twins, had shared close kinship and, as twins sometimes do, a particularly close friendship as well. About nine months after Kerry's death, Kathy came for her appointment looking more indignant than sad.

"You won't believe what my husband [Jack] wanted me to do this week. He actually wanted me to bake a birthday cake for him! As broken up as I've been over Kerry's death, how could he expect me to bake a birthday cake?"

"Well," I started cautiously, "did Jack ask you not to cry?"

"No, of course not," Kathy responded, aware and annoyed that I had chosen to respond indirectly to her grievance.

"Did Jack ask you to make a big cake with lots of decorations and candles and lots of balloons and gifts?" I continued.

"No—he just wanted a plain chocolate cake."

"Did he ask you to have a big party and invite all the men in his Bible study group along with their wives?"

"No," this time Kathy's response sounded a bit defensive. She could see where I was going and clearly did not wish to go there. "He just wanted chocolate cake for dessert for our family dinner."

"A plain chocolate cake and you could cry while you mixed it? Is this right?" I asked.

"You don't get it," Kathy said. "Jack really was asking me to be happy, and he had no right to do that. I am sad because I lost my sister. It's not reasonable to ask me to make a cake."

Kathy had discovered that her pain could make her powerful; her pain could, out of an unconscious sense of personal entitlement, excuse her from attention to others and participation in events occurring around her. Kathy's loss was enormous. Her grief was deep, and her loss was irreversible. Kerry would never come again, laughing as she ran up the porch steps, waving the balloons she had brought for Jack's birthday party. Kathy's need for others to acknowledge her grief and loss was understandable and appropriate.

Kathy's use of her pain, however, was deeply problematic. It was her use of her pain, not the enormity of her loss, that kept Kathy walled in with her grief. Even at that birthday moment when memory made her loss unbearably real, joy, however small, was still a choice. The loss of her sister could not be undone. But Kathy had chosen to add loss of joy to that irretrievable loss: the joy of mixing a cake in her mother's old blue bowl (even if she cried while she mixed it); the joy of the smell of baking chocolate filling the kitchen; the delight of her children in Mom's famous chocolate cake; joy that, in Kerry's absence, Jack remained fully present, solid, dependable, coping with life and his own grief with quiet, practical skill.

It was neither desirable nor possible for Kathy to deny her grief. However, good stewardship of her pain did require her to learn both to be present with her grief and reach beyond it.

It is not true—at least not in the most difficult circumstances of life—that people are about as happy as they decide to be. It's not that easy. But it is true that even in the darkest times, when the pressure of pain is unrelenting, we have the choice to reach beyond ourselves to find a place, however small, where joy can come.

Will My Life Ever Have Value Again?

When people thought about Ruth, they first pictured her smile. But behind the social mask she wore, Ruth was struggling with a deepening depression. At a casual glance no one would have guessed her inner pain. Ruth (not her real name) was physically attractive, well-educated, and personable. She held a position in a downtown brokerage office where she had been successful both in increasing her sales and in hiding her steadily decreasing enthusiasm for her work.

Behind this successful exterior, however, Ruth's inner world was filled with intense pain and an overwhelming sense of failure. She had recently left an important position in church ministry under difficult circumstances. Ruth was now struggling with broken relationships, a deep sense of personal inadequacy, and a continuing sense of bewilderment: How could anything that began with such promise come to such a painful end? And there were faith issues as well. Was her pain the consequence of misunderstanding God's call on her life? But it soon became apparent that Ruth's pain was intensified by an utter absence of hope. In her pain Ruth had become convinced that there could never be a good tomorrow for her.

"I'll get through this somehow," she said softly one day. She added sadly, "It's not about work. I have an okay job. It's about my life—it feels like my life will never be okay again."

Pain does that to us. Pain that emerges out of loss and change tempts us to abandon all hope for future good. Ruth could logically connect her pain to the recent disruption and loss in her professional life. What surprised Ruth, however, was the way in which deeper, more difficult issues had surfaced as she dealt with her job loss. With the loss of her job, deep doubts about herself and her future had arisen. Ruth felt as if she were no longer the self she had been and that the motivation and skill with which she had once served others was gone as well. In this loss, Ruth now wondered if she had also lost the woman she dreamed of becoming and the possibility of reaching goals she had once set. Was yesterday's loss tomorrow's loss as well? Effective stewardship of pain requires that we meet head-on the challenge that pain poses to our sense of hope and our belief in a productive future.

Pain pushes us to rethink and redefine the basic beliefs about worth and value that form the infrastructure of our lives. At this point we may find that we have unwittingly absorbed the cultural belief that *how I look* and *what I do* equal *who I am*. While commonly held, this is a dangerous idea. Change and loss inevitably come in personal appearance and in levels of productivity as a result of the aging process if from no other life event. If my appearance falls far short of the cultural ideal; if my capacity to produce wealth and power is irreversibly reduced; if I am no longer "good for anything," what basis do I have for hope? Can anything good lie ahead?

In order to flourish, hope, like joy, requires attachment to a reality larger than things that can be changed and lost. Taking hold of hope while we are in pain often requires us to reconsider as well our understanding of the gifting of the Holy Spirit and the issue of human brokenness. We may know that, to use Paul's metaphor, we have the treasure of the indwelling Christ in clay pots (2 Corinthians 4:7), but we are unsure what it may mean, jokes aside, if the clay pot is cracked and broken. What then?

And what does it mean to be filled with pain? Perhaps unconsciously, we can mistakenly believe that our inner sense of well-being acts as a barometer of the Spirit's action in our lives. When we think this way, a loss of happiness leads us to believe that the activity of the Spirit in us has vanished as well. We think, erroneously, that evidence of the Spirit's work in us and through us exists only when we have an inner sense of feeling good. That is not, thankfully, the case, but we are, nevertheless, often confused about the Spirit's willingness and ability to use our failures, our limitations, and our inadequacy.[6] We lose the ground of our hope because we assign meaning to our pain out of a faulty theology of clay pots.

We also become bewildered about the Holy Spirit's gifts when we go through a time of change. When we become unable to express our gifting in familiar ways, we think that change and pain have altered who we are in such a way that the Holy Spirit's presence and gifting action have also changed. And our painful uncertainty at this point is often accompanied by a confused sense about reliable evidence. We think that if by the Spirit's enabling grace we *are* productive, we will then *feel* productive and *look* productive to other people and ourselves. In this way, dangerously, we can confuse kingdom productiveness with people approval, our own included.

Clay pot or not, broken or not, as God's people we carry within us the mystery of the presence of God. We have God's reassuring promise that this remains true, whatever the circumstances of our lives. Pain erodes away our sense of this, however, and leaches away the hope that springs from this reality. Unless we resist this process, we become both unbiblical and self-defeating in the ways that we think about hope. Pain itself does not have the power to wall us away from hope, but faulty thinking about the ground and reality of our hope can leave us prisoners in our despair.

Good stewardship of pain is marked by a conscious, deliberate, disciplined focus on hope. In this sense, hope, like joy, requires a steady choice to reach through and beyond the pain to envision a good tomorrow. Hope is at its core a choice to agree with God, whether we feel like it or not. It is a choice that roots our expectations for the future in what God has said (His promised provision for us) and who He is (unchanging in His love and presence with us). Hope becomes hopeless in short order if we seek to base it solely on our human capacity to perform.

In adopting this worldview, however, those who make redemptive use of their pain remain tough realists. They "let go and move on." They become the experts in the "get past it" crowd. They "get past it," however, *not* by denial of loss or pain but by moving through the pain and toward a different place, a new time. They accept that on arrival the hopeful tomorrow toward which they are moving (despite their pain) will look quite different from their yesterdays. They believe, nevertheless, that this tomorrow, although now in embryo, is also a part of God's story,[7] and in it, by God's appointment, they have yet a useful part to play. Those who make redemptive use of their pain choose hope as a framework for meaning in their pain, but they frame this meaning in authentic hope, not wishful thinking.

We begin to make productive use of our pain when we acknowledge, realistically, that the basic structures of life may fall apart, and, like Humpty Dumpty, they cannot be put back together again. But this realization is framed in the knowledge that shattered dreams and the disintegration of the framework of our lives' events do not have the power to forestall or stop God's transforming work in our lives. We recognize our own frailty in faith and life, but we trust, as Paul reassured the church at Philippi, that God will continue to give us the desire to obey Him and the power to do those things that please Him (Philippians 2:13). Hope comes most easily when we keep in mind that while we may not know about our tomorrows, we do know about the One who journeys with us. He is neither frightened by our frailties nor inhibited by our limitations. And, knowing Him, we may safely hope in the future. Sensed or not sensed, God will be there, with us and for us. When hope is built on this foundation, it stays steady, even when the winds of adversity reach hurricane force.

Hope confidently expects that in our tomorrow God will not waste our gifts any more than He will waste our pain. For the weaver, God will supply the thread. Hope is a logical choice as a way of living when, like joy and faith, it rests on the reality of who God is, and not on the circumstances through which we are called to live.

In a pragmatic way, survivors who make good use of their pain think about hope in a way that is something like this.

My experience of pain and loss is what it is—pain and loss in the events of my life today. Today's experience of pain and loss is not evidence that tomorrow has been emptied of all work that has value. It is not proof that tomorrow's dreams will never come true. This is today, not tomorrow.

I choose for the ground of my hope the reality of God's story. My hope does not lie in those things that can be changed and lost. I am a part of God's story; my tomorrow is a part of God's tomorrow. I take as my own God's promise to His ancient people of Israel that beyond disaster He has a plan for my tomorrow, a future that makes hope the reasonable response now here in these circumstances.

I recognize that my story stretches beyond today. The pain and loss I am experiencing today is only one part of my story. I know that in the cycle of life the process of change that has brought me to this place will carry me beyond it to another time and place. Nights of tears can be followed by mornings of joy. Planting done in grief and sorrow can be followed by a harvest brought home with joy.

I know that my failure and brokenness are what they are: my *failure and brokenness. This failure and brokenness are not evidence of a deficit in God's character or His love. My failure and brokenness cannot tempt God to abandon me or separate me from His love. My failure and brokenness cannot shut me away from a good tomorrow He will make possible for me. My hope rests in His love and His presence, not my past or my performance.*

I value my wounds. With God, my failure is the ground of my learning—an invitation to begin again, a step in the making of new things. My brokenness can be the bridge of connection with others whose wounds have left them in lonely places, scarred with shame. My hope emerges from the promised potential of who I can become in relationship with God and with others through and because of this time, this pain, this loss.

I remember that I serve an Eastering God. I remember the horror of that Friday and the terrible silence of the Saturday that followed. But I remember, too, the shattering of that dark night into Sunday's brilliant Easter light. And the

One who talked to Mary in the garden that morning, who sat down and ate fish and bread with His ecstatic astonished disciples, He is the One who walks with me in this journey. My hope for my tomorrow rests in His power to come through the pain and the dark into life and light and His promise to bring me with Him where I cannot come alone.

Guidelines for Pain Management

Growing in grace and in discipleship through our pain requires something more and different from simply "doing what comes naturally." Good stewardship of our pain requires thoughtful choices that grow out of specific principles.

Principle One: Choose Life

Effective pain managers concentrate on life, not on the pain. They know that life and God are bigger than pain, and pain does not have the power to take life away. They trust an Eastering God whose death and resurrection invite His people into life beyond the reality of present pain. They know this God walks with them in the struggle. They choose life. Despite its pain, they believe life is not a burden—it is the gift of God.

Principle Two: Place Loss in Perspective

Effective pain managers name loss for what it is—loss—then hold it in perspective. They know that life is bigger than loss. They understand that in the cycle of life, loss can be the beginning of new things. They look for new life in the spaces left desolate by loss. They assign boundaries to loss and center it in the present. They believe that this loss does not limit God's willingness or God's ability to act in their behalf in the tomorrows that lie ahead. They remember that their God is the God of plans for a hope and future. They remember that the God they serve is the God of the Exodus and the Exile, the God who restores His people, the God who brings His people home.

Principle Three: Act Out of Personal Autonomy

Effective pain managers assume responsibility to influence the outcomes in their life. They know that influence and control are not the same. Since they cannot control other people and life events, they choose to do what is possible—to influence other people and events and manage themselves effectively. They accept the limitations of others and of themselves realistically. They reject perfection as a goal for themselves or for others. They persist in choices that foster their growth and well-being even when pain depletes their strength. They trust the Spirit to empower them and to bring about positive outcomes. They live in the tradition of Abigail, remembering that taking whatever present action is possible can alter future life events in astonishing ways.

Principle Four: Embrace the Tension of Change

Effective pain managers embrace the tension of change. They understand that pain both changes the individual and at the same time leaves the God-created self intact. They both grieve the losses change brings and celebrate the new life that comes with change. When change preserves the old in new contexts, effective pain managers both honor the old and celebrate the new. They hold relationships, possessions, and life itself with open hands. When change erodes away that which seems essential to life itself, they remember Jesus' reassurance: the kernel of wheat that falls into the ground and dies produces many seeds. They know God and life are bigger than change.

Principle Five: Choose Joy

Effective pain managers know that joy can be present in the midst of pain. They choose ways of thinking and acting that finds joy in the ordinary and the familiar. They know, however, that joy, like life, is transient; they do not hold it as a barricade against their pain. They understand that joy cannot be compelled but will surprise those who make it welcome. Effective pain managers keep in mind that joy is not solely their concern. They remember that joy is God's business too. In good times and bad, joy remains the fruit of the Spirit, not simply the product of circumstances. Those who manage pain well understand that time and change are often the servants of joy. They take for today God's promise in the Psalms: Weeping may remain for the night, but rejoicing comes in the morning.

Principle Six: Anticipate Tomorrow with Hope

Effective pain managers know that hope, like joy, can be present in the midst of pain. They understand that the choice to do what they can with what is available nurtures hope. They know too that hope, like the new life that emerges from the rubble of loss, is not achieved by wishful thinking. Effective pain managers understand that hope grows best in the large view of life and the long view of time. They root hope in the context of God's goal for their lives and His promise of the new world to come. Those who manage pain well understand that hope cannot grow from denial of human limitations or longing for perfection. They hold hope as the logical response to God's ability and willingness to deal with broken lives. Hope leads them to value their wounds. They learn from hope that pain can serve as a bridge to new self-knowledge and compassion, to new relationships with others and with God. They ground their hope in the One who came through pain and death into the light of Easter morning. Their hope lies in His ability to lead them through the dark and the pain into a morning that they cannot reach alone.

chapter 5

HOW CAN I LIVE PRODUCTIVELY WITH PAIN?

Choosing life is the first essential step in living productively with pain. Most of us assume that God remains in charge of life-and-death matters, and the idea that life is something about which we need to choose makes us somewhat uneasy. We assume that whether we live or die is a choice that God makes; the buck stops, so to speak, on God's desk, not ours. That being the case, talk about choosing life seems like a figure of speech at best, and, more likely, semantic nonsense. For the most part, we think, the choice about life is safely out of our hands; our choice is to do the best we can with the life we have been given. In one basic sense, this is true.

However, the issue is more complicated than that. People who are experiencing intense suffering find that life often has little appeal, and the process of living may feel overwhelming. While we may be unexcited about the choice of life at such a time, if we are pushed to think further, we will agree uneasily that it is possible to choose death. With few exceptions, most of us know at least one individual who chose death during a time of pain and loss, either by sudden, dramatic means or by long, slow, heart starvation and withdrawal from living. We rarely discuss the choice of death, and we have limited understanding of the events, despair, and rage that lead to such choices. But when we think of ourselves, we assume unconsciously that choosing life is a default position; choosing life is what happens automatically when we do not choose physical death.

The Challenge to Choose Life

God's challenge to Israel provides a severe jolt to our thinking at this point. With His people poised at the banks of the Jordan, the Promised Land a river's width away (Deuteronomy 29), God's challenge to His people placed both life and death as options: "Today I have given you the choice between life and death" (Deuteronomy 30:19). Then, having presented these opposing options, God throws down His gauntlet: "Choose life... that you... might live" (Deuteronomy 30:19b).

God was certainly concerned about something other than the risk of mass suicide occurring on the far side of Jordon. The challenge to choose life was relationally based, emphasized in every aspect of the renewed covenant: *Choose relationship with Me—when you're afraid, I will never leave you or forsake you; when your enemies endanger you, I will deliver; when you celebrate the harvest and your barns are full, I will rejoice with you.* Choose life, God urged them, and in urging this choice, God clearly intended life to be more than physical survival. God wanted them to choose rich, full, productive life in relationship with Him, life as He intended it to be. But this choice was not a one-time event—it was a process of choosing: choosing when the enemy threatened; choosing when the gods of Baal offered their seductive pleasures; choosing to follow God's rules when the neighbors did not; choosing, like Hannah, to trust when obedience did not produce fruitfulness; choosing in Babylon to view exile as temporary, expectantly believing that in His time God would bring His people home. Then, as now, choosing life was both a decision and a process, both of which are paradoxically and simultaneously straightforward and complex.

When we are in pain, disoriented, and "exiled" from the good times, we are faced with deciding what choosing life may mean. For us, as it was for Israel, choosing life is something more than physical survival, more than life by default, more than a refusal to choose death. Yet even in times of pain, we also sense intuitively that choosing life is something more than choosing comfort and managing to avoid life's disagreeable experiences. At the same time, we know as well that choosing life requires something quite different from immersing ourselves in an adrenalin-driven world of sense satisfaction. Pain and the culture can confuse us at both these points, however, despite what we know.

More than Comfort or Pleasure

Comfort remains an appropriate, important goal in times of pain. However, even in difficult circumstances, comfort is not an unqualified good; choosing comfort as a lifestyle becomes dangerous. My grandfather once told me, "You can have more good than is good for you." Too much comfort permits us to settle into a passive stillness that inhibits our capacity to respond. We move inwardly into a slow, inactive place that is the emotional and spiritual equivalent of the inertia that follows over-indulgence at Thanksgiving dinner. For gluttons—either of comfort or pumpkin pie—life's desirable options can be reduced to a long, uninterrupted nap.

Choosing life solely in terms of pleasure is equally hazardous, however. The problem does not lie in pleasure itself, of course. Experiencing joy and pleasure are among God's goals for His people. The Teacher of Ecclesiastes advises, "Go, eat your food with gladness, and drink your wine with a joyful heart... However many years a man may live, let him enjoy them all" (9:7a; 11:8 NIV). However, we may become gluttons for pleasure without understanding that the unchecked pursuit of pleasure is dangerous and can be fatal. Both the Teacher (Ecclesiastes 2:10–11) and the results of modern research warn us of this. In 1953, psychologists James Old and Peter Milner placed an electrode in what became identified as the pleasure-and-reward center in the brains of some laboratory rats. When the rats were wired in a way that let them press a lever and provide themselves a jolt of pleasure/reward, they did so with obsessive frantic repetition until they collapsed. To the amazement of Old and Milner, some rats, unchecked, pursued pleasure to the point of death. While humans are certainly more than rats, this research provides an interesting counterpoint to the culture's unqualified recommendation to "go for the gusto." Choosing life and choosing pleasure are not the same things.

Choosing Responsible Self-Care

But if choosing life requires more than choosing comfort or pleasure, what do we mean when we say that good management of pain requires us to choose life? Stripped to its basic elements, choosing life is a decision we make—and make again—to undertake responsible self-care that enables us to survive and thrive in ways that glorify God. As Christians, we believe that acceptance of God's gift of life in Christ is foundational to self-care. But in the context of this basic step, we understand that we must also work out self-care in the specifics of faith-based living when life becomes messy and complex. In times of pain and disorientation, this is a difficult and confusing task. When we are suffering, it is not always easy to determine what acts of self-care will enable us both to survive and to prosper emotionally and spiritually.

At the outset, it is important to keep clear the distinction between self-care and selfishness. Rightly understood, the idea that choosing life requires a deliberate choice to care for ourselves is neither a recommendation for selfishness nor a rationale for indulgence. The Bible does not encourage either starvation or gluttony (emotional or physical) as a lifestyle. Neither malnutrition nor obesity is good preparation for a marathon. What is necessary for good stewardship of our pain is *self-care undertaken as an act of responsible discipleship.* "Run the race in a way that you will win the prize," Paul told the Corinthians (1 Corinthians 9:24–27). Self-care that enables us to win the race is not selfishness; it is serious, focused preparation to run the race well. It is discipleship.

The self-care that emerges from responsible discipleship is rooted foundationally in the creation narrative (Genesis 1, 2) and the redemptive reality of the church as the body of Christ (1 Corinthians 12:12–31). In discipleship, to choose life is to value and care for ourselves wholly (body and soul) because, *however broken, however flawed, we remain the fragile carriers of the image and the gifts of God.* For the Christian, choosing life in terms of holistic self-care becomes an act of faith in the purpose of God *for* us and the reality of His presence *in* us. Despite the pain and the disorientation we may experience, life is not random nor is it a burden; it is the gift of God infused with His purpose and love. Christians who practice faith-based self-care have as their goal the nurture and development of God's gift of life, choosing to live their lives to fulfill God's purposes. In functional terms, this is what discipleship means.

Practically speaking, self-care as an act of discipleship pivots around our cooperative partnership with the Holy Spirit in the transforming work of God in our lives. Self-care becomes a Spirit-influenced pattern of behavior through which we become ready recipients of the grace of God, better prepared to "do all such good works as thou hast prepared for us to walk in," in the words of the *Book of Common Prayer*. As we live out our faith-centered self-care in cooperation with the Spirit's guidance, the Spirit's presence in us both protects and empowers us to avoid the extremes of indulgence and individualism.

In this cooperative partnership with the Spirit, we soon learn that our dependence on the Spirit is not optional—it is essential. Self-care does not work well as a do-it-yourself project. Authentic, God-honoring self-care requires a level of self-discipline that can be achieved only by the empowering of the Spirit. For some of us, attempting a regular regimen of exercise makes this abundantly clear. We discover, too, that Spirit-led self-care is not just about us. Self-care does indeed require that we pay attention to ourselves. In times of pain and disorientation, self-care can require a high priority that would be out of place in sunnier times. However, even in times of great difficulty, faith-oriented self-care is never a matter of paying attention *only* to ourselves. Self-care undertaken in cooperation with the Spirit does not lead to indulgence or selfishness.

Faith-centered self-care strikes, too, at the root of the individualism so idolized by the present culture. The goal is the preservation of the individual, but it is preservation of the individual in relationship with God and others. We carry His image, we belong to Him, and He is present in us, giving us gifts for our participation in His work in His creation. Faith-based self-care is centered on the individual person who is uniquely gifted and uniquely valuable; but such self-care also views this valuable individual as an essential part in a corporate whole, the living body of Christ (1 Corinthians 12:12–31). Individuals are valued for their unique gifts; they are valued as well for the potential enhancement that their gifts provide for the common good (1 Corinthians 12:4–7). Faith-based self-care is indeed about caring for ourselves; at the same time, it is self-care undertaken not solely for our own sake but also for the welfare of the body of Christ (1 Corinthians 12:12–31) and for the sake of our ability to partner with God in the eternal stakes of the kingdom. When we pray "Thy kingdom come," and we rightly understand what we are praying, we assume responsibility for self-care that enables us to play our part in bringing about God's desired ends.

When we base our self-care properly in discipleship we assume a realistic view about human nature that does not emphasize self-blame, self-condemnation, or self-promotion. Faith-oriented self-care takes into account both personal strengths and weaknesses and places both firmly in the context of God's grace. God knows us, and in His grace He values us just as we are. Similarly, faith-based self-care recognizes our capacity for cruelty and selfish indulgence and places barriers against the temptations pain may bring to act on such impulses. But without false piety, faith-oriented self-care also nurtures our potential, rooted in creation, to love God and our neighbor, to conserve and develop our gifts and our world, and to practice justice and show mercy in ways that bring the "not yet" of God's coming kingdom into present reality. Self-care rooted in discipleship incorporates the tension of the human paradox—it incorporates both our unending dependence upon the grace of God and the parallel paradoxical necessity that we act responsibly on our own behalf.

While discipleship-based self-care is realistic about human nature, it is also realistic about the impact of pain and its power to distort and narrow our capacity to respond. In the darkness and chaos that suffering brings, we sometimes feel unable to focus on anything other than our pain. We may find that we have very little left over to give to others. Self-care rooted in discipleship recognizes realistically these limitations, but insists gently that we can do *something*: If I cannot quite say thank you, I can smile. If I cannot smile, I can give a look of welcome to the person who has come to be present with me. And if today I can only acknowledge another's presence, I can choose acknowledgment and a word of welcome as my goal for tomorrow—or the day after. Whatever my limits while I am caught in the bitter grip of pain, faith-based self-care insists that I act in ways that recognize that my pain is not just about me. Whenever I take whatever small step I can, I gain from my pain. I learn through these small steps something more about following Jesus, who, at cost of great suffering, placed my interest above His own (Philippians 2:1–11).

Being in the Moment

Even in the most difficult circumstances, faith-oriented self-care requires us to take into consideration both our own welfare and the well-being of others. Making any semblance of concerned choices involving others is often the thing we feel most unable to do, even when these choices entail small things. Making such choices is possible, of course, even when we feel like we cannot. This choice becomes much easier, however, if we first learn a sensible but odd sounding skill: We need learn to separate ourselves from our pain, while, paradoxically, staying steadily with it. While a description of this process may sound unusual, the process incorporates the simple logic of common experience: In order to rake the leaves and trim the hedge I must be in the yard, not in my recliner; to clean the kitchen I must be in the kitchen, not on the porch. In order to handle the pain we are experiencing in the moment, we must first be present where the pain is and fully in touch with what is happening in our inner world. But at the same time, in order to handle pain in the context of discipleship, we must be able to detach from the pain we are experiencing in a way that permits *us*, not the pain, to determine the choices we make. In order to develop this skill, most of us find that it is necessary to reclaim the skill of focusing our attention solely in the moment, in the here and now.

The practice of focusing completely on the experience of the moment comes naturally to children, but by the time we reach adulthood, we can drive down a familiar street and have no memory of our journey home, re-entering the present only when we open the garage door. We can eat and not know what or when or how much we've eaten. In a culture that glamorizes the ability to multi-task, the willingness to stop and focus on the roses—their color, their scent—is viewed as wasted time. The culture rewards us for pushing through life, multi-tasking, getting things done, being efficient, and (we think) "doing it right." Then, gradually or suddenly, pain comes, and we need to relearn the skill we've laid aside. In order to handle our pain in ways that support discipleship, we must learn to be both in the pain but separate from it. We must make the distinction that pain is what is happening *to* us and *in* us—pain is not who we are. We can make choices about managing the pain that is happening to us. While I was working on this chapter and thinking about this essential skill I had an interesting opportunity to practice what I wanted to write about.

My day had begun early and ended late. The hours had been emotionally overloaded with both my own and my clients' pain and overfilled with responsibilities, both personal and professional. As I drove home I became consciously aware that my mind was frantically darting between the past (my client's pain-filled childhood and my failure to put the trash out) and the future (staff meetings and my need to do laundry), landing for only brief moments in my present world, the one in which I was on dangerous automatic pilot down a busy boulevard. As I neared home, I pulled into our neighborhood park and stopped. In a moment of clarity, I realized that before I reached home I needed to reorder and bring under control the disordered thinking and sensing I had permitted the day to produce within me. (Theologically, Paul calls this process "[taking] captive every thought to make it obedient to Christ" (2 Corinthians 10:5 NIV).

I knew I needed to clear my mind. But additionally, I wanted to do something else. The snow was covering everything in a thick, soundless blanket, and however erratic my behavior might appear to a casual onlooker, I wanted to see my favorite old pine model its new coat of white, the gift of winter's first heavy snowfall.

Pulling my coat around me, I got out of my car. The empty parking lot was filled with untracked snow; other people were long gone from the park, hurrying home ahead of the deepening dark. I was alone, and my steps, muffled by the snow, made only a whisper of sound.

I stopped under the shelter of a young pine that gave me a clear view of the ancient tree I loved that stood sentinel at the curve in the path. I waited, motionless, hearing the silence, feeling the cold gossamer touch of snowflakes on my face, sensing my aliveness and aloneness in a world of falling snow, breathing in the heavy wet scent of the pines and the deepening dark. Slowly, heartbeat by heartbeat, I began to center in the moment, breathing, present and listening in that windless space, focused on the scent of pines, the cold light touch of snow.

And then my rational mind interrupted with critical abruptness: *And those unfinished reports? Those unanswered phone calls?*

Recognizing an old battle, I moved into the process of bringing my thoughts captive, of assuming—once more—control of my mind. I recognized, named, and felt the pain of inadequacy, the old sense that I never get things right no matter how hard I work, and then chose to detach myself from it, choosing once again to be present in the woods focused on the scent of pines, the sound of silence, and the feel of snow. Slowly, as pain often does when we detach, that pain crested, then lessened and flowed past, carried into the river of my unconscious mind. A bird stirred in the branches overhead. A scattering of snow dropped on my sleeve.

Then, with sly mockery, a voice of unbidden self-consciousness slipped into my awareness: *How ridiculous—standing alone in the snow, getting wet feet, and running a foolish risk in order to see a tree.*

And again I acknowledged an old pain, the separateness of being different, the pain of the struggle to live with my needs, my gifts, and my limitations. Then, choosing to detach from the pain, I focused again in the present, in the here and now of the snowy woods, drinking in the sense of winter night as it came on.

Then a memory, lodged like hidden shrapnel in my heart, broke loose and moved, exploding, into my mind. I was paralyzed by the intensity of the sudden pain that for a moment literally stopped my breath. In that instant there remained only a small, desperate, grace-barricaded place behind the pain where I could separate from it. I sensed instantly I *could* make that choice; I could stand in the snowy woods. Without words I began to focus on breathing, breathing the scent of the pine and sensing the wet, thick silence of the snow, simply breathing and being present in the deepening dark. Then as I began to find words to help me, I said gently, "I name and acknowledge this pain. But I know that this pain came from that other place, that other time. That was then and this is now, in the pines and in the snow." And again, as it does when we detach, the pain began to lessen. I concentrated—breathing in God's promised peace with the clean, cold air—breathing out the pain and old things—*in* the moment yet separate from it, standing steady in that small, grace-kept inner space. After a while the pain ebbed and flattened like a spent wave and moved unmarked into the unshaped space of the winter night. I remained still and quiet, focused on the snow touching my face, on my hand resting against the rough, unyielding trunk of the tree under which I sheltered, listening and watching the thickening snow crowning the ancient pine flake by fragile flake.

And then—I cannot explain how—for a sheer instant of time a tiny epiphany bloomed luminous in the dark—unasked, unmerited, and unanticipated. Like those other disciples traveling to Emmaus, I found my heart was suddenly warmed and my eyes opened. I knew who it was who had made and held that small, safe island of grace where I had stood when the waves of pain threatened to carry me away. I recognized who—before I could call— was already present with me in the pain, to stand with me, by me, in the dark. Then, as instant in its passing as in its coming, that moment of incandescent awareness was gone. But I knew Him—it was Immanuel, God with us, who had gifted me with a sense of His presence as I stood alone in the dark and the snow.

After a while, I walked slowly back to my car. My lungs were filled with the wet green scent of pine, my soul was filled with peace, and my mind was under my own control, by God's grace.

(My feet were, in fact, cold and wet, but in that moment that reality was worth no thought at all.)

Emotions, including our pain, are events that happen in us and to us, but they are *only* events. Sad or glad, angry or peaceful, our emotions are experiences we have; they are not who we are. It is possible for us to be aware of ourselves feeling the pain (or a flood of joy) and at the same time be quietly aware that we are sitting in a chair, lying in bed, or standing in a snowy evening in the woods. And it is out of this experiencing the pain yet detaching ourselves from it that we can begin to choose life and to choose it in the context of discipleship.

In my own experience, after my time in the woods I gave some careful review to the choices I had been making in terms of disciplined self-care. Was I choosing life as a pattern of faith-based self-care? In a practical way, how could I assess my life choices without wallowing in an orgy of self-absorption?

On a quiet Saturday morning, accompanied by my Bible, my journal, and a pot of good coffee, I settled down in my favorite chair to review the past week. I used a checklist that allowed me to evaluate in practical ways how effective I had been in my self-care. The MEDDSS checklist, the subject of the next chapter, is a helpful tool for making sure that we're applying the basic skills of self-care during seasons of suffering. This checklist is oriented toward helping us see what we are *doing,* rather than exploring how we are *feeling;* this emphasis helps us evaluate behavior and our response to the obligations of discipleship. It encourages us to see how faithfully God is making possible valuable experiences beyond and in addition to our pain.

chapter 6

HOW DO I EVALUATE
SELF-CARE?

There are many bad ideas in the world. Spending hours of time focused solely on caring for ourselves is certainly one of them. However, caring for ourselves only after everyone else's needs have been met is an equally bad one. Faith-based self-care as a life pattern works best when we develop a practical, middle-of-the-road routine that requires a minimum amount of fuss and produces maximum positive payoff both in deepened discipleship and our relationship with God.

Finding (and staying with) a productive middle path in times of distress often proves difficult. At such times, the acronym MEDDSS[1] provides a helpful checklist for the basic skills of self-care. It is easy to ask ourselves, "Have I taken my MEDDSS today (or this week)?" and check off the items on the list. The "meds" in the acronym are not pharmaceuticals; they are intentional acts of self-care that increase our spiritual health and strengthen our ability to deal with the life circumstances in which we find ourselves.

M: Mastery

Whatever pain we are experiencing, appropriate self-care begins with understanding and acting out of a place of mastery. Mastery provides, so to speak, a "competency vitamin," the "vitamin C" that strengthens our emotional immunity system against the erosion of strength that pain inevitably brings.

Acting out of a sense of mastery fits well with God's original intent that humans act in protective dominion over His creation. Mastery is *doing* rather than simply saying this truth. On this side of Eden's closed gates, God's design, while broken, still calls us to action in even the most difficult circumstances. The source of this ability to act does not lie simply in human willpower, however; the power to act is the gift of God. Faced with the dissension and disorder in the church at Ephesus, Timothy was not confident about his ability to deal with the situation. Paul, understanding Timothy's self-doubt, simply reminded him of God's gift: "God did not give us a spirit of timidity, but a spirit of power, of love and of self-discipline" (2 Timothy 1:7 NIV).

Pain and trouble cannot reduce us to a place in which we can no longer act or choose unless we make either or both of two fatal errors. One, we can forget or confuse the true source of our power. Or two, we can surrender to circumstances and adopt a passive victim role.

Mastery rests upon our belief that by God's enabling we *can* act. Mastery does not mean, however, that we can do whatever we decide we wish to do. We *can* act, but in our journey through pain this often requires that we first face those things we cannot do. Paradoxically, recognizing our limitations is often the beginning point of mastery in difficult circumstances. Claire's story (in chapter 4) illustrates this. In her first moments of consciousness after surgery, Claire realized that she could not walk or talk or turn her body in her bed. She could not think clearly. She could only move her head slightly and focus her eyes. That was all she could do. But she *could* do that. For Claire, mastery at that moment was reduced to her options to turn her head slightly so that she could focus her eyes alternately on either the door or window—and that is what she did. Prior to her illness, Claire was a successful executive in the corporate world; mastery was not a new idea to her. What Claire gained in her illness was new understanding of the little things around which mastery often pivots in times of pain and loss.

Two years after she had first been declared in remission, we met at a favorite restaurant for lunch. Claire talked about her discovery.

"I leave Friday for London, but I don't measure myself by that kind of thing anymore. My job is exciting, but my job didn't teach me who I am. I learned about myself when I could do nothing glamorous or dramatic, when the things I could choose were reduced to the absolute bare bones of life. I discovered who I was not in the boardroom but in the hospital room when my choices were simple: look at the door or the window, and choose, one more time, to breathe."

Mastery is not about grandstanding nor even about doing the tasks we once took for granted. Mastery is about taking the next right step and doing what we can. But human nature can be devious at this point. Mastery sometimes eludes us because we refuse to act at the simple level to which pain has reduced our capacity to function.

My client Alice was a severely depressed woman who was nearly immobilized when she first came for assistance. She had been an immaculate housekeeper and a gourmet cook, the respected (and envied) "Martha Stewart" of her neighborhood. But by the time her family brought her to me for help, she spent her days sitting in her pajamas in a house of chaotic disorder, surrounded by piles of unwashed laundry, waiting for her seven-year-old daughter to fix hotdogs for dinner.

Initially, I attempted to entice Alice to practice some of her old skills. These efforts were met with a spectacular lack of success. Alice's response to every suggestion was a dreary, "No. I can't do that."

This lack of progress led me to reconsider the problem; obviously I was missing something. I had not responded to the truth my client was telling me: *She could not do what she once had been able to do.* My effort to assist her to reboot her old life, so to speak, was counterproductive and seriously wide of the mark.

The first step out of the dilemma did not lie in the pursuit of past competencies. Progress pivoted around what Alice could do *now.* As soon as I had framed the issue clearly, the question then became *would* Alice do what she *could* do? If not, why not? I decided to try a new road.

"Is your silverware drawer neat and tidy?" I asked at the beginning of an hour together. It was a rhetorical question—we both knew her kitchen was in a chronic state of primeval chaos.

"No. I just can't keep house anymore," she said.

"Well," I said, taking a deep breath, "You have an assignment today. When Jim (her husband) comes home for lunch, he'll put the silverware drawer on the kitchen table. He'll wash the silverware and stack it there by the drawer. It's your job to sort the forks and spoons and stuff into the right spaces so that Jim can put the drawer away when he gets home from work."

"Oh, no, I can't do that," she said.

Looking Alice straight in the eye, I said directly, "No. That is not the truth. The truth is that you *can* do that. You *can* sort the silver. The truth is—at least at this minute—you are choosing *not* to do what you *can* do."

It was a long and difficult afternoon. Nevertheless, by the time Jim came home, the silver was sorted, and my client had taken a significant step toward restructuring her life and her understanding of herself. However awkward my technique, I had helped my client begin to tap into the power of mastery in dealing with her pain. In appointments that followed, Alice examined carefully some possible reasons for her resistance to taking this simple action that held potential for her good. In time Alice discovered that her emotional investment in the "Martha Stewart" role she had once played conflicted with her need to act in ways that incorporated appropriate self-care. If she could not meet the idealized level of performance in the role she once played, she would not act at all, regardless of the adverse impact of her doing nothing. She refused mastery if mastery required her to accept change and the loss of her old way of doing life. It was Martha Stewart—or nothing at all.

Alice—and her husband—discovered something else. Alice was struggling through a very painful place in her life. The pain was clearly pain. But, ironically, Alice discovered that there had been hidden gains in the collapse of her competency role and caretaking behaviors. *Others now took care of Alice.* For the first time since she had left a troubled childhood, Alice had resigned from caring for others. Those who loved Alice now took care of her in ways that permitted her to experience as an adult her long denied need for dependency. Mastery, at even a small step, would require Alice to begin the difficult task of redefining her understanding of love and facing her dependency needs as an adult. How much of the old "Martha Stewart" role could she resurrect and still establish with her family mutual caretaking and a new pattern of expressing love?

Stereotypically (and unfairly) men are often caricatured as behaving like babies when they are ill. In the majority of cases, men do *not* have lower pain tolerances than women; physical illness or emotional pain and trouble do *not* trigger an attack of uniquely male immaturity in men. What often happens, however, *can be* role related. Illness or the experience of pain and loss sometimes gives men emotional permission to lay down their culturally imposed caretaking roles and permit (or require) others to care for them. For either a man or woman in pain, when mastery entails risking emotional nurture and comfort that has emerged as an "unexpected good" in the journey through pain, then that person may resist mastery as a bad bargain indeed.

In a time of struggle and pain, accepting responsibility to do what we can do pushes us to look at ourselves with new honesty. When we say, "I cannot," the truth may well be that, indeed, we cannot, if what we mean is we cannot do something great, spectacular, and marvelous, something that amuses or pleases us, or, interestingly, something that we (and others) could label as "spiritual." We may resist doing anything at all if we perceive that pain and change have reduced our life options from bright and beautiful to basic beige. For this reason, the issue of mastery often plays out in a place where, so to speak, all that we can do is breathe and sort the silverware.

This reluctance to do what we can do sometimes catches us by surprise. If we view ourselves as a person who does important work, we may be perplexed by our reluctance to do anything that seems unimportant, even at those times when "unimportant" things may well be our lifeline. We rationalize our resistance on the principle that chefs rarely sort the spices and clean the pantry shelves; priests rarely iron the altar linens. Such tasks would bore us. Sometimes we are surprised by our reluctance to assume any appearance of competence; we cling to our vulnerability in ways that puzzle us. We (mistakenly) feel that mastery will bring loss of an "unexpected good," the nurture and care of others that has accompanied our pain and loss.

When we cannot do those things we once labeled "important," we learn that what we *can* do becomes the important thing. We learn too that competence need not trump relationships and mutual caretaking. In effective pain management, the significance of mastery lies in the power of choosing rather than the specific content of the choice. Mastery by doing what we can is not denial, disregard, nor disrespect of the gifts we have been given. Present limitations may look quite different in the tomorrow that lies ahead. Mastery, particularly when it pivots around small things, is doing hope rather than saying the word. Soul growth through the dark times is much like gardening: there is usually a great deal of weeding and watering before there are blue-ribbon tomatoes to show at the fair.

Faith-based self-care encourages us to choose life by asking ourselves, "Have I taken my M (mastery) in my MEDDSS today?" When the answer is no, it is helpful both in discipleship and pain management to attempt to determine what lies behind that no. Why have we not, by God's enabling grace, taken the next right step, small through it may be?

E: Exercise

A regular exercise program has been demonstrated to provide significant assistance in managing emotional struggle. Some studies have indicated that systematic exercise can be as helpful as medication in managing certain forms of depression.

For those whose bodies function with difficulty, exercise can be a special challenge. For one wheelchair-bound client, physical mobility is severely limited and movement is sometimes painful, but her courage in doing what she can in exercise inspires us all.

For most people, however, meeting the need for exercise does not require a personal trainer, membership at a local gym, or such measures of sheer courage. Taking the E in MEDDSS requires two basics: a pair of properly fitted walking shoes and acceptance that nothing else can be substituted for exercise in MEDDSS. The link between mastery and exercise is straightforward, but this connection can come as a surprise to those of us who began our Christian experience with a limited understanding of the significance of the body in the life of the soul.

On that Saturday morning when I sat down to inventory my self-care, I was reviewing what had been, without exaggeration, a fiercely challenging week. Nevertheless, I had earned some good marks. I had worked hard at mastery in my inner world and in relationships. I had detached myself from my pain and had not permitted it to dictate my choices. I had named my loss and faced its grief, and at least twice I had experienced some deep joy that had moved unanticipated into my heart. My work had been productive, and my clients were, for the most part, a safe step further on their journeys. And in my own journey there had been some deep moments of prayer and time with the Bible that had fed my soul. Initial review indicated that I had made good progress through a difficult time. Nevertheless, remembering the emotional firestorm in the park, I sensed that I had left something undone, unrecognized, that had increased my vulnerability.

I moved on with my inventory. Had I taken my MEDDSS? I checked off the M for mastery. Then came E: exercise.

Nothing. On not even one day had I taken time to walk around the park. Had I taken my E? No. Not even ten minutes on the treadmill.

It was clear where the problem lay. Failure to exercise had made me more vulnerable to the cumulative fatigue and impact of the emotional lives of those around me in my work. My personal journey had contained its own full measure of pain and loss. My body would have helped process the contents of this week at home and at work, however, had I given it the opportunity to do what it was designed to do. I had chosen, most unwisely, to act as though exercise were an option. I had assumed that if I were prayerful and chose to manage stress and pain through constructive thinking, disciplined feelings, and steady attention to my work, I could choose irresponsibly about my body. What I learned—not, unfortunately, for the first time—is that it simply does not work that way. Mastery work cannot be substituted for physical exercise any more than protein, however essential, can be substituted for water in the metabolic processes of the body.

The ancient Greek disdain for the body unconsciously corrupts our biblical understanding of the nature of our wholeness, body and soul. The body is designed not simply as a disposable container for the soul but as its literal embodiment, through which the soul functions.[2] And in this embodiment, physical exercise becomes the process through which *the body strengthens the soul.* In the process of exercise, the body strengthens our ability to moderate and regulate responses to pain and in quiet, powerful ways aids in "clearing the system," so that rest and renewal happen naturally. I learned early in my life that I cannot afford a disjuncture between work and prayer, that, in fact, there is no such thing as being too busy to pray—the greater the pressure of work, the greater the necessity for prayer.

However, I am still learning that I cannot afford to make an arbitrary artificial dichotomy between body and soul—the greater the demand for thinking and sensing, the greater the necessity for body energy released through exercise. To borrow from the *Book of Common Prayer,* all such good works as God has prepared for us to walk in as His children are by His design works of body *and* soul that cannot be separated. I am called to pray and walk and work and love in the intermingled reality that constitutes the wholeness of body and soul. And when in the struggle to deal with pain and loss we are tempted to fragmentation, taking the E in our MEDDSS calls us back to the wholeness of God's design for our lives. Redemptive management of our pain must be worked out through the complex intermingled reality of the body and soul; in this world, it is the only "self" we have. A young friend shared her story, and she has given her permission to share it here.

> I discovered at age thirty-nine that I could walk my way out of depression. I mean that quite literally. The simple, daily discipline of placing one foot in front of the other and repeating that act over and over empowers me to live freely.
>
> … [But] even after I'd been walking for months and had seen the benefits, I stopped. I was grieving the reality of my difficult marriage and my choice to have no more children. My sister had recently gone through a divorce and had been in treatment for breast cancer. I was in the worst depression I had suffered to date. The turning point came when my therapist asked, "When was the last time you walked?" It had been several weeks. She said, "I want you to put on your walking shoes and walk half as far as you think you should." Appointment over. I did that, day after day. In the midst of learning to take care of myself, I also registered to walk sixty miles in three days in the

fight against breast cancer. We formed a team that trained together every Saturday. My walking became not just about me, but about someone else as well. I was forever transformed into a walker that year.

I cannot imagine *not* walking now. It is as vital to my health as anything I do. It's still not about my weight, nor will it ever be again; but the side benefit has been a steady loss of weight and the ability to maintain a healthy weight without employing the crazy patterns of the past.

I turned my walking into an opportunity to listen to God, to be connected to Him through my surroundings, and to talk with Him about what burdens my heart. My walking friends and I are willing to get up in the dark, in the cold, in the heat, just because we've seen and felt the benefits of community. Our walking matters. We matter to one another and we've got hours of time to build meaningful, lasting friendship.

I cherish what I've learned through the daily act of walking. I honor my body for its strength and ability to endure through pain and difficulty. When I feel tempted to dip my foot into the edge of the pit of depression, I lace up my faithful walking shoes and head outdoors. In this place of power, I am reminded that I am not alone and that when I do my part, God shows up and multiplies my efforts.

D: Diet

Mastery, exercise, diet. Careful attention to food is another aspect of faith-based self-care. Choices we make about food affect our health and well-being and our ability to act in ways that are consistent with discipleship. However, food choices are not just about nutrition; food choices reflect powerful emotional needs and, like exercise, reflect complex body/soul relationships about which we can become confused. When in self-care inventory we ask, "Have I taken my D (diet/food) today?" the answer is not so simple a matter as recording the number of calories consumed in a given day.

The commonsense rule-of-thumb regarding diet is straightforward. In life, and particularly in times of pain and struggle, we need to focus on balanced nutrition and operate out of the Goldilocks principle: not too much, not too little, but just the right amount of healthful foods for our individual needs. Making choices consistent with the Goldilocks principle is not as easy as it may sound, however, when we are caught up in painful life circumstances.

At such times, food can easily become a displaced focus for our pain, a substitute solution for management of our discomfort. And when without conscious awareness we tangle food choices with management of pain, we can make ourselves additional trouble, sometimes in oddly erratic ways. One day we can say, for example, "I am lonely," and handle the pain by refusing to eat, making the absence of food reflect the absence of human companionship. Then another day we can say "I am lonely" and eat a half-dozen chocolate doughnuts using sugar as anesthesia for our pain. And at still another time, we can say, "This is the pain of emptiness," and consume enormous amounts of food in an effort to fill the inner spaces where pain dwells. Clearly, the problem does not lie in loneliness, painful as that reality may be, but in the misplaced effort to use food as the solution to the problem.

With rare exception, problems with food management grow out of unsolved problems in pain management. The pain may be related to the body itself—body image, sexuality, gender identity—or rooted in life events, personal relationships, and loss. But the impulse to use food as a solution to the problem is not generally determined by the specific source of the pain itself. Rather, unconscious, uncontrolled use of food to manage pain generally stems from a lack of ability to separate from the pain and to identify it for what it is—an event that happens in and to us, but an event that is separate from us, from which we can stand apart. When we learn to stand apart from our pain, to be in the moment without being defined by it, we gain the power to choose our responses to our pain. Only from that space apart from pain do we have the freedom to choose. But from that space, we are free to choose food as a part of our pain management, or we are free to choose other means.

For example, I may, in a moment of intense pain, choose the comfort of a cup of tea served in my grandmother's old china cup; I may walk down to the coffee shop and have a latte; I may choose to go to the farmer's market and buy the two most beautiful apples in the bin (and eat them both), or I may choose to listen as I walk to the intricate patterns of Miles Davis or John Coltrane's jazz. I get to choose. I may choose to have food in some form as a part of my pain management. I may not. However, the clearer I am about the nature of pain, the more faithfully I have worked at mastery, the more consistently I have embraced through exercise my body as my ally and source of strength, the easier it becomes *if I choose food* to choose according to the Goldilocks principle—not too much, not too little, but just the right amount of healthful food to strengthen body and soul.

Food, like exercise and sleep (as we will see shortly), serves as an essential tool in pain management, but food requires thoughtful choice. Comfort food is just that—comfort food—and can be a constructive choice. Food clearly falls into the category of those good things that God has richly provided for our enjoyment (1 Timothy 6:17), but like other good gifts of God, food requires wise management. Food is designed to supply life and energy, pleasure, and comfort, but the gift becomes dangerous when we choose food as an unconscious physical solution to managing our pain, whether we choose to eat or refuse to do so.

When in self-care inventory we ask ourselves, "Have I taken my D (diet/food) today?" we are asking the Goldilocks question: Have I chosen today not too much, not too little, but just the right amount of healthful food for my individual need? If the answer is no, we need to ask ourselves another question. In what ways have my food choices reflected my struggle to manage my pain? What alternative choices do I need to explore?

D: Drugs

Self-care has two Ds—diet (food), which we have just considered, and drugs. The drug question, "Have I taken my drugs today?" initially appears to invite a straightforward response: *If the question is whether I took the medication my doctor prescribed, then yes, I did. And if the question is whether I use recreational drugs, then no, I do not. What is the point here?* Actually, there are several points, and probably none of them as straightforward as we would like.

While working on this D section of MEDDSS, I decided one afternoon to do some fieldwork. I went to the pharmacy section of a super discount store not far from my office. I walked up and down the aisles adjacent to the pharmacy itself, paying careful attention to the stock on the shelves. Then I located a seat that let me observe traffic both at the pharmacy and in the area adjacent to it. For the next hour or more I watched people come and go and thought about the chemical Americana that I was observing.

My first response was surprise about the sheer number of goods displayed. I was somewhat taken aback by the volume and variety of non-prescription, chemically based materials available for sale. I was impressed as well with the volume and variety of drugs that filled the shelves in the restricted area behind the pharmacist's counter. It was the people, however, that provided the greatest surprise. At mid-afternoon on a weekday, large numbers of people crowded the aisles and formed long, irregular lines waiting for their turn to be served at the pharmacy.

What is happening here? I wondered, and started cataloging the obvious. People were buying chemically based products ranging from toothpaste, shampoo, and aspirin to life-extending medications that keep tired, irregular hearts beating. They were buying vitamins and cough syrup and appetite suppressants, solutions to soften painful corns, dye to change hair color, and pills to control female fertility. They were buying nail polish and lipstick and insulin and antibiotics and deodorant and mouthwashes and creams to soothe swollen arthritic hands and tiny blue pills that promised sleep. They were buying medications that control depression and calm anxiety, that soothe ulcers and their pain. Chemical choices appeared to be endlessly diverse. As people filled their shopping carts, I listened to their conversations; I watched their faces and listened to the body language that without words filled the emotionally thick space around me. Gradually, slowly, my initial question reshaped itself.

I wondered again, *What do these people hope to take home with them?* Glamour, beauty, comfort, good health—and, for some, the continuation of life itself in the small, carefully labeled amber containers dispensed at the pharmacist's window. People hoped for all these things and more, I suspected. After their packages were scanned at the checkout counter, many people carried with their purchases the culture's half-magic expectation that human longing, fear, and pain in its nameless, unnumbered forms could be brought to the pharmacy and exchanged for the mysterious power of chemicals that would make life different and better.

Important truth underlies this perception. Aspirin does indeed help a headache, and toothpaste reduces cavities, provided it is used regularly. Deodorant makes life more pleasant for everyone. Blonde from a bottle can be beautiful, and vitamins, while not magic potions, are helpful. Antidepressants make it possible for life and work to continue for some who would otherwise be homebound or hospitalized. Drugs used in chemotherapy give opportunity for extended life to cancer victims, and anti-nausea medications help make the side effects of chemotherapy bearable. Insulin permits diabetics to live productive lives. Medications that regulate blood pressure reduce significantly the danger of stroke and heart attacks. It is easily possible to make a long list of the positive byproducts of chemical intervention in our lives. What then is the issue?

Not surprisingly, the problem lies in human nature, not in the chemicals. Buying toothpaste does not automatically result in a disciplined program of dental hygiene. We can purchase aspirin and successfully moderate the symptoms of a stress-producing lifestyle while we are at the same time denying the source of the problem. Purchasing contraceptives does not necessarily produce sexually responsible behavior and relationally ethical choices. Sleep-producing substances do little or nothing to deal with the underlying fears that often drive sleepless nights. And the cosmetic industry's relentless marketing of chemicals links glamorous costly packaging with the implicit promise of increased sexual attractiveness exploiting women's longing to be beautiful and to be loved.

I left the store carrying a small plastic sack, feeling both thoughtful and privately amused at myself. I had purchased baby aspirin, an over-the-counter drug prescribed by my physician as a preventive measure to protect my aging heart. I had also purchased a small beautifully packaged container of hand cream formulated (allegedly) to protect my skin against the rigors of the cold, dry climate in which I live. My fieldwork had given me some helpful ideas to consider. It had also resulted in a small and interesting joke on me. Without consciously planning to do so, I had selected two items that illustrated concretely the complexities that surround the use of drugs in faith-based self-care.

In the present culture in which drugs—prescription, nonprescription, and street drugs—are commonly abused, it is difficult to avoid unbalanced thinking about the proper use of drugs. For the most part we are aware that the culture and the pharmaceutical industry can tempt us to use drugs as an over-easy answer to problems. However, we are less aware that we can as easily, and as dangerously, be tempted to disregard the necessity for drugs. A faith-based life does not eliminate the need for insulin. Neither does a faith-based life automatically correct the insufficient levels of serotonin that in many instances underlie biologically driven depression. In regard to prescribed drugs, the question of "right amount" is not easy for either the attending physician or the individual to determine. Drugs are chemically complex, the biological conditions for which they are prescribed are complex, and the response of a given individual to a given drug cannot be predicted with absolute certainty. Experienced physicians are cautious both as to the specific drugs and amounts they prescribe. But the medical challenge is not the point in self-inventory. The drug question in self-care inventory is designed to focus not simply on drugs as such (prescribed or over-the-counter), but rather on the ways in which our use of drugs affects discipleship-oriented self-care.

Take, for example, the baby aspirin that my physician had prescribed. The drug itself (aspirin) was relatively simple and available over the counter. The prescribed amount had been established through controlled studies and medical consensus. My physician and I knew what I should take and how much and how often. If the inventory question had been simply, "Have I taken my aspirin today?" the answer could have been a straight-forward yes or no. But the Goldilocks form of the question raises a tougher version of the issue: "Have I taken the right amount of this drug for good functioning?" The answer to that form of the question required me to think about more than the aspirin. For my prescribed aspirin to result in good functioning, I needed to add to the aspirin good habits of exercise and healthy choices regarding food.

Was the prescribed baby aspirin all that I needed for good functioning? The answer, unfortunately, was, it depends. Probably yes, if I exercise and eat properly, but only maybe if I do not. The Goldilocks form of the question requires a similar it-depends answer whether the drug is insulin, thyroid medication, or an antidepressant or any of the thousands of available pharmaceuticals, prescribed or over-the-counter. The question is not simply whether I take the given drug at a prescribed or recommended level. The question is whether I take the drug in a way that enables me to function more effectively, whatever the pain and confusion and struggle present in my life. An honest answer to the Goldilocks form of the question does not permit us to weasel. It requires us to look at more than the fact of our action; it requires us to look at *how* and *why* as well as *what* we have chosen to do. "So whether you eat or drink or whatever you do, do it all for the glory of God," Paul urged the believers at Corinth (1 Corinthians 10:31 NIV). Living out that text requires us to use drugs, prescribed or over-the-counter, in practical ways that strengthen our discipleship.

And now some attention to the second item in my bag. Why did I buy that hand cream? When I returned to my office, I opened the gold foil package and set the lovely oval-shaped bottle in the middle of my desk. Then I sat for a while thinking, looking first at the bottle and then at my hands. What had I hoped to bring home?

When I was young, my hands were strong and slender, and, I confess, I was somewhat vain about their appearance. But years have passed, and while my hands are, thankfully, still strong and capable, arthritis has slightly reshaped one index finger and my skin is no longer clear and wrinkle free. As I looked at my hands, I recalled the larger-than-life, air-brushed photo of the model that had hung above the display of hand cream. The photographer had caught the model's image at the moment one of her beautifully shaped hands had lifted the fall of her dark hair away from her flawless face. Her left hand rested in casual elegance on the back of a chair. Her eyes as she looked down at us were filled with implicit promise.

Remembering the image, I smiled to myself. What had I hoped to bring home? That grace? That seductive beauty? Had I indulged in a moment of total silliness and imagined that the physical consequences of aging could be erased by the contents of that elegant bottle of hand cream? Fortunately, I have a sturdy sense of reality not easily moved by advertising images. I felt reasonably certain I had not been silly in that way, but that left an intriguing question. What *had* I thought that I could bring home?

At the moment of purchase, I did not give words to the inner reality of my experience. But in retrospect, sitting at my desk, I realized that standing there with the image of the model looking down at me, I had been sensible. I was fully aware that my hands would never look like hers. But standing there, I had also become aware of something else. For a short wordless second of transient regret, I had confronted one of the irreversible losses that aging had brought. My hands will never again look as they once did when I was young. But without words, in that moment I had also considered my choice. I could not turn back change and loss, but I could have comfort and hand cream in a beautiful package. I could choose life and joy in the reality of my loss, and so I did.

What had I hoped to bring home? Comfort and beauty—in the shape of the bottle, no longer in the shape of my hands—and an odd form of mastery. Choosing to purchase the hand cream was a brief moment of self-comfort and self-care. It was also a choice of mastery: I chose to do what I could with what was available—chemically, in this instance. Both food and drugs can be abused in reaction to pain. But both can be an important part of appropriate self-care that is faith-based and oriented toward discipleship. Drugs, like food, can be appropriated in choices that deal comfortingly with pain and need—whether physical or emotional—and chosen in ways that both strengthen our choice to live and to honor God.

S: Sleep

Self-care inventory incorporates attention to sleep. The Goldilocks form of the question is straightforward: Have I had the amount of sleep—not too much or not too little—that enables me to function well?

For many people, the answer to this question is no. The American Academy of Sleep Medicine has estimated that as many as seventy million Americans experience chronic significant sleep deprivation.[3] In many instances, insufficient sleep is the result of life circumstances and choices that routinely limit time in bed to fewer than the eight hours generally required for effective adult functioning. However, for a large percentage of these people—perhaps for as many as forty million—sleep deprivation is not an unintentional result of the daily routine of life but is associated with some form of sleep disorder often undiagnosed and untreated.

Medical concern is growing regarding the amount and quality of sleep people experience. We know that lack of sleep can lead to serious accidents; sleep deprivation significantly interferes as well with learning and memory and resistance to disease. Increasingly, research is demonstrating a link between sleep deprivation and the development of serious medical conditions such as diabetes. Failure to get sufficient sleep is not a casual omission of an unimportant task.

Experience teaches us that there is a direct link between our emotional stability and our lack of sleep. We know that anger and tears happen more easily and more intensely when we are tired; we know that patience is far more difficult to demonstrate after a sleepless night. A recent study has demonstrated empirically the nature and significance of that link we intuitively understand.[4]

Scientists assigned healthy people to either a normal sleep group or a sleep-deprived group. Participants in the study were then shown a series of images that were initially emotionally neutral but that became increasingly unpleasant and disturbing, including, for example, a dirty toilet bowl, a burn victim, a dying patient, or mutilated bodies. The activity of the amygdala, that part of the brain that triggers emotional responses to potentially threatening cues, was measured as participants viewed the images.

To no one's surprise, both groups experienced greater amygdala activity in response to the more negative pictures. However, the intensity and volume of the response in the sleep-deprived group was unexpected. Dr. Matthew Walker, the director of the study, reported, "The size of the increase truly surprised us. The emotional centers of the brain were over 60% more reactive under conditions of sleep deprivation than in subjects who had obtained a normal night of sleep."

The size of the increased response was only one of the significant findings, however. The amygdala in the sleep-deprived group appeared to be more strongly connected to the brain's primitive impulsive regions and less connected to the more rational prefrontal lobe, which normally keeps emotions and behaviors in check. In short, the amygdala in a typical sleep-deprived individual was not only 60 percent more reactive—*this increased activity asked for response from the most primitive, impulsive part of the brain.* Dr. Walker concluded, "This study demonstrates the dangers of not sleeping enough. Sleep deprivation fractures the brain mechanisms that regulate key aspects of our mental health. Sleep appears to restore our emotional brain circuits, and in doing so prepares us for the next day's challenges and social interactions."[5] I recently passed a church bulletin board that read, "God supplies, but we must apply." God does supply, and often, out of His infinite mercy and love, God supplies on His own initiative without our application. "Before they call I will answer," God promised through the prophet Isaiah (65:24 NIV), and we know that He performs faithfully that which He has promised. Nevertheless, it is also true that the choices we make influence our capacity to receive God's grace, and the application idea points toward this parallel truth. When in the midst of difficult circumstances we apply for the Spirit's fruit of self-control, patience, and kindness, our application requires in practical terms that we make some choices. Praying with integrity requires us to shut off the television (or computer or close a book), go to bed, close down our conscious minds, and go to sleep. God supplies, but our ability to receive His grace and gifting is increased by the practical act of getting a good night's sleep.

But good rest is often much easier to wish for than to achieve. We forget as adults that as a baby we had to learn to sleep—to feel safe in our bed, to know when we were tired and needed to sleep, and to link the rhythm of our rest and activity to the rhythms of the world around us. Learning to sleep included some discomfort, although by adulthood we have forgotten that. However, for some of us, family history may include stories of the trouble we had (and caused) when as an infant we "had our days and nights mixed up." I recently visited a young mother who had just put her infant son down for a nap. As the young mother poured our tea, sounds of serious discontent reached us from the nursery—whines, half-cries, and other loud indications of displeasure signaling her son's clear demand to be picked up. Noticing my awareness of these sounds of distress, the young mother smiled and said, "He's all right. He'll quiet down in a little bit. He's still learning to take a nap and sometimes he fusses himself to sleep."

In circumstances of pain and disorientation we sometimes have to relearn the art of resting, retrain ourselves to take the trusting step to sleep. And what was not easy at the beginning of our lives often becomes even more difficult when complicated by the bad habits of adulthood. As adults in this sleep-deprived culture, we have learned to go without sleep and often do not realize how tired we are. Sometimes we have learned to take a perverse pride in chronic fatigue, viewing exhaustion as evidence of achievement and importance. Sometimes we have an unconscious show-and-tell program going with God, acting as if by exhaustion we demonstrate our commitment to bringing about God's kingdom on earth. Many of us have practiced routine disregard of the biblical principle of Sabbath keeping. As a result we come to a place of needed rest with lack of knowledge, lack of skills, and lack of experience. We need sleep and the restoration that sleep brings, but we do not know how in the midst of our fear and grief to get good rest. All too often the best we can do is the adult equivalent of the behavior of my friend's young son: we wear ourselves out with tears and worry and fragmented praying until eventually, we fuss ourselves to sleep.

Retraining ourselves to rest requires first that we commit to sleep as a basic priority in our lives—not too much, not too little, but the right amount for effective functioning. As adults, establishing a right priority for sleep requires us to deal with the disregard for proper self-care we frequently build into our life routines. We tend to regard sleep, like exercise, as something that has to fit into whatever time is left when the important "have-to-do" things are finished. What is true, however, is that proper rest is not functionally optional. We can schedule our lives as though we can go without sufficient sleep and give ourselves a hundred reasons why this deprivation is necessary and desirable. What we can*not* do, however, is compel our bodies and minds to function when sleep deprived in the way they will function when properly rested. Functioning well in a sleep-deprived state—body, mind, or soul—is not an option that God's basic Eden-level design of humans permits us to have.

The link to discipleship is clear and straightforward. Behaviors demonstrating love, kindness, patience, and self-control are *not* the fruit of sleep deprivation. It is blessedly true that in times of emergency, God can, and does, faithfully supply our needs. However, if we systematically, routinely deprive ourselves of sufficient sleep while asking God to make us into peaceful patient saints, such praying is much like asking God to give us a healthy heart while continuing a regular diet of fries and cheeseburgers at our local fast-food franchise.

Practical preparation for good rest requires that we establish a regular schedule for sleep together with a standard relaxing bedtime routine. Bed, bedding, and bed clothing need to be comfortable. A bedroom that is cool, dark, and quiet provides the best environment for sound sleep. Activities in the bedroom need to be routinely limited to those activities directly associated with sleep. Watching television or reviewing the agenda for tomorrow's meeting is not preparation for rest. If in the night we awaken and have difficulty falling back to sleep, it is best to get up and leave the bedroom; turning and tossing and trying to go back to sleep is usually nonproductive. It is better to read or engage in some other non-stimulating activity for a while and then return to bed. Long afternoon naps do not replace sleep lost at night and can further interfere with establishment of regular sleep patterns. Consumption of food, alcohol, or caffeine close to bedtime interferes with sound sleep and should be avoided. The sleep-friendly behaviors described here are common knowledge, but present levels of sleep deprivation in our society indicate that large numbers of people are not putting into practice what they know.

Getting good rest in times of pain and disorientation is a particularly complex aspect of self-care. There is something about the darkness and stillness of night that permits fear and pain to flourish exponentially. At unspoken levels we are all afraid in the dark, regardless of the number of candles on our last birthday cake. As adults, we no longer believe that there is a bear under our bed, but we know what does come alive in the dark—our regrets, our failures, our losses, the dread and fear of what lies ahead in the days to come. In times of pain and disorientation, these creatures of the nighttime can leave us wounded, stripped of all hope, with little or no courage to attempt another day.

Compline, the service of evening prayers in traditional liturgical worship, recognizes that fact and takes dead aim at our sense of the dangers of the dark. The service begins with a direct petition for God's provision in the night hours.

"The LORD Almighty grant us a peaceful night and a perfect end," the officiant begins.[6] The collect that follows may include these petitions:

> Be our light in the darkness, O LORD, and in your great mercy defend us from all perils and dangers of this night; for the love of your only Son, our Savior Jesus Christ. *Amen.*
>
> Be present, O merciful God, and protect us through the hours of this night, so that we who are wearied by the changes and chances of this life may rest in your eternal changelessness; through Jesus Christ our LORD. *Amen.*
>
> Visit this place, O LORD, and drive far from it all snares of the enemy; let your holy angels dwell with us to preserve us in peace; and let your blessings be upon us always; through Jesus Christ our LORD. *Amen.*

> Keep watch, dear LORD, with those who work, or watch, or weep this night, and give your angels charge over those who sleep. Tend the sick, LORD Christ; give rest to the weary, bless the dying, soothe the suffering, pity the afflicted, shield the joyous; and all for your love's sake. *Amen.*

The closing response runs:

> Guide us waking, O LORD, and guard us sleeping; that awake we may watch with Christ, and asleep we may rest in peace.

God's people have never believed that a good night's sleep could be reduced to a matter of a firm mattress, a cool bedroom, and the installation of a reliable security system. In good times or in bad, in the dark or in the light, our safety and our rest lie in God. But making ourselves into ready recipients for God's provision is a practical matter that, in times of stress and pain, requires us to take some steps that feel at odds with our established habits of sleeplessness.

The first step is both straightforward and difficult. Preparation for rest and sleeping through the night hours requires that we *shut down* the day's activities and *shut out* the world. In order to do this it is necessary to set conscious, specific boundaries around night hours. We must choose to use nighttime for sleep and rest and for restoration, physical and emotional, so that we are prepared to deal with the challenges and work that our tomorrows inevitably bring.[7] Active grieving, certain forms of praying,[8] revisiting and re-examining experiences of betrayal and loss, reviewing injustice, problem solving, finding new options— all these activities are an important part of our experience of pain and suffering. For the most part, however, these are activities that belong in the daylight. They are part of the work and challenges that come with good stewardship of pain, but they are not work to be done in the night. Our human impulse, however, is to make them into night work. We know that our grief and pain are not finished, and our loss may be still new and raw. So when the lights are out and the darkness comes, we continue our work of anger, of grief, of despair as though the coming day will not have sufficient space for all that we yet need to feel and think. We lay our bodies down to rest, but we permit—and sometimes encourage—our minds and emotions to continue to work. We disregard the critical importance of rest and our deep need for a Sabbath from our pain. And, further, we disregard the boundaries that God has given—work for the day and rest for the night.

Jesus was talking to His followers once about the human tendency to worry, and He made an interesting comment. He said, "Do not worry about tomorrow, for tomorrow will worry about itself. Each day has enough trouble of its own" (Matthew 6:34 NIV). Jesus was not lecturing in a Judean sleep clinic, of course; He was encouraging His followers to rest in God's faithful care, whatever their circumstances. But making a conscious choice to be obedient to what Jesus said can lay a solid foundation for rest and, considered from the standpoint of discipleship, can serve as a commitment to mini-Sabbath keeping. We are called to say, "This day is over. I stop. I shut the door. This night I will not work at grief or pain or worry or problem solving. This night I will take Sabbath from my work and from my pain. I will rest in God's protective presence and His faithfulness. And *in obedience, I will leave tomorrow's work and worry for tomorrow.*"

But that is simply not possible, we object. We regard our anxiety, our regrets, our memories, and our grief as elements that lie outside our control and beyond the reach of choice. We regard

Paul's insistence that every thought should be taken captive and made obedient to Christ (2 Corinthians 10:5) as a theological concept irrelevant to our getting a peaceful night's sleep. In the text of the Corinthian letter, of course, it is true that Paul was not dealing with sleep. He was encouraging the Corinthians to think clearly about Christ even when faced with the powerful competing messages of the Greek culture. But that fact of the historical context does not take us *off* the hook; to the contrary, it places us firmly *on* it. Paul insisted that God's people control their thoughts in the midst of the clamoring static of Greek "wisdom" and the false teaching of pseudo-apostles. Are we not similarly responsible to control thoughts and feelings that come in the dark, to resist the inner voices that speak in the night in the clamoring static of our doubt and pain?

Tears *do* come in the night—memories, fears, and the voices of old regret that can seduce us to despair. There is no magic spell by which we can prevent these night visitors from appearing and no magic spell that will instantly banish them with a word. But thoughts and emotions that come in the night, like those that come in the day, are events that happen. They are events, not who we are. And in the night as in the daytime, what we can do is to be present in the moment, focusing on the moment. We can stand behind the thoughts, the feelings, and disengage from them. We can acknowledge their presence and reach through them, through the pain, to sleep. We can decide what we do with what comes alive in the dark. And in this choosing, we act to take captive our thoughts and move toward sleep.

In order to retrain oneself to sleep, it is important to have a plan, then make and take time consistently to follow the plan. At the beginning, the plan needs to include these steps in some form.

Close the door on today. It is useful to say audibly, "This day is done. I have finished working; my mini-Sabbath has begun." *It is important to speak carefully.* We must *not* say that our work is finished—for most of us, our work rarely, if ever, is done. The message is not about the work—it is about us. Whatever the state of our work, *we* are finished working. It is useful to remember that when the Jewish Sabbath began, work stopped; whatever task was incomplete was left incomplete until the Sabbath ended. It is important to remember as well that emotional regulation was included in Sabbath restrictions; being sad on the Sabbath was forbidden to God's people.[9] Developing concrete, practical routines such as closing a desk, turning off the computer, locking a door, or other similar activities are helpful ways to put in action the truth that we are stopping our work. These actions say, "This day is done. I have finished working."

Assign tomorrow's work, both the work of doing and feeling. It is useful to say audibly, "I will identify tomorrow's work. I will assign to tomorrow the work that belongs to tomorrow; I will separate tomorrow's work from this night." As a part of bedtime routine, it is helpful to make a list for tomorrow of both doing and feeling, a specific list that includes things like:

- Tell God again how angry I am that He let this happen.
- Complain to the person who is closest to me, perhaps a friend or spouse.
- Cry. Remember last year this time and be sad.
- Set up committee meeting for Thursday.
- Stop by the bank on lunch hour.
- Call and make doctor's appointment.
- Hate it that life is like it is. Tell God in detail.
- Stop by the grocery; get special coffee and some flowers.

It is important for us to keep clear that this is not simply a "to do" list. It is part of the process of structuring the working/resting activities of our lives and placing a biblically buttressed boundary around them. For a number of weeks one client who was working on resting put the calendar date at the top of her list, then added the Scripture reference Matthew 6:34, where Jesus tells His listeners not to worry about tomorrow. "[The reference] helps me remember what I write is my intended act toward obedience," she told me. When consistently and prayerfully practiced, this simple act of listing has a surprising power to help bring thoughts captive, close the door on the day, and open the door to sleep.

Check your sleep environment. Check the bed itself: Are blankets and sheets comfortable? Check the room itself—the temperature, light, clock, phone. Is this a safe, comfortable place? As much as possible, is it a refuge, a beautiful, quiet safe place in which to rest?

Think through the nighttime prayers you will use. This is not as simple as it might initially appear to be. Preparing for nighttime prayer requires that we recognize the specific and distinctive purpose that has first priority in nighttime praying. Nighttime prayer is aimed primarily at the goal of trusting rest, rest that comes when the cares of the day have successfully been laid aside. These prayers petition for peace and rest and for protection throughout the night hours. As noted above, the service of Compline begins simply, "The LORD Almighty grant us a peaceful night and a perfect end." One prayer that sometimes follows asks with brief powerful simplicity, "Be our light in the darkness, O LORD, and in your great mercy defend us from all perils and dangers of this night; for the love of your only Son, our Savior Jesus Christ."

In times of pain and disorientation, the perils and dangers we face are more likely to come from within than from without. Tears, fears, and dread of tomorrow do come in the night, bringing agitation and wakefulness. When this happens the goal becomes disengaging from them so that sleep and rest can come. Nighttime prayers need to be linked specifically and clearly to this purpose and should be used to help us stay centered in the moment in a place of rest and sleep.

The experiences of my clients, and my own as well, have taught me a practical caution at this point. For many of us, our initial experience of prayer was shaped in a tradition that placed great emphasis upon spontaneous highly individualized forms of prayer. While there is value in learning to come to God in this fashion, there is a surprising risk to this form of prayer when we are dealing with "the perils and dangers of this night" that come from within.

For example, a client was dealing with the loss of her marriage. Her nights were filled with regrets, fear, anger, and grief. The resulting sleep deprivation began to reduce her effectiveness at work and to increase dangerously her vulnerability to depression. I suggested that when she was flooded with these feelings that she use prayer to stand apart from the emotional event and to stay centered in the moment—safe, comfortable, at rest in her bed, secure under God's watchful care.

After a couple of weeks she reported in frustration that praying simply made things worse. I was perplexed until it occurred to me to ask her to describe how she prayed. "Well," she said, "I just talk to God. I tell God how upset I am. I cry and tell God how scared I am, and then I tell Him how mad I am that this happened, and then I tell God all the things I remember that I did wrong, and then I tell Him all the things that Frank did wrong, and I ask God to make things different. I usually don't feel like going to sleep after I pray, so most of the time I just start over and do it all again."

Listening to her description, I had an "ah-ha" moment. This client was using her unstructured, spontaneous prayer to rehearse her experience over and over again. In the process of this rehearsal she permitted her intense emotional response to what she was describing to move her out of the moment (safe, comfortable, at rest in her bed), into the past (what had happened), and into the future (her fear of tomorrow). While appropriate praying, it was not a form of prayer that aided her to lay aside the cares of the day and to move into sleep. Once I realized what was happening, together we restructured her night praying in a way that provided some helpful results.

First, we recognized the validity and value of her prayers and expanded her prayer life to include some of the lament psalms. (This use of the Psalter is described in chapter 9.) Then we discussed the ways in which her legitimate expression of intense emotion was incompatible with her need for peaceful rest and agreed that, for a time at least, this form of prayer would be better moved from night to morning. Then we made a plan to assist her to move her emotional work from night to day. We agreed that she would close the door on the day by making a daily list for tomorrow. We agreed additionally that when making the list for tomorrow's work (including her plan to ask God to "whack Frank—or at least do something"), she would place each specific burden she had carried that day (a stressful new job) in a theoretical "God bag" for God's attention and care during the nighttime hours. ("Let God take care of your job while you sleep," I suggested). All things placed in the "God bag" became God's responsibility; she could safely leave them there.

But when she had placed today's burdens safely in the God bag and made tomorrow's list, what then? The list and the God bag helped her close the door on the day, but we needed a plan for the night. Having decided what she would *not* think about, our plan required an alternate focus for her attention that would encourage her to embrace God's presence and protection in the night. Her unstructured prayer led habitually to rehearsal of regrets and fears that moved her out of the moment of rest, so we chose one of the traditional prayers that people have long used at night[10] and tailored it for her use. Her prayer became:

> Be present in this bedroom where I sleep, O LORD, and drive far from it all things that destroy my rest; let your holy angels be with me to preserve me in peace; let your blessings be on me in this stressful time; through Jesus Christ, my Savior. Amen.

Our plan required some practice. My client found it difficult at first when the tears and fears came to move through and past them into her established prayer. She described these early efforts at prayer as "oops prayers." "God, where's my tissue box? You know what Frank did—*oops*. Be present in this bedroom where I sleep, O LORD, and drive far from it all things that destroy my rest." In a relatively short time, the "oops prayers" became less frequent, and she began to report improvement in her sleep. She developed increasing control of her thoughts. When in the nighttime she awakened and grief and anxiety threatened to flood her mind ("What if I lose my job?"), she became able simply to name what was happening ("I am feeling afraid about my job"), then say, "My job is in the God bag and on the list. That's tomorrow's stuff," and then move into the prayer we had fashioned for her to use.

After a number of weeks of steady improvement in the amount and quality of her sleep, she announced one day that she had revised her prayer for night use. "I still say it like we wrote it out when I go to bed," she explained. "Sometimes I say it three or four times then, but I made it shorter for when I wake up in the night."

"What do you say then?" I asked, curious about the direction of the growth in her prayer life that this revision might reflect.

"Oh, I say, 'Be present in my bedroom, O LORD. Drive away these things that mess up my sleep. Keep me in peace. Bless me in this hard place. *Amen.*'" She paused and then smiled. "Well, you know how I pray. Sometimes I make it even shorter than that. Last night I just said, 'Jesus, don't let my sleep get messed up. I love you.' And I think I was asleep before I said amen."

Practice good sleep habits consistently. Good sleep habits require consistent maintenance. If we are to get good rest, it is necessary that each day we give careful attention to more than going to bed. We need to get ready to go to sleep each day. Taking our MEDDSS as faith-based discipleship requires careful attention to sleep—not too much, not too little, but the right amount for effective functioning for our good and for God's glory.

S: Spirituality

The second S in self-care inventory is spirituality. In the present culture, *spirituality* has become a generic term that covers a nearly infinite variety of activities. Here the intent is to narrow the focus to matters of Christian discipleship.[11] In the context of MEDDSS, the question is straightforward, despite the complex issues involved. In Goldilocks form, the question becomes, "Have I invested time and energy in my spiritual growth—not too much or not too little, but the amount that results in effective discipleship?"

The Bible considers all areas of life relevant to spiritual growth. Whatever you do, do everything in your life in a way that honors God (1 Corinthians 10:31; Colossians 3:17), Paul instructed, and that includes how you manage your sex life (Colossians 3:5–8). Pray all the time (Ephesians 6:18). Give thanks about everything (1 Thessalonians 5:16–18). Don't worry about anything; talk to God and ask for His help (Philippians 4:5–7). Share your money and material wealth (1 Timothy 6:17–19). If you can't figure out what to do, ask God for wisdom, James advises, and He'll tell you (James 1:5). And watch your mouth. Your tongue can make a lot of trouble (James 3:5–6). Love one another, John urged, in the same way God loves you (1 John 4:7–11). And forgive others not because they deserve it but because God has forgiven you, Paul adds (Colossians 3:13). And make full use of the promises you've been given, Peter points out, because these promises make it possible for you to participate in the very life of God (2 Peter 1:3–4). "Listen," Jesus said, "I'll summarize it for you. The most important thing is to love God with all your heart and soul and mind, your passion, prayer, and intelligence. And the second thing is connected closely to the first one—love your neighbor as well as you love yourself. These are the pegs: everything in God's Law and the prophets hangs from them" (Matthew 22:37–40, *The Message*, author's paraphrase).

As a matter of discipleship, Christian spirituality is threaded through all of life. In faith-based self-care, spirituality incorporates matters of mastery, shapes our choices about exercise, our use of drugs, our eating, our sleeping. Spirituality is doing all that we do in ways that honor God and that make apparent to the world around us something of our relationship with Him. In this sense, answering the MEDDSS question about spirituality requires that we look at each aspect of self-care and examine our choices for their congruence with discipleship. We ask ourselves simply, "Have I in each area of my life made choices that deepened my relationship with God? Such evaluation pivots around faithfulness—our faithful response to our faithful God. It is not at any time about a search for perfection or about the pursuit of excellence; it is about faithful acts of discipleship. But times of disorientation and loss bring us to a distinctive challenge. Pain limits our capacity to function and confronts us with our brokenness and failure in new and evident ways. Investing in our spiritual growth requires that we learn to embrace our failures in ways that deepen our experience of God's grace and mercy. Investing time and energy into our spiritual life becomes a matter of assigning all of life, failures as well as successes, a significant role in our relationship with God. In practical terms, we are called to evaluate our responses to grief and failure and loss as well as our choices of breakfast cereal and patterns of sleep in terms of their impact on our journey. All aspects of life are considered in terms of our relationship with God.

Some specific activities, however, merit mention in self-inventory of our spiritual life. Journaling is a valuable tool in gaining self-knowledge and is particularly valuable in times of disorientation and pain. While journaling is helpful at any phase of life, many people first undertake journaling when crisis pushes them to do so. Practice increases skill at journaling, but the value of the journaling process is, thankfully, not related to writing skill. It is the process of journaling itself, not the literary quality of the material that is produced, that aids in effective pain management. Some technically oriented people find journaling on a password-protected computer to be a helpful way of talking with both themselves and God. Others find that the slower process of journaling with pen and paper deepens the honesty and vulnerability with which we face our inner world. Whatever the form, journaling can deepen self-knowledge, increase the effectiveness of our prayer life, and, over time, provide a helpful record of our journey.

Specific attention to worship is important. For many individuals, the organized church provides a place of refuge and comfort in time of struggle and pain. Communal worship brings an increased sense of God's presence and caring concern. Church attendance provides social support through connection with other people who encourage and comfort and at times express their concern through acts of practical help. However, in many instances, pain and grief are accompanied by a sense of alienation from God and dislocation from any formally identified community of God's people. One client explained, "I'm not sure where God is right now, but church totally fell off my radar screen a long time ago. I fell off their screen too. He paused a moment, then added bitterly, "They showcase winners." The tendency for wounded, distressed individuals to withdraw from church in times of crisis is a phenomenon with which clergy as well as therapists are sadly familiar.

In such a time when communal worship feels emotionally and socially impossible, spiritual well-being requires specific attention to and provision for worship in other forms. Emotional inability to attend church need not prohibit an individual from participation in communion, the ancient liturgy of the broken bread and wine, and profiting from the comfort and encouragement that this act of worship can bring. Many clergy if requested to do so will gladly administer communion to individuals at home; some churches have designated lay persons who will bring communion elements to those who for whatever reason cannot attend regular public worship. Most clergy have a clear understanding that it is possible to be emotionally homebound when the physical act of walking is still possible. In times of emotional turmoil, requesting this ministry is often difficult, however. Asking represents an acknowledgment of our struggle and need in a form that leaves us socially and emotionally vulnerable.

When pain and disorientation are most intense, however, worship may become reduced to something as simple as sitting on the porch, counting how many beautiful things we can identify in the world around us, and giving God credit and thanks for this world. It may mean sitting alone by the fire reading the Psalms. It may mean lying quietly in bed, watching the early hours of dawn and saying, "I cannot sense your presence, God. Today I do not sense that you see or cherish me. But as I face this day, I choose here in these moments of early light to acknowledge your promise that you are with me and that you love me. And through my acknowledgment of your promise I worship and count your promise true." Self-care inventory includes finding a form of worship that fits the place on the journey we find ourselves.

Spiritual evaluation also includes specific attention to what we are putting in our minds and emotions through books and music, film, and other media. Scheduling systematic time to read Scripture and books that focus on comfort and traditional avenues of spiritual growth is one aspect of paying appropriate attention to our spirituality. For some individuals, in difficult times it can be helpful to read books that deal directly with the issue of pain.[12] This must be done cautiously, however, since such books can open the "why" question in ways that may not prove to be helpful. But the greater challenge grows out of the fact that at times, "Christian books," like formal church services, can become intolerable, and feeding our spiritual growth requires rethinking the material we are going to read or the films we are going to view. One of the good things that can come out of such bleak times is a much broader understanding of the ways through which our spirits can be nourished. Reading Flannery O'Connor's work or Wendell Berry's novels can, if we permit it, push us to think more clearly about the human experience, about the complex issues of good and evil in our world, and about God's part (and our own) in the mix. And viewing a film such as *A River Runs Through It* offers greater insight into the complex issues embodied in family relationships and the opportunity to consider lingering questions about ourselves. The issue is not, "Have I consumed traditionally approved religiously oriented materials?" The issue is, "Have I read/seen/listened to material that fed and challenged my spiritual growth at this place and time on my journey?"

Choosing life for the Christian includes at its core self-care that is a part of our discipleship. Such self-care is not a program of self-indulgence. It is a series of actions designed to value and to nourish the person. Self-care is not in and of itself about our feeling comfortable or pleased with ourselves and the world. Self-care is about taking seriously the mystery that no matter how scarred and broken we may be, we carry the image of God; we are the recipients of His gifts, no matter how indifferent we may be to their presence.

Self-care is about living faithfully out of the reality of who we are—chosen children of a loving God—whether we sense that reality or not. In times of pain and disorientation, life and adequate self-care can appear to require more faith, courage, and strength than we are able to gather together. At such times, it is important to have a plan that is based on small steps. MEDDSS outlines basic steps: mastery, exercise, diet (food), drugs, sleep, and spiritual growth. In this simple, faith-oriented framework we can work out a plan for self-care that permits us to choose life one step at a time as an act of discipleship.

chapter 7

WHAT SHALL I DO
WITH FAILURE?

Self-care rooted in discipleship forms the practical foundation of pain management. If we are serious about effective stewardship of our pain, we need to take our MEDDSS. Successful completion of the journey with (and through) pain requires additional skills, however. We must practice endurance and learn to prize it in a biblical context. Life with joy throughout the journey requires the development of a keen eye for epiphanies and skill in savoring the goodness of a half loaf. Perhaps most importantly, it requires us to learn to deal with the pain of failure and to manage its consequences in ways that lead to peace and productivity.

Prizing Endurance

Joy, James says, is linked to perseverance and endurance (1:3). Peter has the same uncomfortable idea (1 Peter 1:6–9). In order to prize endurance in this biblical sense we must clear out any remnants of an old Greek idea out of our minds. The Greek Stoics believed that the pain and struggles of life were the outcome of an assigned destiny over which humans had no control. Since they believed that "whatever will be, will be," the Stoics concluded that refusal to respond to whatever happened, good or bad, was logical. Their measure of maturity became a highly developed emotional indifference in which life events evoked neither joy nor pain.

Mistakenly, we sometimes think like Stoics and view endurance as a call to deny our pain. Most of us learn this idea, however, not from Greek philosophy but from environments that teach us to disregard and hide our pain. For most of us, our upbringing and the patterns of our adult relationships cause far more problems than the long shadow of those old Greeks.

Sometimes the idea of denial is taught directly. Children are told, "Don't cry... Don't be so sensitive... Don't make such a fuss... Don't be a baby." Responses like this teach powerfully that those who are strong and mature do not openly express their discomfort and pain. Adults are also given such messages, no less directly but in different language. Adults tell other adults, "Keep a stiff upper lip... Get over it, and move on."

The most powerful instruction regarding denial of pain, however, comes not from what people say but from what they do in response to the pain we feel. When a child is sad or tired or hungry or afraid and no one responds to these emotions, the child learns that pain is not important and does not merit attention or help, even though no verbal message may have been given. When in friendships or intimate relationships adults' pain is chronically disregarded, adults too conclude that maturity requires them to cover their pain and give little or no attention to their needs. Emotional neglect is a powerful teacher, whether the students are children or adults; it teaches without words the denial of pain. Neglect by others encourages self-neglect in place of appropriate self-care. Self-neglect interferes seriously with our learning to bring our pain clearly and directly to God in prayer as well.

Those who believe that endurance and perseverance require denial of pain and neglect of self-care demonstrate a serious misunderstanding of the biblical point of view. Endurance in the Scriptures is linked to growth in which strength is developed in interaction with adversity. James is quite specific at this point. "For you know that when your faith is tested, your endurance has a chance to grow. So let it grow, for when your endurance is fully developed, you will be perfect and complete, needing nothing" (James 1:3 NLT).

Peter similarly links endurance to growth. He urges those in the faith to utilize God's rich and wonderful promises so that faith will result in a life of moral excellence. This process, as Peter describes it, is one in which self-control leads to patient endurance, and patient endurance leads to godliness and to love. As a result, Peter explains, we become productive and useful in the kingdom (2 Peter 1:3–8). Persevering through the hard places does indeed require acceptance of life circumstances, but biblically it entails *interaction with those circumstances in a way that, by God's grace, results in productive growth.* Those who are good stewards of their pain learn to take joy from their endurance and the strength that they gain in the process of living through these circumstances.

There is nothing glamorous or heroic about this process. Endurance, in practical terms, boils down to taking our MEDDSS. Endurance is exercise when we don't feel like it. Endurance is doing what we can with what is available. Endurance is counting on God's presence when we feel alone and lost. Endurance is worship in response to sadness and despair. Endurance is undertaking the discipline of sleep when worry threatens to flood our minds. Endurance is learning to take our anguish directly to God. Endurance is being present in the moment, in the pain, and reaching through the pain to hope. Endurance is naming our pain and accepting the disorientation and loss in which we find ourselves. Endurance is managing our pain and disorientation day after day while maintaining our eating, sleeping, working, loving, and praying. Endurance is expecting that God is transforming our lives through the process of our ordinary living when there is little sense data to support our belief. When we do what we can do, our growth into maturity follows.

Growth may occur at times in indiscernibly small increments, but as we endure, growth comes through God's enabling grace and empowering promise and our obedience. Endurance is about us and our obedience, whatever our small steps. But, gloriously, the end product of our endurance is about God and His faithfulness. God is at work in us, and He will complete the work He has started, Paul reassures us (Philippians 1:6; 2:11). "Listen," Jude writes exultantly, "God will keep us from falling and present us before his glorious presence without fault and with great joy" (v. 24, author's paraphrase). Endurance, from the human standpoint, is the unglamorous process of left foot, right foot, left foot, *breathe;* right foot, left foot, right foot, *breathe*—a slow pilgrim's progress toward a certain goal of great joy. But the joy is not just a tomorrow thing; there is a measure of this joy on the journey as well.

I grew up on a Kansas farm during the Depression. Everyone, including young children, helped with chores; milking the cows was a part of the daily routine. The barn was some distance from the house, so when the milking was finished it was necessary to carry the milk to the house down a long lane that in the winter was full of mud and snow. My father would carefully pour as much milk as possible into the buckets he carried in order to lighten the load for my sister and me. At best, however, carrying the milk to the house was hard work. The buckets of milk were heavy, and when my boots were heavy as well with mud and snow, the task required all my strength. I have no memory of that task ever bringing any joy.

Over the years, however, something happened. The buckets stayed heavy. The mud and snow stayed heavy. And on those nights when the wind blew out of the north the long length of the lane never shortened. The weight of the milk pails and the cold of the Kansas winter did not change. But I did.

One winter night my father was delayed on the other side of the barn caring for a cow and her newborn calf. Impatient to get to the house where it was warmer, I picked up the two buckets of milk nearest the barn door and started down the lane ahead of him. It was slow, heavy going in the mud and manure. I stopped and rested when I reached the shed and again when I reached the water tank, turning my back to the driving wind and snow while I caught my breath. When I reached the house I was cold and wet, and my muscles were shaking with fatigue. But I arrived with two full pails of milk and an inner sense of exhilaration I could not then explain. I now know it was a moment right out of the book of James: What I experienced was joy in my endurance. In the face of the wind and snow I had carried all the way from the barn to the house a load that once had been too heavy for me to lift. That's the biblical sense of endurance—actively "shouldering the load," as my father phrased it, and growing in the strength and joy and productivity that come as a result.

I remember that night as one of the marker events in my journey into adulthood. When my father arrived at the house, he said, "You should have left the five-gallon pail for me. That's too heavy for you."

"Not any more," I said.

He smiled. So did I.

Epiphanies and Pickle Jars and
a Walk in the Woods

Pain at its worst is brutally insistent; our awareness of the world becomes narrowly focused within the parameters of our suffering. Overwhelmed, our sense of reality becomes distorted and our attention preoccupied with the experience of our pain. However, at some point, those who make good use of their pain discover that something else besides suffering is happening, and they learn to pay attention to it. I call this the epiphany-pickle jar principle for reasons that will become clear.

A client, whom I shall call Miriam, came for help with her grief and the disruption of her life after the sudden unexpected death of her husband, Jim. Jim and Miriam had one of those rare and beautiful marriages in which two individuals come close to a perfect fit. They did everything together, not because they could not do things independently but because they preferred each other's company at work and at play. Jim and Miriam had chosen not to have children. They owned their own company and had the freedom and economic resources to do life on a rather large scale. Without conscious awareness, they assumed that their easy life would blend seamlessly into an easy old age. Then, shortly after his forty-seventh birthday, Jim died of a sudden massive coronary.

Miriam was devastated. Early in our work she told me, "I can't even make coffee. In the old days, I made the coffee while Jim took the dog out. I start, and then I think, *Oh, not so much coffee. There's only one of us to drink coffee no*w. Then I cry so much I can't see to make coffee or drink whatever the stuff is I manage to make. And the dog whines because she wants out and she's upset because I'm crying."

Her friends reported with astonishment that this capable woman had forgotten how to turn the sprinkler system off; got lost while taking the dog to the vet; delegated (dangerously) her executive functions at the company; and in hundreds of ways, big and small, behaved as though loss of her spouse and partner had incapacitated her. Her pain appeared to deprive her both of her capacity to think and her will to live. But without her conscious awareness, Miriam began to experience something in the midst of her pain in addition to suffering.

Miriam came in one day with an air of something close to cheerfulness.

"Tell me what's happening," I said.

"Well," Miriam said, "I reprogrammed the thermostat and turned the air conditioning off. And do you remember that woman who came by and helped me rake leaves? Well, I think I might like her, so yesterday I walked down to her garage sale and found this neat shirt to wear with my jeans. Do you like it? And last night I got the pickle jar open by myself."

She paused. Then her eyes suddenly filled with tears. "The aspen in the front yard is just beautiful this year. I wish you could see it. Autumn was Jim's favorite time of year. It will never be the same without him."

Miriam's grief was painfully present to her and to me. But in the midst of her pain something else was happening as well. Miriam was beginning to develop new relationships and new skills and to use new strength to shape her life without Jim. But caught up in her pain, it was difficult for her to see that. At that moment Miriam was far more conscious of her grief than of her growth.

I often work with a piece of scratch paper on my desk and a pen in my hand. I handed Miriam a tissue and waited quietly until she had wiped her eyes. When she threw her tissue in the wastebasket, I picked up my pen and wrote PICKLE JAR in large letters on the paper and turned it so that Miriam could read it.

"Pickle jar?" she read, a puzzled note in her voice. "*Pickle jar?*"

"Well, let's think about your pickle jar," I said, drawing a very odd-looking object that was supposed to depict a pickle jar on my paper. "This pickle jar tells me that pain is not the only thing happening in your life. Solving the pickle jar problem is going on. Programming the thermostat is going on. A possible new friend is in the making. You have a new shirt. The aspen tree has made a mint of gold leaves again in this autumn. You have its beauty even though Jim is gone."

I paused. We both smiled at the ridiculous shape of the drawing I had labeled "Miriam's Pickle Jar" on my scrap paper. Then I added, "I'll admit my picture doesn't look like much, but this is an important pickle jar nevertheless. It is possible in fact that this pickle jar stands for an epiphany." Then I explained.

In early autumn, the year after the devastating fire that swept Yellowstone, a friend and I revisited the park. What we remembered as acres of towering trees and grassy meadows now resembled the barren lifeless surface of some remote planet. Staying carefully on the boardwalks that had been laid across the black burned earth, we walked through acres filled only with charcoal skeletons of burned trees, cinders, and the tons of ashes that formed the grim remains of that devastated world. But as we reached the end of the walk, we saw beside the path a cardboard sign jerry-rigged by some visitor who had preceded us. On the sign, a crooked arrow pointed toward the black scarecrow carcass of a great tree some distance from the path. Under the arrow the sign maker had written the single word *tree*.

"Well, it was a tree," I said. "But that's strange—that's an odd sign to put up here."

My friend had better visual skills than I, and after looking carefully for some time said, "No. You're looking at the wrong thing. Look down—there on the ground about fifteen feet to the left of that charred log. There's something green there—about five inches high." There was indeed.

In the lecture that followed our walk, the park ranger explained that life was returning to the burned sections of Yellowstone in ways that sometimes astonished even the experts. He noted that some seeds that had lain dormant for years had begun to sprout as a result of the fire's heat and the sunlight now filling the spaces cleared by the fire.

"It could have been a tree," the ranger said when my friend described the sign, "but more likely it was a weed."

My first response to the ranger's comment was instant indignation. In a moment of misplaced romanticism, I wanted that green to be a young tree, already rising triumphantly to replace the giant whose spectacular death was visibly present, its black skeleton etched against the sky. *Weed, indeed,* I thought crossly.

But later I came to think differently. The limited vision of the sign maker had skewed my understanding of the miracle I had seen. The sign rightly should have read *life.* Whether tree or weed, there was life arising in that devastated landscape where death and destruction appeared to rule.

At those times when loss and suffering appear to fill all the spaces of life, those who make good use of their pain learn to pay attention to something other than their pain. They look for life, accepting the reality that it may first arise in small, unglamorous, and utterly unromantic forms. The green they glimpse may not be a tree; it well may be a weed. But it is the miracle of life, God's gift of a new thing. It may be a shirt at a garage sale. It may be the open pickle jar.

Those who become good stewards of their pain learn to see epiphanies that come through oddly common things.

Valuing Half a Loaf

Our consumer-oriented culture assumes that our value lies in what we have. If we assume that this is true, serious consequences follow. If our value lies in what we own, then scarcity and deprivation have great destructive power. Loss carries not only pain but also danger. We fear its power to destroy joy and hope and love and, ultimately, to destroy life itself.

In the great cycle of life, loss *is* real. And loss *does* hurt.

That is not distortion. Good stewardship of this pain accepts this reality, but in doing so it raises some careful questions. How much is lost? And what is the value of those things that remain in the face of our loss? And—the troublesome core of the issue— can what remains be enough? As we discussed earlier,[1] in the struggle of moving through the pain of loss we find ourselves re-working our definition of *enough* in nearly every aspect of our lives.

An old proverb taught what would seem a self-evident truth: a half loaf is better than none. However, in the actual process of dealing with loss, the value of the half loaf may not be as self-evident as the proverb suggests. We find ourselves wondering: Is half a loaf always better than none? Can half a loaf ever be enough?

As with most issues surrounding pain, the choice of perspective from which we evaluate our loss is not a simple matter. The significance of our loss is shaped by the way we view what remains in the context of the rubble of devastation left behind. And in turn, the way in which we view the half loaf is shaped by the circumstances of our loss. We are likely to feel quite pleased with our half loaf if initially it came when we had nothing at all—and expected nothing at all—and were given half a loaf. In this case we see the half loaf as gift and grace and certainly better than the nothing it replaced. But we may have a quite different response if we had baked a table full of loaves and then lost them all to a thief who left only a sorry misshapen half loaf behind. In that case we may view our half loaf as a bitter remnant that mocks our past plenty. A half loaf that replaces nothing is gift; a half loaf that is all that remains of a lost whole loaf will usually appear, at least initially, to be something other than a gift—more likely a bitter icon of our loss. But regardless of the nature of our loss, we have a choice: We can focus on what remains; we can celebrate its worth.

As a child I went with my father to visit a neighbor whose farmstead had been destroyed by a tornado. Seeing the storm approaching, the family had taken shelter in the cellar near the house and had survived without injury. But barns and sheds, the house and its contents, and the family's car had been destroyed. This was Dust Bowl country still lying in the shadow of the Depression; the loss was enormous. My father and his friend sat on the running board of our old truck and surveyed the devastation in silence. Finally my father said with careful gentleness, "Looks like it didn't leave much."

"Nope," said his friend. Then after a while he added, "But like I was telling the wife this morning, we still got our health and this good earth, and we can build again."

Valuing the half loaf is easiest for those who work steadily and consistently on mastery. Just as mastery requires that we do what we can with what lies at hand, the half-loaf principle requires that we celebrate what we have in the context of loss.

Recalling the woman whose post-surgery choice was limited to looking at the window or the door, she could grieve (and fear) the loss of her strength *and* be grateful she could see.

A friend's life circumstances resulted in the loss of a country home she loved. We had lunch one windy spring day at a restaurant overlooking a city park. Looking with interest at the flower beds that edged the walks, she remarked wistfully, "I miss my garden, especially now that it's spring. But watch those daffodils in the wind!" It was possible for her to grieve the loss of her country garden *and* celebrate that wild dance of daffodils in a city park.

The distortion that results from pain can make loss feel greater than it may in fact be. Privately, we smile at the young man whose "life is ruined" by the breakup of a romantic relationship. But we smile briefly. We also know that at times, all that we can see of life as we have known it *has* been lost. At such times our sense of devastation reflects a hard, unyielding reality, not distortion. Nonetheless, in these times, by choice and God's enabling grace, we can focus on what remains. We can take hold of what remains present for us in the moment, however small. We can celebrate the half loaf that we yet hold in our unsteady hands.

Managing Failure

Given our human brokenness, the number and types of ways we can fail probably exceed our ability both to count and describe. What we know clearly, however, is that the pain that accompanies failure is complex and intense. We know too that this pain is persistent and strongly resistant to constructive use. A client once remarked, only half jokingly, "I've been a failure most of my life, and now I'm being a failure at being a failure." Most of us know from experience how easy that is to do.

Perspective becomes difficult. If we wish to manage our pain well and profit from our experience, we cannot simply dismiss failure glibly as "no big deal." On the other hand, it is not helpful to regard every failure as a contemporary rerun of a great Greek tragedy. Redeeming the pain of failure requires us to embrace the failure and to learn from it, an idea that many of us first heard from our parents and grandparents and may have passed on in turn to our own children as well. There is little that is mysterious about this process, but two things make it particularly difficult.

One difficult issue is the faulty thinking in which failure becomes identified as the person we are rather than the consequences of what we have chosen to think and to do. The second interrelated issue is the shame that often becomes commingled with the anger and despair of defeat and the self-blame in terms of the "bad" or "inadequate" person then rears its head. This "bad person" thinking, of course, serves to reinforce the faulty belief that failure is a person rather than an event.

Other aspects of dealing with failure and its pain are challenging as well. We are often confronted with truth we would rather dodge and faced with limitations we would rather not recognize. Dealing productively with failure requires us to examine the goals we have set for our work and for ourselves and, at times, to revise them in the light of reality and God's grace. There is nothing mysterious in this process, but, unfortunately, it requires a great deal of hard work, some of which requires a clear look at ourselves we would rather not take.

To embrace failure is to face it at our deepest level of awareness, call it by name, and deal honestly with what we find. The first thing we find, of course, is pain—the despair and anger of defeat, accompanied often by the raw, bitter acid of shame. The pain of failure is so commingled with shame in many instances that the initial struggle to assess the failure event realistically can be compromised. Shame is powerful and will hi-jack the management process given any (and every) opportunity to do so. To prevent this, it is important to acknowledge from the outset that strong feelings (including shame) are part of the failure event and to accept these feelings as part of the reality with which we must deal. Feeling what we feel and calling these feelings by name is an essential part of embracing the failure. But in the triage process of managing failure, dealing with these powerful feelings must come in its proper place.

Good management of failure first focuses attention to the failure event itself, not solely on the feelings of pain and shame that accompany it. Knowing how we feel and that we feel ashamed is one thing; knowing what happened—that is, *understanding the failure event* itself—is quite another. Good management depends ultimately, of course, upon clear understanding of both. Shame, anger, despair, hopelessness—all are recognized in their place. Skillful management of failure begins, however, with the failure event, and does not permit emotional responses to sabotage this step in the management process.

Sorting for self-understanding

At times when we begin to think through failure the impulse to blame ourselves and others is difficult to resist. However, good management begins with a gentle, non-judgmental sorting process that focuses on our own choices and behaviors and the part they have played in the failure with which we now struggle. Productive thinking looks something like this: "I recognize my feelings, but I choose *first* to focus on what happened and what I have done. When I can see (and say) what has happened, when I understand what I have chosen, what I have done, then I will think about who I am; then I will consciously attend to the feelings I have." To focus on behavior while shame is clamoring for self-condemnation sometimes requires every ounce of energy and self-control that we have. To blame others whose behavior has played into the undesirable outcome with which we are struggling feels justified. However, thinking that links self-condemnation and blame of others ("I am a failure, but it is his fault") leads only to an unproductive dead-end that short-circuits God's intervention and redemptive action in us and in our circumstances.

As we will see, dealing with failure often leads us to face truth about both ourselves and others that we previously have not understood or have chosen to disregard. Nevertheless, the initial sorting process requires us to face and name *our* choices, *our* attitudes, and *our* actions in whatever way we understand them at this beginning place. If we are wise in dealing with failure, we begin by locating the spade, naming the spade a spade, and then, gently, acknowledging that this spade is the object with which we have dug ourselves into a large hole (recognizing in the process that the hole is comparable in size to the Grand Canyon, if that is, in fact, the case).

When we do this sorting with gentle, rigorous honesty, shame begins to recede. We may be surprised to find that the "what happened" portion of the sorting process reduces shame, but there is a logical reason for it. As a quintessentially human experience, failure inevitably entails a complex mixture of *both* good *and* bad. Indeed, our difficulty in rightly understanding our experience of failure often pivots around this frustrating moral complexity. In embracing a given failure, for example, we might find ourselves pushed to acknowledge that we used *both* the spade of goodness *and* the spade of greed to dig the hole in which we find ourselves. In such an instance, it is not only necessary to call *both* goodness *and* greed by their right names, it is also important to recognize our anxious ambivalence about the reality of their co-existence. Handling failure productively requires us to resist our human tendency toward black-and-white thinking, despite the fact that we much prefer the pattern of either black or white over the more complex option of both black and white with several shades of gray into the bargain. However, the game is worth the entry fee: Shame does not flourish where *both* good *and* bad are recognized and called by their right names.

The goal of the initial sorting process is neither self-congratulation nor self-condemnation, however. The goal is the development of self-understanding that leads to new patterns of behavior and thinking. The sorting process is a soul-stretching experience, but undertaken in good faith, it leads through the pain and shame of failure into a place of peace and productivity. This process does not come automatically or easily and requires time, energy, and effort.

Failure saps both energy and motivation at levels that encourage hiding and sleeping (or at least putting our heads under our pillows) rather than performing emotionally difficult work. At times, doing nothing not only feels reasonable, it feels like the only possible response. Success at the task often requires the help of a trusted friend to keep us steady with the sorting process when it feels too painful (or shameful) to pursue. But eventually, however initially uncomfortable the process may be, necessity and common sense come to our rescue. We begin actively to engage in the sorting process. We ask ourselves, *What in the world happened here?*

What happened, of course, was that failure occurred—an undesirable and painful outcome that fell far wide of our original goal. Whatever our level of perfectionism—indeed, at times precisely because of it—we acknowledge that failure occurs. We may be surprised at this particular failure, but failure itself doesn't surprise us. However, when we begin to ask what happened *here*—in this specific place at this specific time—what often does surprise us is the power and pivotal role of choice, our choices and the choices that others too have made.

When we are wet and cold from the rain, it is a quite unpleasant experience to be reminded that we played a significant part in bringing the roof down on our heads. It feels much more agreeable to assign responsibility to the wind, bad construction, and malicious neighbors. In a somewhat parallel fashion, when sorting out a failure event, we are rarely pleased to recognize our choices and behaviors that contributed to the failure we now grieve. We are wise to keep clearly in mind from the beginning, however, that the Janus-face of choice looks two ways. It is true that the power of our choice was a crucial factor in our failure. However, this same power of choice becomes a comforting fact when we consider that the consequences of failure are determined not by failure itself but by the ways in which we can choose to use it in the days that lie ahead.

This is good news, of course, that we can influence the consequences of failure even though we cannot control them. We can integrate the experience of failure into our lives and relationships in ways that produce growth and wisdom. We can choose to embrace failure with an unsparing honesty and personal awareness that lead to a redemptive use of the experience itself and of its pain. But from the outset, we must also keep in mind that this is not unqualified good news—choice wears a Janus face. We can use failure in the service of godliness and growth. However, we can equally well use failure to license self-pity, to dilute the demands of discipleship, and to deny responsible use of our gifts.

The dilemma lies, as always, with God's refusal to compel us to do the thing that is good for us. He will give us wisdom and He will empower us, but He will not unilaterally turn our failures into growth and goodness without our freely chosen cooperation. Out of His unfailing goodness, God showers grace upon us in times of failure. Indeed, He sometimes floods us with grace and mercy at such times. That is who He is. That is the unchanging character of the God we serve. Through His Spirit He will gently encourage us to take hold of our failures and pain. In His comforting presence we can take courage and look them full in the face; God forgives—and forgives again. He will bless our steps as we seek to begin again. But God will not compel us to confront our failures and to grow through their pain. That is a choice that we must make and make—and make again. God works to bring about transformation, but He does not work unilaterally. He does not force goodness in us. We get to choose.

Separating the person from the failure

Those who productively manage failure maintain a careful distinction between the *experience* of failure and the *person* who is experiencing the failure and its pain. *Effective pain management does not personalize failure.* Whatever the nature of the failure may be, the undesirable outcome is assessed with honest realism in relation to factors that have influenced it. Honest sorting takes into consideration factors such as choices, goals, available information and skills, available resources, perseverance, vision, and other relevant attitudes and their consequent behaviors. These factors are named carefully in a logically consistent way. A bad choice is confronted squarely as a bad choice and labeled as such, but it is the *choice* that is labeled bad, not the person.

Good pain management does not avoid the unfashionable and uncomfortable practice of calling contributing characteristics like greed and selfishness by their right names. Neither for comfort's sake does it avoid facing (and naming) the consequences of such attitudes. Attitudes, and the choices they influence, may be dishonoring to God and destructive to the person, but productive pain management *insists that the essential value of the person is not contingent upon good or successful behavior.* No matter how bent and broken, no matter how flawed, the person suffering the pain of failure remains the fragile carrier of the image and gifts of God.

As Christians, dealing with failure biblically requires us to cling fiercely to our foundational belief that God created us in His image. Faced with our failures, we may confront our laziness and the resulting erosion of opportunity; our dreary relentless addictions; our despairing sense of helplessness in the face of temptation; our greed; our chosen inadequacies; the destructiveness of our uncontrolled rages; the sin of trustless despair—indeed, we may be called to see and name all this and more. Nevertheless, in the face of all that we have done and have failed to do, we are confronted, in the final analysis, with God's radical, overruling truth: *We remain, just as we are, carriers of the image and gifts of God.* Redemptive management of failure and its pain stands solidly on this foundation of faith. In God's economy, the value of the person cannot be equated with the events that have happened in the individual's life. Failure does not tell us who we are; God does, and He says we carry something of Him in us that failure cannot erode away.

Failure is an event. It is something that happens, an undesirable outcome that we profoundly influence and for which we must become honestly accountable. But those who deal productively with failure place this undesirable outcome in a realistic social context, recognizing that we are rarely, if ever, the only player on the field. Honest accountability requires us to take into consideration those other players and their choices as well as the condition of the field. Embracing failure means embracing *my* choices and *my* behaviors and their consequences without blaming others. It means at the same time embracing *only* my choices and becoming accountable for them. Embracing my failure does not entail assuming responsibility or accountability for someone else. Effective assessment of failure does not permit me in unconscious omnipotence to assume that my environment is irrelevant to my choices or to assume in some grandiose fashion that I am the only player on the field whose actions count. None of us can honestly assess our appropriate share of responsibility for outcomes or deal effectively with our pain if we presume immunity from the powerful forces of the environment in which we live. Neither can we deny the profound influence of the people with whom we live and work. My failure is about me, but it is about my functioning in a world peopled by individuals and institutions that do not necessarily have my best interests at heart. While my failure remains my own, the context of my failure is a world in which the choices and behaviors of others have consequences as well.

Personalizing failure is dangerous and self-defeating. Assigning oneself the label of "failure" is a complex, destructive form of self-blame that intensifies the pain and closes down the development of constructive options.[2] If I *am* a lemon, my options are severely limited. Who I am (*my unalterable lemon-ness*) requires me to remain yellow and sour and to move only when someone moves me. In contrast, suppose I am God's image bearer, with the power to choose, and find myself faced with a pile of lemons I have sinfully—or mistakenly—picked, or have maliciously been given. As a choosing image bearer of God, I have a number of doable options: I can make pie, custard, lemonade, or potpourri; I can create a centerpiece in a crystal bowl, adding yellow candles that I love; I can arrange my lemons with oranges and apples into the subject for a painting or for a photograph; I can place my lemons in a basket and share them with my neighbor who loves lemon pie. I can act as a chemist and use my lemons for raw material for "natural" cosmetics. My options are limited only by my inventiveness and ability to think outside the box. What I choose to do does not require me to alter my identity or to change the parameters of the self. It is true (thankfully) that who I am can be altered over time by what I do. However, in times of failure, focusing on what I can do is the place of beginning again that ultimately enables me to reconsider and reshape the self I am.

Evaluating initial goals

People who use failure successfully become ruthlessly honest in evaluating their original goals. They ask, "Now, what was I actually attempting to achieve here?" A strong dose of honesty at this point frequently produces some initial discomfort, but truth clears the space for change and growth to come.

When we raise this question, we often find that our failure incorporates an initial choice of what was an essentially faulty goal. For example, among many other reasons, a relationship may fail because the initial goal was to change the other person or to control the other person's behaviors and value system. Most of us understand that people can indeed change. At the same time, we also know that in the final analysis change is a one-person process—the only person I can change is myself. Despite the fact that intellectually we are aware of this truth, we sometimes set out to change and control others with little conscious awareness of this faulty goal. In such a case failure of the relationship can have great value if we honestly acknowledge the faulty goal and set about learning different patterns of behavior. While the pain of a failed relationship cannot be erased, it can be lessened when we begin to act on the potential for change. Today's failure can lead to a tomorrow in which new goals and new behaviors lead to new joy.

Some goals and their resulting failure reflect faulty understanding of our gifts and abilities. The experience of learning through failure what we *cannot* do has the potential to open the door to a new understanding of what we *can*—or can learn—to do. However, redeeming the pain of failure in such instances requires us to face clearly limitations we may formerly have chosen to deny. I sometimes use a ridiculous story I have invented to open up this issue with my clients.

"Suppose that my passionate life goal is to sing *Madame Butterfly* at the Met." At this point my client usually smiles. Since my natural speaking voice is quite low-pitched, the listener has immediately understood that I lack the essential basic qualification for this project. I do not have, and cannot acquire, the type of voice required to sing *Madame Butterfly*. Whatever my passionate desire, this natural limitation dooms my plan to certain failure. The story as I fabricate it on any given day goes on to include ridiculous denial of the facts, devious and preposterous manipulation, and an absurdly unreasonable investment of time and resources. The end of the story climaxes in a spectacular failure in which my performance results in a riot at the Met. I then explain my failure by blaming it on a number of factors. I blame the audience—they were musical morons who did not appreciate the artistry of my performance and the beauty of my voice. I blame the conductor—he caused the orchestra to play my major aria in the wrong key, much too high. I blame the weather—I have a particularly sensitive throat and it was such a cold day. I blame my rival understudy—out of jealousy and spite she bribed the critic from *The New York Times* to say terrible, untrue things about my performance. The variations that clients contribute to the story in its process become quite entertaining at times, but eventually we move from story to real life script. "Let's think about this," I propose seriously at some point. "Do you suppose that this circumstance, this failure that is causing you so much pain, is not so much about you as it is about your goal? In some way did your goal have something in common with my goal of singing at the Met? What *was* your goal? Was it a doable goal in light of your gifting, your training, and God's calling— *and* in the social context of the world in which you live?"

A faulty goal is often a crucial element in failure. This fact is not always easy to see, however. This faulty goal may have been set early in life and worked out consciously through a long series of events. Once we can accept this possibility, however, we can begin the slow and painful process of exploring the ways in which dishonesty, denial of limitations, and distortion of gifts have woven together to mask this faulty goal. We can take our courage in hand and examine the ways in which blame for the failure outcome has been assigned to self and to others.

It is difficult and painful to deal straightforwardly with the tangle of denial, distortion, and blame that this sorting process may uncover. Many times the most difficult work of all lies in the necessity to face squarely the relationships that have been wounded in the pursuit of a faulty goal. Persisting in this difficult process does not make the pain of failure magically evaporate, of course. Nevertheless, pain of failure significantly lessens when new truth and understanding lead to growth and change and hope for a new tomorrow. The pain that came with failure has not been erased, but it has been redeemed for good.

The impossible dream

Thinking about our goals requires that we learn to name our expectations accurately and to recognize the danger and seductive quality of what are essentially impossible dreams. When failure is connected with an impossible dream, redemption of that pain is particularly difficult.

The problem does not lie in dreams as such—dreams are good things. They encourage us to set goals that lie tantalizingly beyond easy reach and apart from rational expectation. For example, I was the first in my extended family to dream of college and a professional career. The expectations for women in my rural environment coupled with the financial limitations of my immediate family made this dream well beyond easy reach. From the viewpoint of those around me, it was certainly irrational planning as well. Much more sensible, they thought (and said) to dream of marrying a young farmer who would inherit several sections of good land. But after considerable time and a number of painful failures, the day came when my shingle—Gay Hubbard, Ph.D.—marked my office door. Dreams can come true, and achievement of a dream brings a special joy. However, Janus-like, the pain that comes with a broken dream carries an edge and intensity all of its own as well. Without question, failure of a dream raises the bar on pain management skills. But the pain of an impossible dream brings suffering that is particularly difficult to sort, understand, and manage.

In the novel *Don Quixote* by Miguel de Cervantes, the title character, a Spanish nobleman, accompanied by his faithful squire Sancho Panza, set out as a knight errant, determined to right the wrongs of the world. The world into which Don Quixote rode, however, was a world in which he saw objects around him through an imagination that defied reality; he saw windmills as giants, a flock of sheep as an enemy army, and a country inn as a castle. The farm girl, Aldonza, was transformed in Don Quixote's imagination into the Lady Dulcinea, in whose honor Don Quixote undertook his chivalrous quests. Unfortunately, Don Quixote's distorted view of the world linked with the impossible nature of his quest made his goal one that lay forever beyond his reach.

Cervantes' novel became the basis of the Broadway musical *The Man of La Mancha*. Something close to a magical moment comes in the production as Don Quixote sings his last passionate embrace of his quest in the memorable song, "The Impossible Dream." The lyrics list a number of noble, yet impossible tasks such as fighting unbeatable foes and righting unrightable wrongs, and the song ends with Quixote singing passionately that his quest is to "follow that unreachable star," even though he recognizes the hopelessness of the quest.

Even when we think we know better, there's a moment when, caught up in the magic of the music in the dark of the theater, we're tempted to think, "Yes! Yes! That's what life should be about—trying with our last ounce of courage to reach an unreachable star." However, when the lights come up and we are dealing with the realities of the parking lot and downtown traffic, the lyrics we have just heard seem patently absurd. A note of caution is in order, however. Our quick abandonment of that magic theater-based moment for a traffic-based sense of reality can lead us away from an important insight. In the tangle of traffic we ignore the fact that for a moment, sitting in the anonymity of the darkened theater, we half-believed Don Quixote's point of view and his conviction. For a moment we half-agreed with his definition: The truly glorious quest means reaching for an unreachable star and following it, no matter how hopeless the quest, no matter how far, no matter how exhausted we become in the journey.

In dealing constructively with failure, it is important to understand the heroic quality we humans often assign the quest for goodness and truth when undertaken in the face of insurmountable odds. If failure has come as the aftermath of an effort to right an unrightable wrong, to reach an unreachable star, or to fight an unbeatable foe, how are we to understand it? Is failure the price of heroism? Is attempting the impossible against insurmountable odds sheer lunacy, or is it walking by faith? However stimulating such questions may be in dinner conversation after the play, the way this idea translates in real life leads to a sense of failure that can complicate the sorting process enormously and break our hearts in ways we do not understand.

Janice was the only child of a man who was himself the only remaining male heir of a family dynasty stretching over six generations. Her impossible dream was achieving value in her father's eyes. He had told her, with no hint of a joke in his voice, that he would never forgive her for being female, that he would rather have died childless than to die without a son to carry on the family name. Greg was a capable, high-achieving man, the only son of a widowed mother. Greg's impossible dream was to gain his mother's emotional permission for him to fall in love and to give another woman a wife's priority in his life and affections. Rena's impossible dream was to persuade her alcoholic father to enter treatment. Katherine could never remember her mother saying that she had done something well; her impossible dream was to "make my mother proud of me." All of these people—competent, responsible, brave people—had unknowingly set out like Don Quixote to reach an unreachable star. Janice could not become the son about whom her father obsessed. Greg could not alter his mother's self-absorbed, controlling desire to be the "wonderful mother" and keep Greg the adoring son who could not get along without her. Rena could not change the alcoholic behavior of her father and his persistent alcohol-distorted choices. Katherine could not alter the hostility and untreated personality disorder that fueled her mother's rejection of her. And, contrary to Don Quixote, pursuit of the impossible dream did not produce peaceful, calm hearts in these people. It produced a sense of failure, and with it, a sense of anger, shame, and despair that was complicated by the goodness of their goals.

"It's a good thing to try to help my father stop drinking," Rena said.

"It's my responsibility to care for my mother; after all, I'm all that she has," Greg argued.

"Mother is just a perfectionist," Katherine offered in defense of her mother's behavior. "Mother just wants me to get it right."

"What my father really wants is love," Janet said. "If I can just love him enough it won't matter that I can't be his son."

Who can argue with such goals—love, sobriety, excellence, responsibility, loyalty—all good in themselves? However, in the context of the relationships in which these people pursued these good things, their goals were the content of an impossible dream. For these individuals, managing the pain of failure required honest assessment of their goals, followed by honest assessment of the ways in which these goals needed to be revised in the light of reality and the grace of God.

"You can marry," I said gently to Greg one day, "and you can at the same time continue to care for your mother. However, it is not likely that you will be able to do both with your mother's approval."

"You can make a very fine birthday dinner for your mother that *you* can feel proud of," I pointed out to Katherine one day, "but I doubt that you can ever make a meal that your mother will not criticize in some way."

"You may point out to your father the destructive pattern of his drinking and the consequences of his drinking for himself and others," I said one day to Rena, "but you cannot choose sobriety for your father. Only he can do that."

"You can love your father," I told Janice, "but your love cannot change your father's distorted sense of gender value. Love can influence, but it cannot eliminate your father's obsession with a male namesake. Only he can change the way he thinks."

It is our belief in the heroic value of pursuing the impossible dream that tangles us in managing our pain when we fail, as we inevitably must. For a long time each of these people chose the pain of continuing failure rather than face the loss and disorientation that accompany relinquishment of an impossible dream. They found, as do we all, that it is far easier to choose an impossible dream than to let go of one, whatever the failure we may suffer in pursuing our heroic quest.

Embracing failure requires us to accept the painful distance that lies between our intended goal and the circumstances in which we find ourselves. Constructive management of failure and its attendant pain require us to sort and acknowledge honestly our behaviors and choices—good *and* bad—that brought us to this place. We learn to view failure for the event that it is and to distinguish the event from the person. Bad choices produce bad consequences—not people without value. Whatever the failure, we continue nevertheless to carry the image of God. Dealing with failure productively requires us to refuse the immobilization of shame. Truth in honest accountability for our actions and attitudes—*good and bad*—protects us from shame and strengthens our sense of gifting and hope. Inevitably, failure throws clear light on our goals, whether heroic, dishonorable, or plain mundane. Often failure brings us face to face with unspoken goals that we have hidden even from ourselves. Failure confronts us with our needs, our longings, our gifts, and our limitations. When we become caught in our own impossible dreams, dealing with failure confronts us with the painful necessity to relinquish our heroic illusions about our ability to reach the unreachable, to fix the unfixable, and to straighten the stick that cannot be straightened (Ecclesiastes 1:15). We are required to deal with truth about ourselves and about others that we may not have understood or have chosen to disregard.

Failure makes clear the powerful forces of the environment in which we live. We are sometimes frightened by what we see when we understand the profound influence of the people around us with whom we live and work. Failure sometimes makes clear in an unavoidable form a truth we have chosen to disregard—we live and function in a world that includes people who have little or no concern about the outcomes of our lives. This peopled world may include some who, in fact, may desire our injury and may act to promote our failure and defeat. Failure teaches us that we may be our own enemy. Failure also teaches us, however, that while we often are our own enemy, we are rarely the only enemy that we have.

And, if we permit it, failure around an impossible dream can aid us in sorting out a common tangle in our faith. God is—and thankfully remains—the God of the impossible. However, in His freedom to be God, God chooses the place and time in which He demonstrates His omnipotence. God promises to transform us through and out of our failures (surely an impossibility from our human point of view). God promises that when we are weak, even in the weakness that follows failure, we are strong (that paradox is also sheer impossibility from our human point of view). And in His decisive, Eastering word about impossibility, God insists that Friday-death is not an end but a beginning. In that Sunday-empty tomb, the God of the impossible demonstrated that He is the God of life, however impossible Friday's bloody death makes that appear.

But granting His irresistible power, we are wise to keep clear God's sovereign reservation about how His power is to be used. God has never agreed that if I set up an impossible dream He will make it come true to demonstrate to my small world that He is my personal God of the impossible. Failure of an impossible dream can confront us with the embarrassing reality that we sometimes seek to use God to our good ends. At times we enlist Him without His permission or approval in a project that has at its heart our pursuit of an unreachable star that we have defined as our heroic "Christian" quest. Such an act does not stem from faith; it is presumption growing out of our human longing and need and does not reflect response to the Word and calling of God. And in God's refusal to participate in our impossible project, we gain valuable insight to the character and heart of God if we become open to the truth. God is compelled only by that which is within himself—His infinite, exhaustless, eternal love. If we seek to coerce God into making our impossible dream come true under the guise of advancing His reputation, protecting His image, or demonstrating that we are one of His favored children, we discover that God is remarkably unmoved by the threat of what "people may say" if our "Christian" impossible dream fails. He is tragically familiar with slander, misrepresentation, and half-truths about himself; He is well acquainted with that Dark Angel who is the father of lies. We forget that God cares about the quality of our relationship with him. And if, out of God's desire for honest relationship with us, He permits our impossible dream to fall flat on its pretentious posterior, it is a failure that in the final analysis carries embedded in it His gift of love, His commitment to our good, and His longing for honest relationship with us without manipulation, heart to honest heart.

Effective management of the pain of failure pivots essentially around accepting the pain of the truth we find when we sort out our failures honestly, then following this truth with honest action that this truth requires. Dealing with ourselves as we really are and with those around us as they really are—the good *and* the bad, the better *and* the worse—require us to learn to utilize both spiritual and human resources in new ways. If we permit it to do so, failure leads us to new understanding of our need for community and new skills in prayer. Dealing with what we find in the rubble of the ruins takes courage. Acting out of new understanding of ourselves and of God is a task best undertaken in community (chapter 8) and with recommitment to deeper levels of intelligent, focused prayer (chapter 9).

WHAT DIFFERENCE DOES
COMMUNITY MAKE?

We are tempted to hide when we are hurt, to hide our pain—and ourselves. In many respects this is an instinctive response to the vulnerability that comes with pain. Taking a broken heart to a party rarely appears to be a good idea, either to the broken-hearted one or to the host. But at many levels, our desire to keep our pain private and secret reflects our distrust and lack of experience in community.

Some of our distrust stems from beliefs about pain. While we may not put our ideas in words, we think that our pain will cause others to judge us negatively. We fear that they will think that our pain is our fault and that we are getting what we deserve. We are afraid that people may see our pain as evidence that we are incompetent, ignorant, careless, or, at best, totally inept at managing life. We know that we are vulnerable. Even the possibility of criticism seems more than we can bear.

And we sense—often rightly—that our ability to think clearly and to function socially is compromised. We are afraid that we will be unable to respond in an appropriately protective way to things that people may say and do. We cringe at the prospect that some well-meaning soul, seeing our pain, may say, "Don't make such a big deal out of things." How can we respond to that? We shrink too from the question that this may raise in our own minds. Can it be that this pain that feels so catastrophic is in reality only a small thing that we are making big? Is the enormity of our pain an artifact of our own making? And how can we respond if someone implies (or says directly) that our pain is simply a poorly disguised bid for sympathy and attention? We long for someone to see our hurt and share our pain. Then we wonder: In truth, is this longing only a childish desire for attention? We sense that we need connection with people, but we fear it as well.

Our reluctance to risk community stems too from the culture's obsession with what may be fairly considered the cult of the individual. Without realizing we have done so, many of us absorb the idea that if we are strong, competent, and courageous we can—and will—manage life, including our pain, alone. We adopt as a life script the myth of the rugged individual played out in Western movies where the cowboy hero rides off alone into the sunset. Metaphorically speaking, we say to ourselves, "If I am 'doing it right' I will settle my Stetson firmly on my head, gather up my horse's reins, and ride off alone into the social equivalent of empty unfenced range." According to the myth of the rugged individual, the ultimate level of human courage, competence, and emotional maturity is demonstrated by the ability to disengage from people and to function in isolation. By default, community then becomes defined as the holding place for the incompetent, the weak, and dependent. Affiliation with a group is viewed as a crutch for the emotionally crippled, who are unable to "go it alone."

Christians are not, unfortunately, immune to the impact of this cultural myth. Scripture, however, regards this myth as serious error. At the point of creation, God declared Adam's aloneness "not good" and took direct divine action to correct the problem (Genesis 2:18). The apostle Paul explained at length that God's action in relation to the church has made aloneness impossible for His people. By divine fiat, we have been made a part of an organic whole, the body of Christ. In that body we have each been given distinctive gifts (1 Corinthians 12:4–31). We continue to have a choice about the way in which we use these individually crafted gifts—or fail to use them, as the case may be—for the better or the worse of the body as a whole. However, Scripture gives no indication that as Christians we have a choice about our connectedness with others; we *are* a part of the body of Christ. That fact has been settled by the sovereign choice of God.

While God has insured our connectedness in the body of Christ, He permits us to live in functional defiance of His truth. *He does not prevent us from acting as though we are alone.* Bent and broken as we are, we can read Genesis, preach from Corinthians, and then in times of suffering and disorientation, act like cultural cowboys and ride out alone with our pain and grief.

It is not always the cultural myth that pushes us into isolation and aloneness, however. Most Christians have a large fund of war stories reporting the wounds they have received from other Christians, and, particularly, injury that has occurred in their experience with the social institution of the church. It must be admitted that there is an intensely, uniquely painful aspect of church-related woundedness that defies ready description. Gossip; criticism; social cliques; ridicule; demeaning attitudes and disparaging acts; rejection; abandonment; betrayal; sexual exploitation; physical injury; failure to comfort; failure to form committed, caring relationships; failure to be emotionally honest and present; failure to respond with practical help in times of need; failure to practice justice and to extend grace—a list of the ways in which we fail each other and wound each other within the body of Christ can extend a long tragic length beyond this short list. Learning to manage church-related pain is a separate issue in itself for clergy and those in church leadership that lies beyond this discussion. Here the concern is more narrowly focused. When those who profess to follow Jesus wound us, or when they look past us and disregard our wounds, we conclude that we need to hide our pain (and ourselves) as much as is possible from all people, at all times. We think our experience teaches us that the only way to be safe is to be alone.

Nevertheless, despite the barriers of distrust and fear that they must surmount, those who become effective pain managers are active participants in community. Such a healing community is far different and far more than a casual collection of acquaintances, however. It is a chosen community that reflects two basic facts. One: No one can do it alone. Two: Not everyone can help. Those who mean to make the soul-searching journey through pain productive neither overstate their human capacity nor underestimate the potential impact and consequences of pain. They understand as well that they must choose close companions for the journey carefully. Not everyone who wishes to help is qualified to do so. And we discover that some who can help—indeed, some with whom we learn to trust our lives—need to be invited into community; not all who are qualified to help volunteer.

The fear and distrust that block participation in community are best handled by confronting them face-on. Our fear of further injury from people reflects an unpleasant reality. There is no such thing as an injury-proof, fail-safe relationship. However, in matters of community as with other matters of pain management, our safety does not depend upon our power to control but lies in our ability (and willingness) to influence relationships and the environment in which we live. The community we gather around ourselves consists primarily (although not totally) of those with whom we choose to be in relationship. We can choose to make close community with those who are least likely to injure us and most likely to help us on our journey. We can ask God for wisdom to choose wisely (James 1:5).

We need His wisdom too in shaping our relationship with those acquaintances who may share our life space but who are not good pain managers themselves. We may continue to interact with these people whose lives intersect with ours in significant ways without permitting them to enter into a place of personal intimacy. We have choices about both the individuals with whom we relate and the degree of intimacy in a given relationship. Making careful choices at both these points reduces our degree of risk and increases our safety. But we are dangerously mistaken if we think that the absence of relationships can serve as a safety net. Relationships may—and do—entail risk. But aloneness does not ensure safety. Being alone carries at many essential levels the greatest risk of all.

If we choose to live through our experience of pain and loss outside of community we risk many things. We risk loss of perspective; loss of faith; loss of a sound sense of reality; and loss of a check on our pain-enhanced sense of narcissism. We lose the opportunity to become givers as well as takers in and through our pain. We risk loss of the human comfort of a friend's voice, a smile, the warmth of human touch. We lose accessibility to practical assistance. We lose the gift of someone to laugh with us, and, at times, to encourage us to laugh at our own absurdity and pain-inflated sense of self-importance. We forfeit the joy of having a present crowd of witnesses who can and will celebrate with us each halting step. And we lose the vital collective memory bank that community supplies. In losing that we lose an essential source of knowledge about ourselves. We can become confused about our worth. We can lose our place in our own story and forget the song that God has given us to sing. We risk losing that song forever if we have no community. Community helps us hear our story, keep our place, and remember our worth. Community sings our song back to us again when we have forgotten both the words and the tune. Alone, we risk the loss of essential parts of ourselves, the knowledge of who we are, and the value of our gifts.

The Community of the Walking, Working Wounded

When we talk about community, in a general sense we are referring to a group of people who are connected to each other. This connection that forms community may be strong or easily broken. It may be marked by close or loose affiliation. Members of the community may share deeply or superficially, forming connections that consist of varying degrees of intimacy. Community connection includes mutual commitment to common interests and goals, but the strength of that commitment may itself also vary widely in intensity, from passionate to near indifference. Some communities are long lasting; some have a short life and are soon forgotten. Most of us function simultaneously as members of various communities, all of which vary in goals and in strength of connection and in the degree of intimacy we experience within the group. We may simultaneously belong to our church community, a business community, the geographical neighborhood in which we live and vote, and various special interest communities of people with whom we have chosen to affiliate. Each of these communities has a different life expectancy, and we may function as a longtime resident or a brief visitor in each.

The community of the walking, working wounded is an important, loosely connected group that can provide crucial assistance in pain management. This community consists of people who have experienced a soul-stretching journey through pain and developed effective management skills in the process of their journey. They are connected primarily through their common experience as survivors and the repertoire of skills they have acquired on their journey. They have an unpublicized, often unverbalized goal: They mean to live effectively using their experience with pain as a tool and are willing to help others do this as well.

In one sense, these successful survivors are anonymous. These men and women form a borderless unidentified community; there's no entry in the yellow pages that identifies these people. They are not listed on the tax rolls. We have to find them—or be found by them, as is sometimes the case. But while the search to find and to be found requires time and effort, the gain is enormous. If we can connect with them—the community of the walking, working wounded—we can share their stories and skills in ways that support our courage and increase our ability to manage our own pain well. And, not incidentally, these men and women encourage us to function as *both* givers and takers in the world of pain.

The good news is that we can find members of the community of the walking wounded scattered throughout the various communities in which we function, and, at times, briefly present in incidental one-time interactions in daily life. The not-so-good news is that we don't necessarily find these people readily. They rarely advertise their skills or publicize the journey on which they acquired them. To the contrary—most of these individuals do not wish to be identified by the pain they have survived. Many of them, particularly those successful survivors who are men, prefer an audit by the IRS to personal disclosure of what they have learned (sometimes through tears) in dark hard places of life. Men or women, the walking wounded tend to be private people. Nevertheless, in the search, it pays to look twice at the clown. While it is difficult to see the clown's face through the greasepaint, it is wise to keep in mind that a clown's mask may cover valuable scars and old tracks of tears, marks of a hidden but successful journey through pain and loss.

When we begin to look for the community of the walking wounded, we discover that there are no two alike; as individuals, they are incredibly diverse. They all have skills, but they have traveled different journeys. They have not developed the same skills equally. Some may have particular skills in endurance, and some have great ability to deal with loss; some know how to use distraction and laughter with great effectiveness. Carl (whose story is in chapter 2) was an ardent baseball fan. One day while we were talking about Carl's need to build community, he described this combination of common skills and diversity in this way: "Oh, I get it. These people you want me to connect with are like a ball team. Some guys are good at bunting, some are great out in the field, but they all know how to play ball." Exactly.

The search for those who are members of the community of the walking wounded is further complicated by another characteristic. Effective pain managers are not only diverse; they are discreet. Connection with them requires the risk of cautious self-disclosure. Successful survivors tend to share their own story only when they sense some indication from us that there is a worthwhile reason for them to do so.

Finding and connecting with effective pain managers requires energy for the search. In order to develop more than a surface connection, it requires the risk of cautious self-disclosure as well. Time, energy, motivation, and the social discernment required for cautious self-disclosure are often in short supply in the midst of our struggle with pain and loss. And, particularly at the beginning stages of our learning curve, we "don't get it right." We attempt to conserve our energy through isolation and to discount the dividends we can earn by investing energy in community. We struggle with the issues of how much to say, and how to say it. We sometimes assume the stiff-upper-lip posture and say nothing. Then at times we respond to a casual inquiry with far more information than the questioner wants or is prepared to handle. We sometimes use our awareness of not "getting it right" at times to rationalize retreat behind closed doors, ignoring the fact that doing nothing does not make us safe.

Risk in relationship is a fact of life. Although we can manage the degree of risk we choose, it remains a fact that if we enter into relationships with people we risk further pain. But having acknowledged that truth, those who become effective pain managers understand that it is aloneness itself that poses the greatest risk of all. In the woundedness that inevitably accompanies aloneness, there is potential fatal risk to the self. Community is worth the energy and the risk required to seek it out.

Drawing Boundaries in Community

Nevertheless, there are some whom we would do well to keep at a safe distance when we are struggling to live productively with our pain. Not everyone who wishes to help knows how to do so.

Catastrophizers

Effective pain managers avoid catastrophizers. These are the "Oh-isn't-it-awful" people who are more than willing to assure the sufferer that what is happening is the "worst thing they've ever seen" and, further, having an eye to the future, they are confident that "things are certainly bound to get worse." Effective pain managers understand that interacting with people who think catastrophically can intensify their sense of pain and distort their sense of reality. They remember the story of Chicken Little and keep at arm's length anyone who behaves like the characters in Chicken Little's story, with the important exception of the Lion King. Chicken Little's adventure is worth retelling in short form because, while it is regarded as a children's story, it makes this adult point about catastrophic thinking quite clear.

Chicken Little's adventure began on an ordinary morning when in his usual, ordinary way Chicken Little set out to find a fat bug for his breakfast. It was a splendid morning, and Chicken Little was feeling quite pleased with himself and the world until—as it often does—pain came unexpectedly in a way that Chicken Little found difficult to account for.

This is what happened. Chicken Little bent over to catch an exceptionally fine bug he had spied in the grass. At that instant—POW!—something hit Chicken Little on the head. This startled Chicken Little, of course, and made him jump. It made his head hurt as well. Chicken Little became very cross. He looked around to see who had hit him, but there was no one in sight. All that Chicken Little could see was the sky.

"Ah, ha," said Chicken Little to himself, "I know what has happened to me. A piece of the sky fell down and hit me on the head. That is what happened."

Then as Chicken Little thought more about that piece of the sky falling on his head, he began to feel quite frightened.

"A piece of the sky came down and hit me on the head," thought Chicken Little to himself. "This is terrible. The sky is falling. I must go at once and tell the other animals. *The sky is falling! The sky is falling!*" And off he went.

At this point the children's version of the story recounts Chicken Little's journey and his conversation with a large number of animals (Henny Penny, Ducky Lucky, Goosey Poosey, and many others with equally distinguished names, depending upon the inventiveness and energy of the storyteller). Eventually, however, Chicken Little and a long procession of animals who believed his story came to the Lion King to tell him the terrible news.

After he had listened to Chicken Little's story, the Lion King suggested that they all go back to look at this place where the sky had fallen on Chicken Little's head. Led by the Lion King (who was wise and powerful and had a great deal of common sense as well) the animals returned to the scene where something had hit Chicken Little on the head and frightened him and made his head hurt.

No one could find a piece of fallen sky.

The Lion King, however, found a very large acorn lying in the grass.

As humans, storytelling is one of the most powerful things we do. We are changed by telling our story with its fear and loss and grief and changed by the response of those who listen. In times of pain and disorientation community provides the essential gift of listeners, those who are willing to be present with us and to hear our story and its pain and to respond. But listeners differ in important ways, as Jesus pointed out in one of His stories (Matthew 13:18–23), and catastrophizers come in several forms. Those listeners who encourage a dreary repetitive rehearsal of our painful circumstances do not themselves understand redemptive pain management and unwittingly encourage us to tell our story in a way that intensifies our sense of hopelessness. Those listeners whose hearing is marked by avid curiosity and a spectator's interest exaggerate and exploit the presence of our pain for their own entertainment. These listeners distort our sense of perspective, and in using us for their own purposes, increase our sense of vulnerability. Those listeners who carry deep levels of fear in their own lives are dangerous listeners. Like Chicken Little's friends, they meld their fears into ours and magnify them when our story touches their lives. Effective pain management includes gathering around us in close community those who can be present with us and listen to our stories. However, those who become good stewards of their pain do not invite those listeners who through mindless repetition, exaggeration, or fear, lead us away from understanding the story we are in and managing its pain.

There are others who wish to help but whose efforts are counterproductive. The Fixer, the Entertainer, the Explainer, the Understander—all of these, with rare exception, are people with good intentions; they are, nevertheless, potentially unsafe as close companions on the journey.

Fixers

It is quite difficult to avoid entanglement with Fixers because they want to so much to help and are so convinced that they know how to do so. Fixers are confident that they can identify the problem and tell you how to fix it, or, better yet, fix it for you themselves, so that your pain—and the pain your pain causes them—will go away. From a safe distance, it is easy to see that Fixers dangerously combine good intentions with a reductionistic view of pain. From their point of view, pain is nothing but the result of an unsolved problem. Therefore, all things are simple—identify the problem, solve the problem, and then live life in merry ease. Reducing pain to "nothing but" evidence of an unsolved problem oversimplifies issues whose very complexity is, of course, part of the problem that they pose. Accepting our pain in both its complex content and context is an unavoidable step in good management.

Fixers, unfortunately, tempt us to shortcut this process. Because they tend to be "take charge" people, we can find ourselves entangled with the Fixer's definition of our problem and his or her plan of action for us before we realize what has happened. At such times we often lack the energy and social skills necessary to refuse the "help" we have been given.

This happened to my client whose daughter had committed suicide. Sarah was a deaconess in the church my client attended and a dedicated Fixer. Sarah came to visit my client some time after the memorial service for her daughter. I suspect that Sarah had decided that my client had been sad long enough and viewed her family as overly tolerant of her pain. At any rate, when Sarah arrived she explained to my client that her problem was grief and that the solution to the problem was to read the book that Sarah had brought. Sarah explained further that the book was a "Christian book, and the author believes in prayer, so I'm sure it will help. I'll try to stop by next week, and we can talk about it."

Part of my client's pain was certainly her grief over the loss of a child, but to reduce her pain to "nothing but" grief that could be handled in six steps from a self-help book was to make problems, not solve them. Fixers often inadvertently cause hurt feelings at a time when those in pain have no energy and little motivation to work at mending the damage that has occurred. My client experienced this as well. "I don't want this book," she told me, dropping it into the wastebasket by my desk, "and to tell the truth, I don't want to talk to Sarah, or see her again for at least five years. How can I keep her from coming next week?"

Fixers can, unwittingly, cause other problems as well. Pain blurs boundaries, and it is easy to become confused about how much problem solving is enough. With a Fixer's encouragement, we can perseverate on problem solving in a way that increases anxiety and decreases sleep. Even more dangerously, we can focus on problem solving in a way that distracts us from the spiritual essentials that keep us balanced and steady. For example, with rare exception, Fixers have a near total blindness to epiphanies; we, in turn, are less likely to glimpse one if we permit ourselves to become caught up in problem-solving in the way that a Fixer recommends. Certainly in times of pain and disorientation there are problems to be solved, and attention must be paid to solving them. The difficulty results from the tunnel vision and faulty priority system that we acquire when we follow the Fixer's advice. Ironically, the Fixer's assumption that problem solving pleases God has merit. God does indeed have a vested interest in helping with our problems. However, when Fixers function on this basis they assume further that God's priority is something like their own and that reaching a practical solution to life's problems comes first on God's agenda as it does for them. They assume as well that the problem-solving process forms a logical and sufficient basis for relationship with Him.

At an adult level, this thinking mirrors that of a child who works to complete a crayon drawing in anticipation of a relationship with a parent. The child thinks, "When I have my picture done I will show it to my father and then my father will be pleased." As our loving eternal parent, God is, blessedly, interested in our pictures. But in times of pain and struggle we are not at all sure about the picture we are drawing. We have lost the blue crayon we love, and the others are broken. At these times, it is essential to keep focused upon the fact that God's vital concern *is being with us while we are drawing.* He is pleased to help us with the picture. He will celebrate with us when it is complete. He will help us, and He will like our picture even when we have no blue crayon for the sky. But managing our pain well requires us to keep clear that God's primary interest lies in us, not in a picture for His eternal refrigerator door. His joy in our picture lies in the fact that it is ours. He knows how hard that picture was to draw. God prizes our picture, but He *loves* us and wants to be with us always. Narrow concentration on the problem-solving process can lead us away from this reassuring sense of the presence of Immanuel, God with us in our pain.

Effective pain managers know that pain management is certainly not as easy as the problem-solving formula suggests. At a self-evident level pain is certainly a problem and brings other problems with it as well. But effective pain managers know that the Fixer's solution-based response can distort in an essential understanding of pain itself.

Pain is an event that happens to us and in us. Pain is the side effect of living through the dark, mysterious, unwelcome segments of the cycle of life, those times that include loss, grief, rage and fear, sadness, disappointment, and disorientation. Pain is not simply a fly that can be spooned out of life's soup. Pain is a by-product of the process of living through a slice of life we do not like. Pain is just plain messy; it exists within fluid, shifting boundaries that cannot be made to fit into a box. Pain is a problem, but it is, nevertheless, a problem whose solution does not lie solely in problem solving. As an artifact of life itself, pain must be lived—effectively and triumphantly or in miserable, bitter hopelessness. We have a choice about how we live our pain. While acknowledging this, however, effective pain managers reject categorically the concept that pain is nothing but a problem to be solved. They understand that viewing pain as nothing but a problem leads to a despairing dead-end when problem-solving efforts fail.

When dealing with interpersonal relationships, it is helpful to remember that fear often drives the Fixer's problem-oriented way of thinking. In order to feel safe, Fixers act out of the illusion that we humans, if we are "spiritual," can find a solution to every challenge and discomfort. The Fixer wants to believe that there is no pain we cannot cause to go away, provided that we work on the problem (and are spiritual, of course). As a consequence, deep, persistent pain rattles the way Fixers think about reality and the theology they have developed to accompany it. Chronic, persistent pain, the pain that cannot be budged, provides unwanted evidence of a world in which there are sticks that cannot be straightened and losses that cannot be recovered (Ecclesiastes 1:14, 15). The presence of such pain contradicts the gospel of emotional prosperity and points to a theology in which living with and through the pain is the road of fellowship with the crucified one. Sarah, the Fixer who visited my client, was deeply frightened by the possibility that her belief in the certainties of her "Christian world" and her definition of the

"Christian family" could be toppled by the hard evidence that "Christian parents" could experience the brutal loss of a "Christian child" and an unsettling grief that challenged their souls and shook their faith. *Sarah* needed for my client's grief to be little and fixable at once in six easy steps. Sarah was genuinely concerned about my client, but she was also deeply concerned about *her* need to maintain *her* illusionary world through *her* solution to my client's pain. This unspoken agenda explains why Fixers can be so annoying at times. They walk over our boundaries; they insist on "helping" when we have neither asked for help nor necessarily think that we need it. While we are attempting to make our world more manageable, Fixers can tread heavily upon our toes in their effort to keep their own worldview stable and intact. In the majority of cases, they are apologetic but confused if someone points out the pain that their efforts to "help" have caused.

Entertainers

Entertainers are poor companions too. Like Fixers, Entertainers are acutely uncomfortable with our pain and presuppose that, like a parent with an upset baby, we will stop crying if they provide us with something else to look at, something else to be interested in, something that will entertain us away from our pain. Experienced parents know, however, that no stuffed bunny is a match for the pain and tears that come with colic in the night. In much the same sense, experienced pain managers know that distraction, while useful, has its limits and its dangers.

Effective pain managers understand both the Entertainer's truth and error. It is true that we must learn to look at something in addition to our pain and learn to look through our pain in hope to what lies ahead in the journey to come. But ironically,

Entertainers are dangerous precisely because they unknowingly short-circuit this necessary process. Entertainers do not encourage us both to be present with our pain and with that which is present in addition to it. Entertainers believe that the distraction process leads to the elimination of pain. The Entertainer's error lies in a belief in an illusionary either/or—if laughter is present, pain cannot be. It is not a matter of the Entertainer refusing to recognize the elephant in the living room. Entertainers see the elephant; however, they mistakenly believe that if they stage a really good play in the living room, the elephant will go away. This idea incorporates a complex from of denial that can be tempting. Perhaps, we think, the Entertainer has found a splendid way out of our pain. We will laugh and have a good time, and while we are at the party pain will fold its tents and fade away. While laughter and distraction are valuable tools in managing pain, they become destructive when we use them to deny the reality of our inner world and to avoid facing the disorientation of change. The Entertainer can help us smile and attend to things other than our pain. However, Entertainers function poorly as close companions on the journey. Laughing at a joke in the morning is a good thing, provided that we do not expect the joke to eliminate the afternoon's tears nor substitute for them.

Explainers

Explainers are also poor companions and difficult to manage. Like Fixers, Explainers are confident that they can help and certain that they know how. Fixers provide solutions; Explainers provide answers—serious answers. Entertainers can (and often do) make a problem with their distorted sense of the value and power of laughter. Explainers often make a problem at the other end of the continuum—they have little sense of the value of the light touch in dealing with issues of pain. And Explainers have a further problem; their explanations rarely explain despite their earnest intentions to do so. The reasons for pain and directions for managing it that are offered by Explainers unfortunately fall wide of the mark both emotionally and theologically in most instances. The prospect of an explanation that doesn't explain delivered with heavy-handed seriousness can drive even the experienced pain manager to leave church by the side door when an Explainer is heading her way.

Jane (my client who suffered from infertility issues and whose story appears in chapter 3) had an Explainer in her community, who was a fellow church member. One Mother's Day shortly after Jane had suffered spontaneous abortion of the only child she had been able to conceive, the Explainer (Ella) cornered Jane on her way out of church and said, "I've just heard your bad news. Now, Janie, you've just got to realize that God wanted your baby more than you did. You've just got to surrender your life to God's will and be brave and cheerful." When talking with me about this wounding experience, Jane said tearfully, "I'll be polite because Ella is mother's friend, but I will never really talk with Ella ever again."

Explainers tempt us to focus on the "why" question at a time when clear thinking is difficult and increase our sense of vulnerability without any understanding that they have done so. At times an Explainer's comments may carry criticism, implied or directly stated, that triggers difficult bouts of self-blame as well. A client whose husband had physically injured her was told by a church staff member that her injury was her own fault, the result of her failure to be sufficiently sexually responsive to her husband. It required a long period of careful, knowledgeable assistance before this woman could discriminate between Christians who were best kept at a safe distance and those whom she could trust in close community to help her live through and beyond her pain.

Understanders

And then there are the Understanders, those people whose invariable response to our pain is the classic, "I know just how you feel." They do *not* know, of course. No matter how empathic we may be, we can never understand fully the world with which others are struggling and the burden of their pain. However frustrating we may find these people who "understand," we need to remember that they intend to help. Their goal is good. It is their method that makes the problem. Their method itself is a frustrating mix of half-helpful and downright disastrous. Understanders set out to reassure us that we are not alone. ("I know just how you feel.") Then they undertake to prove that we are not alone by sharing an experience that they believe to be like ours, preferably their own. ("When I lost my mother, I cried for weeks.") They assume that this reassurance and shared experience will ease our pain and perhaps provide some good advice into the bargain. They are then perplexed and hurt in turn when someone points out that their "understanding" is neither helpful nor comforting.

Their motivation is not the problem. The difficulty lies in the frustrating combination of truth and error out of which Understanders operate. They have one piece of truth absolutely correct: *We cannot do it alone*. It is equally true in a paradoxical way that no one else can do it for us. Nevertheless, the Understanders have this point correct: If we are to make truly redemptive use of our suffering we need others. We need the companionship of the walking, surviving wounded and access to their stories in order to understand and live our own. That is the powerful, compelling truth of community.

The thing that Understanders do not understand, however, is the nature of those supportive connections and the way in which those connections are formed. Understanders report *their* experience and think that by reporting *their* experience they are sharing *our* wounds. It is not possible for them to participate closely in another's journey in this way, however. Reporting is a process of talking-about rather than sharing-in. As reporters of human experience (their own and that of others), Understanders function as spectators—concerned spectators, admittedly, but spectators. They remain watchers, historians who preserve and report accounts of pain. They believe that recounting the history of *their* pain (or that of others whom they know) consists of an act of sharing in *ours.* This fatal confusion keeps them members of the group that experienced pain managers hold at respectful arm's length. Their "understanding" walls them away from our pain in ways that we find difficult to explain and they do not comprehend.

Undertaking the Search

It is easier to identify those who are unhelpful companions on the way than to describe the process of finding those who are willing and able to help. Making friends with whom we can share deeply both our failures and our triumphs is not a matter of following a formula. There are no guaranteed procedures for making connection with those who have a repertoire of pain management skills that they are willing to share. There are, however, some steps that increase the possibility that such a connection can occur.

We can demonstrate an attitude of willingness to be responsible for ourselves. Being responsible entails two steps: First, we need to agree with both ourselves and God that we can't do it alone, that we need companions on the way. We need then to keep clear at the same time the kind of help for which we're searching. We need companions who can encourage our learning and insight and foster the skills necessary to manage our anger and despair. We need those who can teach us to keep our balance in this time of disorientation and change; we need too those who can (and will) encourage and challenge us to do what we do *not* wish, in some senses, to do at all—to live with and through our pain.

Settling these issues early (both with ourselves and God) enables us to demonstrate a willingness to be responsible for ourselves that attracts those who can and want to help. It is well to keep in mind that the people who are most able to help us usually do not "need" us—we need them. The walking, working wounded are people who are now doing well in most respects. They are willing to help because, in concern for the common good, they want others to do well also. Additionally, they are willing to help because they remember that somewhere along the way in their dark journey someone helped them.

They do not need to help us to demonstrate their gifts, prove their moral goodness, or earn our gratitude (and obligation) for rescuing us. They do not need us to be helpless so that they can be powerful; they do not need us to be beaten up so that they can play Good Samaritan to the applause of the watching crowd. They help because they believe that their gratitude for life is best expressed by supporting life in others; they help because, out of their own experience, they know that adding some of their strength and courage to whatever remaining strength we have and are *willing to use* is the best and definitive investment they can make of themselves and of the life they have been given. My grandfather was annoyingly fond of the cliché "God helps those who help themselves." In the context of searching for companions who can help, this old proverb might be paraphrased to say, "Those who make an effort to help themselves (no matter how small the effort) are more likely to receive offers of help from others who are effective."

We can go where people are rather than waiting for others to come to us. Particularly in the early stages of dealing with pain and the disorientation it brings, we often find that choosing to be with people requires energy that is in scarce supply, and we are quite willing to go along with that part of ourselves that wishes to isolate and withdraw. A client who was a gifted quilter had been absent for several meetings of the quilters club to which she belonged. While initially resistant to my urging, she eventually agreed to try one meeting with the stipulation that she could leave early. She shared with me about her experience.

"It was unbelievably difficult to make myself go. But after I got there, it was so good to have a needle in my hand again. Something about taking one tiny stitch after another was comforting. But the thing that happened at the end was the best. I said to Helen—she's always so quiet—I said, 'I'm going to go. I'm just worn out.' Helen smiled and hugged me, then she said, 'Grief wears anybody out. I'm glad you had the good sense to come, and I'm glad you've got the good sense to go home early.' I couldn't believe what I heard! Helen gets it!"

Indeed, Helen did understand for reasons that she shared slowly and cautiously with my client in the weeks that followed. Helen's initial coaching (good sense to come; good sense to go home early) was the first of many practical pieces of wisdom Helen shared out of her own journey through her personal tragedy. I doubt that this remarkably helpful relationship would have developed, however, if my client had not taken her courage and limited energy in hand and gone where the quilters were.

We can cautiously, carefully disclose something of our journey. In this limited, protected self-disclosure we can give opportunity for someone hearing our disclosure to respond and connect with our journey.

Carl discovered this at a baseball game. Carl and Ginny had held season tickets to the local baseball club. Now, after the accident, it seemed too painful to Carl to go alone, and he was considering the option of selling the tickets. However, in addition to the relationships Carl had formed in his recovery group, he was developing a significant friendship with a business acquaintance, Rex, who shared his interest in baseball. Carl decided one day to invite Rex to attend a doubleheader at the local ball park.

Carl reported this to me and added, "You know, I didn't really want to go to the game, but I'm glad I did. I learned something about Rex. He's lived through some hard stuff. He's lost somebody too even if it wasn't his own fault, like it is for me. But I see what you mean—I can learn from him. What surprised me is that I didn't guess [that Rex had experienced the painful loss of his wife]. I just thought he was a darn good tax accountant and a Rockies fan."

Initially Carl thought that he had made a bad choice. Going to the game with Rex required Carl to cope with crowds when he felt like staying home. When Rex sat down in the seat where Ginny had once sat, Carl thought for a moment that his memories (and his pain) were more than he could manage publicly and considered leaving before the game began. However, Carl's decision to make the emotional effort of staying paid off richly.

"Does your wife like baseball?" Rex asked as they settled into their seats.

Carl hesitated, and then said, "Well, I'm not married. I'm a single dad. Glad you could come tonight—this ought to be a good game." Following a long pause, Carl risked a significant but guarded self-disclosure, "My wife was killed in a car accident a year ago."

Another long pause followed. Then Rex risked in turn, "That's tough. My first wife died from breast cancer when she was thirty-two. I've been working on putting my life together again for five years now."

That was all. Neither man shared more at that time, but with Rex, Carl had made a connection with someone who could help him in turn work on putting his life together again.

A word of caution is needed at this point, however. Like Rex, the person who appears to be a tax consultant may be a Rockies fan, a C.P.A., *and* an honored member of the community of the walking wounded. In building community, what we hope to find (a pain management expert) may not be what we see on the surface, at least initially. And the converse is equally true: What we see (the competent C.P.A.) may be an interesting, responsible person and a delightful companion at a ballgame but at the same time is an individual with no dark journey, few pain management skills, and no interest in acquiring any more. Developing community requires commitment to its value and to the persistence and risk it demands, knowing that we do not hit a homerun every time we come to bat.

This search becomes easier when we realize that community is not just our concern. It is God's concern as well. Whether we sense Him or not, God walks with us through the wilderness of our pain. When we choose to fellowship with Him there, community becomes His project too. In our connection in community we come to know ourselves—for both the better and the worse that lie within us. We come to know God and His love and grace; we experience His presence as well. God chooses in the context of community as the body of Christ to be present with us in particular ways. Jesus promised specifically that where we are gathered together, even when there are just two or three of us, He is with us in a special way (Matthew 18:20). We tend to think too narrowly about Jesus' promise. He was talking about far more than Sunday morning church.

When we find those who can help us it is important to remember from the outset that *this community embodies the very brokenness we ourselves carry.* We gain strength and courage and, thankfully, common sense as well as wisdom through our connection in community. We learn, in Christian community, from saints in process of becoming. But what we do *not* gain is the companionship of the already perfected. We enter the fellowship of those whose journey still continues. For some of our companions, the worst of their dark places lie behind them, but they continue, nonetheless, to live with their memories, their scars, and the wounding process that produced them. Unless we understand from the outset that the community of the walking wounded is one of embodied brokenness, we will ask for what it cannot provide.

This community cannot compensate for our losses; it cannot absorb our rage or dissolve our grief. It cannot serve as a surrogate parent or a substitute self. This special community does not lessen the disciplines of discipleship nor decrease the demands of maturity. In the fellowship of the walking wounded, brokenness—our own and that of others—is neither celebrated nor denied. Brokenness is embraced simply and straightforwardly as one of the relational places in which human spirits can connect with each other and connect with the presence of God. The community of the broken is the place of the "already" but "not yet," the place where the already-redeemed work out the not-yet-complete process of their human journey. But out of the "already" but "not yet" we—all of us—can learn to live triumphantly with what we cannot change.

We assemble this community of the walking wounded from individuals scattered throughout the communities of which we are a part. Connecting with these individuals in our various communities requires, however, that we resist the temptation of isolation and go where the people are. It requires as well that we go carefully, however, choosing people and activities where we can be cautiously self-disclosing, and listen for responses in which we can hear echoes of another's journey. We walk with friends, we play ball, we go fishing, we swim, we barbeque. We go to lunch, we share coffee, we carpool, we go about those pieces of living that we can manage. But we pay new attention to those we come in contact with, asking as carefully as we can the questions with which we are struggling. We do this trusting that among those who hear us are some who, hearing, will recognize the questions, remember their journey, and reach out to us.

While we are searching, sometimes someone from the community of the walking wounded finds us. A friend tells a story of such an experience from her own life.

Lisa was alone at a time when the structure of her life had disintegrated around her. The intensity of the pain of her losses had exhausted her energy and distorted her sense of realistic options for restructuring life in the years that lay ahead. She felt utterly disoriented in the flood of change that had carried away relationships built through thirty years of living, and—for all that Lisa knew at that moment—had carried away broken fragments of herself as well. She wandered into a neighborhood restaurant one evening near closing time, aware, belatedly, that it had been a number of hours since she had eaten. She ordered a bowl of soup, and, while waiting for her order, counted out cash from her purse to cover her bill. Her hair was a mess of disordered tangles; her face was swollen from crying. The waitress eyed her sharply when she brought her order but made no verbal comment. Lisa remembers eating slowly. Each swallow of soup was a struggle; she remembers thinking that she had swallowed so many tears that day that now there was no longer any room for soup.

When the waitress brought the bill, she first glanced cautiously at the manager busy at the front register and then slipped into the booth opposite my friend.

"Listen, honey," she said in a voice that had learned to talk in Texas, "I can tell you're in trouble. Been there and know the look." Then, as she eyed the cash lying on the table, "Do you have a place to sleep tonight? I know a place that's clean and safe and don't cost much."

Lisa, telling the story, said, "Tears came to my eyes. But my tears weren't about being lost and my dreams broken. My tears were about being found. Somebody had seen me. Somebody would help."

When she could speak, Lisa said, "Thank you so much for paying attention. But I have a place to go. I will be all right. I can manage. I can do it." For a long moment the two of them looked at each other across the table. Then, nodding her beehive hairdo, the Texas waitress smiled and said, "Yep. Bet you can. You go, girl," picked up her tray and vanished behind the kitchen's swinging door. At the worst times in the difficult months that followed, Lisa remembers saying to herself, copying that Texas-tutored voice as best she could, "Yep. Bet I can do this. Bet I can."

Lisa did do it—and out of her life now discreetly, quietly, without obvious fanfare, she watches in turn for those who "have the look" and who need to be seen where they are on their journey, who need to hear someone say, "Yep. Bet you can do it. Bet you can." The community of walking, working wounded is not a collection of sentimental "wannabe" rescuers. Like Lisa's waitress, they offer help without assuming responsibility for outcomes that are not their own to determine. Their offer of assistance is given to supplement the strength that is there, no matter how small. They do not say, "I give because you cannot do it without me, and by this act I rescue you." They give because out of their own journey, remembering, they believe that with some help, we can do it. Their gift is their bet that we can.

Finding and Being Found

Connection within the community of the walking wounded comes as a result of both finding and being found, from both choosing and being chosen. Since this is a community scattered within other communities in which we function, connection requires the wisdom to say no to those who wish to help but who cannot and the self-knowledge and humility to say yes to those who can. It requires too that we develop the discernment to know what it is that we need so that we can recognize it when it comes unexpectedly, oddly packaged, and given in a way that requires us to stretch and reach in order to receive.

Who do we want to find us? What is it that we need?

Presence

One of the most important things we need is people who can be present with us, who can simply be with us in our pain, those who can be fully aware of the intensity of our grief and loss yet feel unafraid, those who can come into our chaos and disorientation without becoming in turn disoriented by it. We need people who can see with the eyes of their hearts, so to speak, and understand that to be present is to lessen the aloneness and help us hold a space where hope can come. Those who bring the gift of presence have an inner matter-of-fact calmness and patience in the face of pain that permits them to come and "sit a bit" until things "settle out," as a country neighbor once said to me. Those who are effective in being present are, for the most part, unpretentious, unassuming, and totally disinterested in theatrics. They are attentive and watchful; they often know that we need them before we know it ourselves. They will come alongside, but in order for them to "sit awhile," we must have accepted our need for community. If we signal nonverbally our desire to be alone, these people will respect this. They are not Fixers. They simply offer to bring themselves into the space of our pain share that space—they do not presume to pick up our pain. If we do not wish to have them present, they will go. They have an unsentimental commitment to presence that they do not confuse with problem solving. It is not that they are disinterested in our welfare—far to the contrary—but if pushed to explain, they would say that the problem solving is up to us and God. Ann Weems, whose work we have discussed earlier, has written about presence in a way that captures something of this gift. She writes:

> I see your pain
> And want to banish it

With the wave of a star
But have no star.

I see your tears
And want to dry them
With the hem of an angel's gown
But have no angel.

I see your heart fallen to the ground
And want to return it
Wrapped in cloths woven of rainbows,
But have no rainbow.

God is the One
Who has stars, and angels and rainbows,
And I am the one
God sends to sit beside you
Until the stars come out
And the angels dry your tears
And your heart is back in place,
Rainbow blessed.[1]

The presence of someone who has come simply to sit until the stars come out makes the darkness into a place of beginning hope. It is a healing experience to find—or be found by—someone in community who can simply come and be present in our pain.

Listeners

Our need for listeners grows out of the odd human fact that what happens to us is not finished until the story is told. For runners the climax of the race may be that last desperate effort and the moment when they cross the finish line, but the race is not over until the story of the race is told—heartbreak hill and that moment when they hit the wall. And for those who go fishing, there is that moment of sheer adrenal rush when a big fish takes the bait and the line begins to sing as it spins off the reel. There is the fish and—we smile—then later there is the story of the fish. We know that stories change in the telling. We are less clear that the stories change us—teller and listener alike. We are changed by telling the story, both our own and that of others. We are changed too by listening to the stories of others and by listening to our own story even as we tell it. Telling and listening to stories is one of the most powerful things that we do as humans, and it is a primary means of pain management.

Telling and listening are serious acts that require careful attention. In our society we provide designated listeners for those who have survived times of grave danger and whose stories contain great risk, threat, and terror. These stories sometimes contain experiences of torture and horror the storyteller cannot bear to remember but can find no way to forget. Sometimes we refer to this formally designated listening as debriefing. In other settings this listening becomes part of the formally designated responsibility of a therapist. But often an individual who functions in a healing way as a hearer is an undesignated volunteer, a listener from the community of the walking wounded. Whatever the setting and roles involved, this portion of managing pain has at its core storytelling and listening. Someone tells a story. Someone listens and hears. And in ways we cannot yet fully explain, pain is lessened, some of the horror is leached away, and a space is made where the storyteller can stand safe and apart, released (at least for that moment) from the trauma in the story that has been told. But this space and its quiet safety come only when the story is told to a listener who hears.

If we want someone present with us in community, we must abandon our aloneness and embrace the risk. If we want a listener, we must additionally resist the temptation to edit our story to make it safe (or nice) and embrace the vulnerability that telling our story brings. This vulnerability is a difficult choice for a logical reason. Stories, and the telling of stories, can be frightening at times in ways we cannot control and may not anticipate.

My family did not have radio or television. On Halloween my sister and I, with ghoulish enthusiasm, would provide what we considered to be the proper quota of stories about ghosts from books or from our imaginations. One year my sister's friend came to stay with us overnight. At bedtime the three of us settled under the blankets and decided (with delighted shivers of anticipation) to tell some "really scary stories" before we went to sleep. When it became my turn to make a story, I invented a dreadful tale filled with corpses and graveyards and ghosts that came through locked doors and windows. I earned satisfying shrieks from my sister and her friend and was quite pleased with my literary efforts. However, in the night I myself awoke screaming in the middle of a nightmare. My father, awakened by the noise I was making, lit the lamp and came to see what was happening. I explained that I was having a bad dream. My father said, "Must have been a mighty powerful story you told. Scared yourself, didn't you?" He was right.

We are cautious about own stories for good reasons, among them the fact that parts of our story can make us feel frightened—the ghosts we describe may rise to haunt us. However, fear is not the only problem with which we have to grapple. The complexities of our stories make them difficult to tell. Even when we are brave enough to do so, we feel unable to describe the road we have traveled, to say plainly where we have been and how we have come to this place. We feel confused by the disjuncture that exists between the enormity of our pain and the mundane, ordinary portions of our lives that are also part of our journey and a part of this present place and its suffering. We are not sure how to put the different pieces of our story together.

"I didn't think you'd believe me," a client whispered the first time she risked telling me a portion of her story. "I'm a teacher, a plain ordinary teacher, and I go get my hair cut and go to the grocery store and then I go home and... Things like this don't happen to teachers." But they do. Tragically, they do. But in times of pain and disorientation it seems impossible to assemble all the disparate parts of our story and to seam them together with meaning. At this point we must trust our story itself. In the telling itself, the pieces of our story will come together in ways we need not anticipate.

To begin requires courage as well as trust, however. We feel afraid of what we may hear as we listen to ourselves. We sense intuitively that while we are hearing our own story we may be confronted with things we do not wish to know or feel. We may be afraid to look straight-on at our losses, to face the consequences of our choices. We may feel ashamed and afraid of what we feel now and what we felt then. We may feel diminished and dishonored by the choices of others. We may feel depleted by our failures, disoriented by change. We may be afraid of the seismic shifts that are occurring in our understanding; the "truth" in our story may seem less sure and our story, chameleon-like, may seem to be changing. We are not sure of our story or of what we will learn there.

And we are afraid too of what we *can* feel here again in the present if we tell our story—more grief, more rage, more shame, more hopelessness and despair. And we are afraid of the conflicting senses of reality that our story can produce. We know our story happened *then* and that we are telling our story *now*. But we know too that the story that happened then can *seem* now. We are afraid of the power in our story to draw us again into the reality it both embodies and evokes. We sense that our story has the power to shift portions of the past into the present in ways we may not always be able to control. And we know too that a portion of our story that is past reaches into today and stretches ahead into tomorrow in ways that we cannot anticipate. We are unsure about our story's beginning, its middle, and its end. Telling our story, and hearing it as we tell it, is no simple task, but it is vital for us to take our courage in hand and do so if we wish to manage our pain well. Jesus said once to His disciples that truth would set them free (John 8:31–33). At the time, Jesus was talking about himself, but the principle is far-reaching. One vital way of knowing truth that can free us in times of pain and disorientation is to tell our story and learn the truth it teaches. But this is not something we can do alone. We must risk telling our story, but we must risk with a listener who can be present with us and who can hear the story we need to tell.

Listeners who provide a safe place for us to tell our stories are lifelong learners. They listen to our story—the circumstances, the loss, the pain, and disorientation—because they are interested in us and in our story and in *what our story means*. They want to hear our story because at the core they are responders who respond to our story looking for the truth they can see. They are not Explainers or Fixers. They are not sentimental sympathizers or empathic hand holders, even when we might wish them to be. It is their commitment to the truth that our story points to that makes these listeners safe people to tell and hear our story. They can hear our pain, and it does not frighten them. They can see our disorientation, and they do not lose their balance. But their pain management skills make them focus on the next right step—the truth that can be said and acted on, although they rarely think of their responses in this way. Carol, whose husband was imprisoned for embezzlement, had a wonderful listener in her friend Ilene. After listening again one day to Carol's story with its pain and anger, Ilene said, "If I were in your shoes I'd be twice as mad and ten times as scared as you are. What do you think your options are?"

Telling me about the conversation, Carol said, "For a second, I was mad. Then it just washed over me—what a gift Ilene is. She gets it—she really gets it that I'm so mad and so scared that some days I can barely get to work. She took the kids to school Wednesday and kept Kerry overnight. But Ilene understands that I need to think about my options." Carol's truth was straightforward. Her anger and fear were reasonable responses; her need (and option) to choose how she would respond to the chaos in her life was also part of her story. Ilene's response helped Carol hear her own story in all of its parts—her rage, her fear, *and* her power to choose.

Sometimes the important truth to be looked at is less straightforward. Listeners can hear a story that is filled with cruelty and pain and chaos but see at the same time a place in our story where there was strength, however small, and the choice to survive. We may not know this part of our story until we tell it with a listener who can see this truth and tell it back to us. Listeners can hear parts of our story that we have made too small, have shrunken and minimized, and can tell it back in better proportion. One of the healing moments in a client's life came when, after some careful preparation in our work together, she chose to risk a portion of her story with Joan, one of the community of walking wounded who was also a member of a women's prayer group my client attended. My client's story included an abusive parent, and at the end Joan said gently, "You talk like it was your fault your father spanked you so hard. No matter what you did, that kind of hitting is not ever okay." I had said this to my client numerous times, but when Joan—as a listener—said, in effect, "Here is the truth in your story you didn't see," something shifted in my client. Telling me about her time with Joan she said, "I know you've told me that, but somehow, when Joan said it, something changed. I thought, 'My father was wrong to spank me like that.'" She paused, and then added shyly, "I think Joan thinks I was brave. I never thought about that."

Sandy, the listener to whom Jane first told the story of the loss of her baby, sat silently for a long while. Then, wise beyond her years, Sandy simply touched Jane's hand and said, "There isn't anything to say that will help." Sandy was right: The truth of Jane's story at that point was that there is grief that lies beyond saying and changing; it must be lived through. Talking to me about the conversation later, Jane said, "Sandy helped. She didn't try to make everything all right. She just listened." In her listening response, Sandy affirmed Jane's sense of her story and her pain—and validated the truth that parts of Jane's story lay beyond that place where words can alter pain's intensity or express its meaning.

Challengers

Listeners are one of the gifts of community that make redemptive management of our pain possible. And community also provides those who are Challengers, those who, if we are willing, aid us in managing our pain in ways that inhibit our tendency toward helplessness, distortion, and self-absorption.

In one sense those who can be present with our pain and struggle provide audience and encouragement that we can survive our story, whatever the circumstances in which we find ourselves. Listeners provide audience and encouragement that our story is about truth as well as pain and that there is truth in our story even when that truth is fragmented and disjointed, and we see through the glass of our present experience with cloudy confusion. Challengers provide encouragement and perspective. Their input discourages obsession with ourselves and our story; they keep us anchored in a world that is bigger than ourselves. Their response to our story and to us as people, not victims, fosters a sense of proportion that discourages theatrics and encourages competence.

Challengers may well be thought of as the blessed half-interested. They are interested in our story and in us. But they are interested in more than the struggle. They pay attention to our competence, our potential, our gifting, our ability to make the world a better place—all of these aspects of who we are, not just the pain and disorientation with which we struggle. But they are only half-interested in the struggle—they are interested as well in what else is happening in our inner world and in what may lie beyond today's reality. The challenger's disinterest in making our pain the whole story is a gift and an unconscious correction of the temptation to narcissism that accompanies pain.

Shirley had been legally but unjustly terminated from her job just before she became eligible for retirement. One day while she was trying to work out her options, a friend left a message on her voicemail saying, "I'd like to take you to lunch Tuesday or Wednesday—let me know what works for you. And this is a head's up—I want to talk to you about mercy. How you think this experience has influenced your use of your gift of mercy? Do you think the injustice you're struggling with has changed your definition of mercy?"

Sometime after her lunch with Jan, Shirley remarked to me, "At first, to tell the truth, I was annoyed and a little bit offended. I wanted Jan to take me to lunch and let me tell her—again—how terrible this has been and how I have been injured. Instead, Jan had the nerve to expect me to be thinking about how I was going to come through this—how I might think and act if I made good use of this experience. We had a good lunch, and in a way it was comforting. We had a great debate over a definition of mercy, and at one point I think we made the waiter wonder what was going on. Never did agree. But probably the best thing was something Jan said that has really stayed with me. She said, 'Good grief. Did you think this had the power to take your gifts away?' You know, I think without knowing it, I did think that. I think I thought that when they fired me I lost not only my job but my ability to make a difference anywhere anymore."

A friend who was struggling with the chaos and economic disaster that had followed her highly conflicted divorce had a wonderful challenger in her life. This woman co-opted Alice into volunteering with her in a program providing support for children who were HIV positive. Talking with me about the experience, Alice said, "Nobody but Marsha could have got away with that. But we've been friends for twenty years, and Marsha just said, 'Come on. I need some help.' And I thought—peevishly, I admit—well, *I'm* the one who needs help. But looking back, Marsha was right. I needed the challenge to do something. I still volunteer two days a month. Helps me keep my perspective. I'm alive, and, God willing, I'm going to be alive for a long time yet. And there's a lot of stuff in this sorry old world that needs doing that I can do without much money and without a husband. Good to remember that."

Challengers are often people who, in their own journey through pain, have become experts at mastery. They have great skills in doing what they can with what is available, and they understand the principle of the half loaf. They expect that good pain management, whatever the pain, will involve doing something with the strength that is available and holding fast to the half loaf we have. Challengers, because of their skills in mastery, also have a good sense of timing. Not surprisingly, after the loss of her child, Jane rejected the invitation to work in the newborn nursery at her church. Jane's challenger, Julie, was gifted with both common sense and intuition. Julie strongly encouraged Jane to walk regularly with her in a park that had a large beautiful lake and walking trails. After a few weeks, Julie said, "Let's have every Tuesday be a pick-up day. On Tuesdays when we walk we'll pick up stuff and take cans to recycling and everything else to the dumpster." Jane became a walker that summer. She said later, "Julie kept me moving on days when that was all I could do. And on Tuesdays, there was the recycling thing. I suppose, looking back, when I was walking with Julie I was moving on and picking up the pieces of my life even though I didn't think about it at the time."

Because of their commitment to mastery, Challengers often confront us with the use of pain itself. Jane's story is about this too. In late autumn, after the summer of recycling, Julie called Jane one day and asked her to meet with a young woman from her office whose sister's much-wanted child had been stillborn. Julie was matter-of-fact and to the point. Jane, telling me about it later, said, "Julie doesn't ever dance around things. She just said, 'I thought you could tell Linda how to help her sister. You could tell her the things that made you crazy when you lost your baby and the things that helped. I think you can help Linda help her sister.'"

Eventually, all of these contacts led Jane to connect with Ginny, the woman whose child was stillborn. Jane had no easy words to say to Ginny, no simplistic superficial comfort; her own pain was still too raw, too real. Telling me about it, Jane said, "We walk early in the mall on Saturday, then usually go have breakfast. We don't actually talk much about her situation or about mine, but we just walk together and talk about whatever. I just try to keep us both moving."

Community is the Petri dish in which we grow through our pain. In community it is easier to keep our perspective and to remember that our pain does not make us the most important player on the stage. Community is the antidote to the hidden aloneness that breeds bitterness and festering self-pity. In community we find those who can be present with us, who can listen and help us hear our story, those who can and will help. And in community we find those who challenge us in turn to help and to remember that pain does not take away our capacity or our responsibility to give. Community makes it easier to resist the temptation to become famous (at least in our own eyes) for our pain or to let our pain become our identity. And community, if we permit it to do so, provides applause. The members of our community celebrate with us. On Jane's birthday, Julie gave Jane a tiny pair of silver-plated walking shoes to attach to the zipper on her briefcase. The note in her card read, "Happy birthday to one of the strongest walkers I know." Julie was talking about more than their trips together around the lake.

chapter 9

HOW CAN I PRAY
IN THIS PAIN?

Pain erodes away the internal boundaries by which we habitually organize our lives and govern our emotions. These weakened structures make us vulnerable to impulse and excess, to great rage and paralyzing fears, and, at times, to disorientation and distortion of reality. As pain weakens internal boundaries and our sense of perspective, relationships become strained and can be severely injured. In difficult situations, this stress sometimes reaches the point where relationships disintegrate. For example, the trauma associated with the serious injury or death of a child is sometimes followed by the collapse of the parents' marriage. We are aware that pain raises risks to relationships in the process of daily living in ways that cannot be completely avoided. However, we also know that if we pursue consistent honest communication we can lessen this risk.

Pain and disorientation bring risk to our relationship with God as well. Ultimately we are dependent on God's faithfulness to sustain our relationship with Him during times of pain and crisis. Nevertheless, in our relationship with God, just as in human relationships, we can choose to manage our pain in ways that deepen our relationship or act in ways that foster a sense of disconnection and alienation. Increasing the depth and intimacy of our relationship with God requires first, honest communication, and second, careful choices about the role that we assign to God in our story. It is our story, with our pain and failure, but it is not just our story—God has a story, too.[1]

Learning to Pray in and Through Our Pain

While the practice of prayer is vital to pain management, learning to pray in and through the compelling presence of pain is no small challenge. In times of pain, prayer can become reduced to self-focus in a way that poorly serves the goal of spiritual growth.

In the struggle to name our pain, prayer can become narrowed to a repetitive rehearsal of our injuries and grievances in a way that intensifies our suffering and our sense of ourselves as victims. In the difficult times of life, there are legitimate questions regarding God's justice and sovereignty that need to be raised in honest communication with God. However, in our anger and sense of alienation, our prayer can be become bogged down in a long bill of particulars comprised primarily of the details of our charges against God. This repetitive enumeration of our personal grievances against God soon moves us away from constructive protest against injustice and legitimate questions regarding God's sovereignty. At this point, this form of prayer easily degenerates into religious whining focused on what we believe to be God's neglect of our entitled comfort.

In times of danger and exhaustion when we are overwhelmed, we sometimes reduce prayer to an instinctive repeated call for help, a desperate appeal to a power greater than our own. Most of us know from experience that in despair we can reach a point where all that we are able to say, is "Help!" Appeal for God's assistance is certainly a controlling motivation and core component of prayer in times of trouble, and, thankfully, this cry for help moves His loving parent help. Nevertheless, if over an extended period of time our prayer life continues to be limited to crying "help," this oversimplified, repetitive appeal does little to facilitate spiritual growth and redemptive management of our pain.

Prayer in times of pain requires attention both to honesty and to structure. The most effective pattern for prayer in difficult times lies in the psalms of lament. These psalms teach us to express our pain honestly to God and to confront Him directly with our doubts and needs. The structure of the lament psalms expresses more than pain and anger, however. In most instances, these psalms lead also to praise. Even a cursory reading of these psalms leads us to voice the full extent of our pain and the terrible urgency of our requests directly to God. But in ways that are profoundly significant for healing, we soon see that these psalms move through this pain into praise. This movement toward praise shapes our focus on our pain in a fashion that protects us from ourselves. In their turn to praise, praying the pattern found in the psalms of lament turns us so that in our relationship with God, our interaction with Him is not just about pain, and the focus in the relationship is not just on us and our needs.

"Happy" Songs and Laments

The book of Psalms has long been a rich source of inspiration for God's people. However, selective religious use of the Psalms has led to a misleading emphasis on their positive content. As a result, people commonly view the Psalms as a book of "happy songs" praising God and reflecting a world in which, to borrow Browning's often quoted lines, "God's in his heaven—All's right with the world!" At those times when our experience reinforces our awareness of God's goodness, we are fond of reading these "happy psalms." We quote the happy opening phrase of Psalm 23: "The LORD is my shepherd, I shall not be in want" (Psalm 23:1 NIV) and stop well short of those uncomfortable references to enemies and to the valley of death. We treasure the promises given in Psalm 121:

> The LORD himself watches over you!
>> The LORD stands beside you as your protective shade.
> The sun will not harm you by day,
>> nor the moon at night.
> The LORD keeps you from all harm
>> and watches over your life.
> The LORD keeps watch over you as you come and go,
>> both now and forever. (Psalm 121:5–8 NLT)

These "happy psalms" become less appealing, however, when the reality of our lives becomes defined by loss and want. When experience indicates that God has *not* kept us from harm and that He has failed utterly to watch over our coming and going, what then? How can we speak honestly and openly to God about our circumstances in the face of what appears, as Walter Brueggemann has phrased it, to be God's "doubtful and unreliable fidelity?"[2] The answer is blessedly straightforward: We can set our feet solidly on the Scriptures and speak out of the content and the patterns given us in Psalms. But encouragement to do this lies in a portion of the Psalms to which many of us are relative strangers.

Because we read selectively, even those who read Scripture on a regular basis are sometimes surprised to learn that nearly half the Psalms are songs of complaint and lament. These psalms contain anguish, rage, and despair and often voice a direct expression of disappointment with God. Some of these psalms express as well a fierce desire for vengeance that raises uneasy feelings in us. What are we to make of a prayer in which the psalmist asks God to let burning coals fall upon the heads of his enemies, and, further, that his enemies be thrown into the fire and fall into miry pits never to rise again (Psalm 140:9–10)?

These are not the psalms commonly read in public worship.[3] These are not the psalms for which we have developed a familiar fondness. These psalms make us uncomfortable, particularly when on one of Browning's lark-singing, dew-jeweled mornings in spring we are feeling quite pleased with ourselves and satisfied with God's performance as God. We do not wish to consider the alternative reality that these psalms present: a world of doubt, great trouble, and pain. Additionally, we are uncertain how we should respond to the psalmist's honest conversation with God. This is no polite commentary on God's goodness; it is an indictment in which the psalmist bluntly expresses his anger and despair and directly confronts God with what he views as God's failure. If we have a limited understanding of God's purpose in the Psalms, we can become confused and overlook the significance of the psalms of lament and fail to utilize the power of these psalms to help us in our pain.

As Walter Brueggemann has demonstrated, the Psalms were designed to function as "the voices of faith in the actual life of the believing community."[4] As such they provide voice not only for the times of stability and joy but also for the anguish, loss, and disorientation that mark the dark side of life. With some important exceptions,[5] the lament psalms are not primarily the voice of God addressing us; they are rather the gathered voice of our suffering humanity come to address God. The psalms demonstrate a faith and an honesty that encourage us to approach God without pretense so that we may receive mercy and find grace to help us in our time of need (Hebrews 4:16).

In this context, the lament psalms are reassuring. When we can find no words to carry our suffering and confusion to God, it is encouraging to find that God himself has provided words for us. In giving us the Psalms, God has not left us voiceless or speechless in our pain. And, in faithful commitment to His relationship with us, God has provided in the Psalms a pattern through which we can learn a deeper level of communication with Him, if we choose to do so. But praying the Psalms in this way requires that we bring our experience to the Psalms, and, in doing so, bring our experience to God.[6]

At many levels we are afraid of our experience of pain with its threat of disorientation and chaos. We are afraid of the intensity of our experience and its implicit threat of continued pain and lack of control. We think that if we start crying, we can never stop and that if we fully express our sadness, we will never experience joy again. And we are reluctant to bring the negativity of our experience before God. We believe that our grief and rage and despair are not religiously respectable responses. We suspect—at times, we know all too well—that we harbor a strong impulse to wound in turn those who have wounded us. We feel embarrassed about our "unchristian" reactions and their potential destructiveness; and, to be honest about the matter, we feel concerned about the possible repercussions if we were to present what we feel and think openly and directly to God. We are not at all certain about what might happen if we "told God like it is" (or at least as we perceive it to be). And, further, we prefer to keep hidden even from ourselves whatever doubts about

God and His trustworthiness we may inwardly entertain. At the same time we are also uneasy about this inclination toward secrecy, so we hide it as well. We say, "Of course I can talk to God about how I feel. He already knows. Of course I can talk to Him." But what we often present, when we *do* talk with God, is a carefully managed, carefully laundered, religiously proper report *about* our experience; we rarely risk a no-holds-barred sharing of the real thing.

We are afraid of ourselves. But we are afraid of God, too. We are afraid that God cannot—or will not—deal constructively with the force and negativity of our feelings. As a result, we deal with God in an overly polite manner, as though He were fragile, delicate, and easily offended.[7] We approach God as though He were an elderly, easily-shocked Victorian maiden aunt. In what Brueggemann has termed fraudulent piety,[8] we behave as though God were too nice for the raw, powerful, dangerous reality of our human experience. And we secretly distrust the scope and reality of God's grace. We feel uneasily uncertain about the possible consequences of coming without pretense before God. While we prefer not to acknowledge this concern openly, we privately fear it may be possible to place ourselves beyond the boundaries of God's mercy and grace. Thankfully, the psalms of lament can lead us out of this religious posturing into a place of healing reality if we will permit them to do so.

The psalms of lament follow a broad general pattern with three major parts. Not every aspect of this pattern is found in every psalm, nor do these elements necessarily occur in every psalm in the prescribed order or in equal proportion.[9] But, however represented in any given psalm, lament psalms, with rare exception, incorporate these three elements:

- Protest—Life is not good and here is what is wrong.
- Petition—Here is how I want my situation changed.
- Praise—By faith, I affirm God's loving kindness and celebrate God's past action on behalf of His people; I acknowledge God's past goodness to me; I trust His presence and deliverance to shape my tomorrow.

Psalm 88 provides an important exception to the praise element, and we will consider it later. These elements are readily apparent in Psalm 13 (NLT).

Protest

O Lord, how long will you forget me?
  Forever?
How long will you look the other way?
How long must I struggle with anguish in my soul,
  with sorrow in my heart every day?
How long will my enemy have the upper hand?

Petition

Turn and answer me, O Lord, my God!
  Restore the sparkle to my eyes, or I will die.
Don't let my enemies gloat, saying,
  "We have defeated him!"
  Don't let them rejoice at my downfall.

Praise

But I trust in your unfailing love,
  I will rejoice because you have rescued me.
I will sing to the Lord because he is so
  good to me.

Protest: The Act of Faithful Complaint

When we focus our attention on the protest element in the lament psalms, two things become readily apparent: the power of the protest, and the nature of the context in which the protest is consistently expressed. When we lay our cautious expressions of pious politeness alongside the passionate protests of the psalmists, we are startled. We find ourselves thinking, "The psalmist said *that*? To *God*?" Yes, indeed, and our hope and our help in managing our pain lies in understanding both the power of the psalmist's protest and the structure of the relationship within which the psalmist boldly confronts God.

The power of the protest provides an immediate challenge to our practice of emotionally withholding from God. Protest in the lament psalms consists of direct unedited expression of the raw reality of the psalmist's experience. In this protest there is no "making nice" for God's benefit and emotional comfort. The sufferer's anguish, doubt, and rage are clearly and at times brutally expressed. But it is important from the outset to keep in mind the purpose of this protest. This cry of pain and despair is more than a cathartic eruption of uncontrolled human emotion. This is no dramatic monologue through which human suffering is emptied into some indifferent existential abyss. Nor is this a social complaint addressed to the ear of a sympathetic peer. This protest is the strong opening statement in a dialogue between the sufferer and God, the Holy One, the God of Israel. While the act of protest carries an uncensored expression of pain, it is a communication addressed to a living being, to someone the sufferer believes to be *covenant-obligated to hear and to respond*. And the sufferer believes further that this covenant partner is concerned about the *disrupted relationship* that is a part of the disorientation and pain that the sufferer is experiencing. The sufferer risks utter unqualified honesty before God, but this honesty frames a faith-based protest made in confidence that the God with whom the sufferer lives in relationship is concerned and will answer.

Learning to read ourselves into the text begins with hearing what the text says, although initially its boldness and passion may feel foreign to our daily pattern of speech. There is clear expression of pain.[10]

> Have compassion on me, LORD, for I am weak.
>> Heal me, LORD, for my bones are in agony.
> I am sick at heart.
>> How long, O LORD, until you restore me? . . .
> I am worn out from sobbing,
>> All night I flood my bed with weeping,
>> drenching it with my tears.
> My vision is blurred by grief.
>
>> (Psalm 6:2–3, 6–7a NLT)

> Turn to me and have mercy
>> for I am alone and in deep distress.
> My problems go from bad to worse,
>> Oh, save me from them all!
> Feel my pain and see my trouble,
>> Forgive all my sins.
>
>> (Psalm 25:16–18 NLT)

> Save me, O God,
>> for the floodwaters are up to my neck.
> Deeper and deeper I sink into the mire;
>> I can't find a foothold.

I am in deep water,
  and the floods overwhelm me.
I am exhausted from crying for help;
  my throat is parched.
My eyes are swollen with weeping,
  waiting for my God to help me...
You know of my shame, scorn, and disgrace.
You see all that my enemies are doing.
Their insults have broken my heart,
  and I am in despair.
If only one person would show some pity;
  if only one would turn and comfort me.

(Psalm 69:1–3; 19–20 NLT)

This expression of pain is linked to God's apparent abandonment and unreasonable absence. The sufferer charges God himself with responsibility for this trouble.

O Lord, why do you stand so far away?
  Why do you hide when I am in trouble?

(Psalm 10:1 NLT)

O Lord, how long will you forget me?
  Forever?
How long will you look the other way?

(Psalm 13:1 NLT)

My God, my God, why have you abandoned me?
  Why are you so far away when I groan for help?
Every day I call to you, my God, but you do not answer,
Every night you hear my voice, but I find no relief.

(Psalm 22:1–3 NLT)

You have laid me in the dust and left me for dead.

> (Psalm 22:15b NLT)

I eat ashes for my food.
My tears run down into my drink
because of your anger and wrath.
    For you have picked me up and thrown me out.

> (Psalm 102:9–10 NLT)

There is the bitter reminder to God that if His failure to act results in death, He too loses. There can be no praise or worship from the grave.

For the dead do not remember you.
    Who can praise you from the grave?

> (Psalm 6:5 NLT)

I cried out to you, O Lord,
    I begged the Lord for mercy, saying,
"What will you gain if I die,
    if I sink into the grave?
Can my dust praise you?
    Can it tell of your faithfulness?"

> (Psalm 30:8–9 NLT)

Are your wonderful deeds of any use to the dead?
    Do the dead rise up and praise you?
Can those in the grave declare your unfailing love?
Can they proclaim your faithfulness in the place of
    destruction?

> (Psalm 88:10–11)

And there is the challenging matter of justice, the protest of innocence, and the obligations of covenantal relationship.

O Lord, hear my plea for justice.
　　Listen to my cry for help.
Pay attention to my prayer,
　　for it comes from honest lips.
Declare me innocent,
　　for you see those who do right.　　(Psalm 17:1–2 NLT)

O Lord, I give my life to you.
　　I trust in you, my God!
Do not let me be disgraced,
　　or let my enemies rejoice in my defeat...
The Lord leads with unfailing love and faithfulness
all who keep his covenant and obey his demands.
　　　　　　　　　　　　　　　　(Psalm 25:1–2, 10 NLT)

Did I keep my heart pure for nothing?
　　Did I keep myself innocent for no reason?
I get nothing but trouble all day long;
　　every morning brings me pain.
　　　　　　　　　　　　　　　(Psalm 73:13–14 NLT)

Bend down, O Lord, and hear my prayer;
　　answer me, for I need your help.
Protect me, for I am devoted to you.
　　Save me for I serve and trust you,
　　You are my God. (Psalm 86:1–2)

We may be surprised by the intensity of the protest portions of these psalms, but we cannot be confused about their
content. The sufferer has brought to God an account—raw and
uncensored—of the devastation and disorientation in his life.
The psalmist includes, along with the report of these circumstances and pain, a straightforward challenge to God: "Where

are you, God, and how could you have let this happen?" From this challenge to God the psalmist then moves into petition for His intervention and help in the situation.

The Petition for Help

The psalmist's protests against God's absence and the threatening disorder of circumstances are accompanied by equally strong petitions that entreat God to come and intervene in the situation that resulted in the protest. These petitions are the voices of "those who find their circumstances dangerously, and not just inconveniently, changed," as Brueggemann noted,[11] and these voices urgently insist that God's intervention is essential. The petitions make clear that God's help is not simply a religiously desirable option; it is viewed as the only option remaining for survival. In the presence of powerful enemies, in the midst of anxiety, betrayal, rage, despair, and the threat of death, the solution never wavers: It is God, the Holy One of Israel, He whose power can defeat all enemies and whose justice, mercy, and lovingkindness can set all things right. The purpose of the petition is to persuade this God to come and act on the petitioner's behalf.

> Return, O Lord, and rescue me.
>> Save me because of your unfailing love.
>>> (Psalm 6: 4 NLT)

> Do not stay so far from me,
>> for trouble is near,
> and no one else can help me. (Psalm 22:11 NLT)

> O Lord, do not stay away!
>> You are my strength; come quickly to my aid!
>>> (Psalm 22:19 NLT)

Lord, hear my prayer!
　　Listen to my plea!
Don't turn away from me
　　in my time of distress. (Psalm 102:1–2)

Like the protest sections of the lament psalms, the petitions reflect the desperation of one who is living at the ragged edge of human experience in the cold darkness of the perceived absence of God. The plea pivots around the need to secure God's presence and the speaker's insistent effort to gain God's attention: *Come, God—come in love, in mercy, in kindness, in justice, and judgment—come quickly. All that I need and my life itself is utterly dependent upon you. Rescue me from death; preserve my life; make me safe; protect me from shame and disgrace; show me the way; make it clear what I am to do; protect and shelter me; do not let me get lost—come, and do what you alone can do.* There is petition for forgiveness of sins. There is the longing request for restoration to gladness (Psalm 5:11, 12), for blessing (Psalm 31:16), and for long life (Psalm 61:6), but all that is needed is seen as contingent upon the presence of God, who can supply all things.

It is striking that while the petition sections of the lament psalms ask—insistently—for God's presence and His intervention in circumstances, *they do not ask for restoration of the status quo.* Paying attention to this practice is structurally helpful in managing our pain. In times of disorientation and loss, we know with deep certainty that life can never be the same again. Nevertheless, we often long to return to those times and relationships that have been swept away, and, in our pain, we can be moved to demand that God restore the lost and mend the shattered. We can face the hard reality of change and deal more redemptively with our loss, however, if we shape our petitions in the pattern of the Psalms. These prayers encourage us to ask, and to ask urgently, for life, for wisdom, for forgiveness, for rescue from our enemies, for protection and shelter, for blessing. We may ask for comfort (God is, blessedly, the God of all comfort [2 Corinthians 1:3–4]), for courage, and for ultimate restoration of gladness. We may ask, even as David did, for long life. We may ask for restoration and provision and praise the God who indeed restores our souls and prepares a table for us in the presence of our enemies.

We will find no precedent in the lament psalms, however, for asking God to return us to what, with a distorted sense of nostalgia, we may remember as the "best years" of our lives or the "good old days." He is the God who does a new thing, who indeed restores the years the locusts have eaten (Joel 2:25). When citing this text, however, our human tendency is to place considerable emphasis on the "restore" and move quickly past the reality underlying the phrase, "the locusts *have eaten*." God's restoration includes His relentless, loving insistence that we first live through the loss of those times when around us lie only the empty fields and bare-limbed trees the locusts have stripped.

But there is another thing for which we may ask. The protest portions of the lament psalms teach us that there is nothing in the raw dark anguish of life that cannot be expressed uncensored to God. And with equal blessed clarity the petition portions of these psalms show us that the most dangerous desires of the wounded heart can be brought unsanctified to Him. While pain distorts reality, pain also reveals a dark-side desire in us that frightens us. We understand all too well the feelings that underlay David's passionate request that God break his enemy's arm (Psalm 10:15)— and worse. These feelings shame and frighten us. But in His mercy, God knows and has made provision too for this response that often comes in times of woundedness. To our astonishment, our bewilderment, and initial discomfort, the lament psalms teach us that we may ask for vengeance, for the wounding of those who have wounded us. When we discover this dark impulse in ourselves, we need not resort to shamed secrecy; we can bring these feelings, too, raw and uncensored, directly to God.

The issue of vengeance

Perhaps the most uncomfortable aspect of the lament psalms is this agenda for retaliation. We do not know what to do with "religious literature" in which God is directly asked to humiliate and disgrace wrongdoers, to make their paths dark and slippery, to let sudden ruin overtake them, and let them fall to destruction in the pit they dug for others (Psalm 35:4–8). This does not fit with our concept of Christian spirituality. Have we not been commanded to love mercy (Micah 6:8) and, indeed, to love our enemies (Luke 6:27)? What are we to make of things when David, who by God's own description was a man after God's heart, asks God to take vengeance on his enemy's *children*—to make them fatherless, evict them from their ruined homes, let them wander as beggars without help or pity, and die young so that his enemy's family name is blotted out in a single generation (Psalm 109:8–13)? And in the context of David's venom, hatred, and privileged status with God, how are we to understand the God who overtly accepts such prayers and who appears tacitly to condone their content?

Such a prayer shocks and offends us. But there is a way through the expression of vengeance in the Psalms, although, as Brueggemann has pointed out, it is a way *through* and not around, and it is not an easy way.[12] The book of Psalms is the voice of the raw, powerful, dangerous reality of human experience. And the way through the psalms that cry out for vengeance requires that we face and acknowledge something about ourselves—that the hunger for vengeance that is present in the Psalms is also present in us. Despite our fearful denial of our dark side, that dark side remains inwardly present whatever the contrasting outer façade our spirituality may portray. No one can avoid completely pain from wounds that are intentionally or carelessly caused by someone else. In these circumstances we find that our own impulse to wound in turn or to ask God to wound another in our behalf can be powerfully and dangerously present. This impulse to "pay back" and to "even the score" does not magically disappear because we are embarrassed by it or afraid of its presence. Although we would like to deny it, we humans are vengeful creatures, and while, thankfully, this characteristic can be Spirit controlled, this control does not come automatically or easily. It is at this point that, shocking and offensive as they may initially appear, the psalms that seek vengeance are God's gift to His people in pain.

As these psalms teach us, it is deeply reassuring to know that there is no human desire that we cannot bring directly and uncensored into the presence of God. He knows and He takes us as we are, where we are. He is able and willing to hear whatever we need to say.

George came to see me at the insistence of one of his friends who thought he needed help with an anger problem. He did, indeed, need help, and for good reason. His fourteen-year-old daughter, Sarah, had engaged in sexual relations with the male live-in partner of George's former wife (and Sarah's mother), Nancy. Nancy accepted her partner's account of the incident in which he blamed Sarah for the sexual encounter, insisting that Sarah had seduced him. Sarah, embarrassed, confused, and traumatized, had begun to believe that she was responsible for what had happened;

she refused to talk further about the incident or to testify against her mother's boyfriend. At the time George came to see me, the case appeared likely to drop through the cracks in the legal system. It was quite possible that neither Nancy nor her boyfriend would ever be held accountable for their actions.

"I want to kill him," George said grimly. "Sometimes I feel like I'd like to hurt somebody he loves the way he hurt Sarah. And I'd like to beat the stuffing out of Nancy because she didn't take care of Sarah. I don't plan to do anything crazy, but I'd sure like to. My friend is afraid I will."

As we worked through George's sense of rage and guilt and helplessness regarding his daughter's injury, one day I risked sharing something of Psalm 109 with him. "Listen," I said, "here's what one man whose name was David said to God about a bad situation." Then I read verses 7–13, stopping to paraphrase each verse and encouraging George in turn to paraphrase in his own words as well. When we finished, we sat quietly.

After a while George said, "I didn't know there was anything like that in the Bible."

"Most of what is inside people is inside the Bible somewhere," I commented, and then asked, "Is there something in what David says that's like what you feel?"

"Yep." Silence.

"How do you think God felt about what David asked Him to do?" I asked.

George gave this some thought and then said, "Well, I don't know about that. Don't imagine God planned to do what David asked, but I expect David felt better after he asked. Probably helped him keep his cool."

George had understood two important aspects of the psalms that request revenge. First, vengeance is *God*'s business—it *really* is. The Bible makes this quite plain (Deuteronomy 32:35; Psalm 94:1; Romans 12:19; Hebrews 10:30). But vengeance is *not* human business. The Bible makes this equally plain, whatever our human inclination to the contrary. Vengeance is God's responsibility to define and to administer in the context of His sovereignty, justice, and mercy. George understood that God could listen to David's feelings, receive David's insistent request for revenge, and then, *as God,* could choose how He as God wished to deal with the matter. Bringing his hunger for vengeance to God was, for David, an act of faith, however ugly the honest content of his prayer. David was rightly bringing to God what was, in fact, God's business.

And second, George intuitively had understood something of the power of language in dealing with the reality of our inner dark-side world and the significance of the context in which that language is expressed. In the text, an unapologetic David stormed into God's presence with his rage and desire for revenge uncensored. David asked fully and forcefully for the vengeance he wanted*, but he expressed his desire directly to God, not to his enemy.* George could see that if David told God how he felt and what he wanted, this action was likely to produce quite different results than if David had told his enemy the same thing in a face-to-face confrontation. In following sessions, as we returned from time to time to this text, George slowly began to believe that his rage and his desire for revenge could also be safely expressed to God. It took time for George to learn to bring his desire for retaliation to God, but as he did so, he became able to consider other options to manage his pain and anger in everyday life. George found that talking to God did indeed help him "keep his cool," and more. George began to consider his desire for vengeance in terms of its impact on Sarah. Had his anger and desire to injure Nancy's live-in boyfriend, however justified George felt it to be, added to Sarah's desire to bury her experience, unexamined and unresolved? If George left revenge up to God, would it free George as Sarah's father to support Sarah's healing in new ways?

Theologically the psalms that ask for vengeance remain difficult and problematic and raise issues that cannot be considered here. But in the context of human suffering, these psalms serve as valuable assets in managing pain, despite the theological challenges they pose. Many of my clients—those who are parents of raped children; of murdered children; victims of domestic violence; and women and men who have been assaulted, robbed, cheated, and charged with crimes they did not commit and unjustly injured in a thousand wordless, undefended ways—these suffering ones intuitively understand that these psalms aid them to bring their yearning for vengeance fully without reservation to God. They find too that their pain and their rage and desire for revenge, once fully expressed, can be safely yielded to the sovereign mercy and justice of God. And many find that once the desire for vengeance is dealt with in a safe holding place with God, they can begin to think the unthinkable—that somewhere in their journey they may begin to forgive the person who wounded them, however unrepentant and undeserving that person might be.

The Turn to Praise

Regularly in the pattern of the lament psalms, when the psalmist has voiced the anguish and the anger and the desire for revenge, a turn comes. Unexpectedly, oddly, as though the anger and pain had been stilled, as though the rescue had already been achieved, the speaker moves from petition to praise. Praise in the lament psalms, however, is distinctive. It does not echo the praise found in those "happy" psalms that celebrate the times of prosperity and peace. It is not the ancient equivalent of modern worship music led by a praise band in a church auditorium. This praise did not begin as praise; it began in hurt, rage, and direct confrontation of the psalmist's perception that God was inattentive. It is praise crafted in the context of danger and uncertainty. It follows and is intermingled with the dangerous risk inherent in the speaker's demanding insistence that God is covenant- and character-obligated to hear and to intervene.[13] This praise is a profound expression of trust, but it is trust that has been arrived at, as Brueggemann has pointed out, as a result of testing; it is not the outcome of resignation, passivity, or blind acceptance.[14] This is hard-won trust forged through the encounter of desperation, praise for the God found available and responsive and trustworthy in the context of pain-filled urgent confrontation.

However, in the movement from protest through petition to praise, praise does not represent a fairy-tale conclusion, a happily-ever-after outcome. Praise in the lament psalms is a knowing act of doxology. The content of such praise does not reflect a naïve belief on the speaker's part that all things everywhere are well nor that the things that are now well will be so forever. Rescue from today's enemies does not ensure peace forever. This praise does not assume that the covenantal relationship will never again experience crisis or that there will be no future confrontation between the speaker and the Holy One of Israel. To cite Brueggemann's apt illustration, praise in the lament psalms can be compared to the joy in the restored relationship that may follow a power struggle between husband and wife, even though both participants understand that the harmony may be unstable and momentary.[15] At the same time, however, the lament psalms contain unambivalent praise that affirms God's character and reaffirms His power. It is praise that remembers and celebrates God's intervention in the history of His people; it is praise that joyfully affirms God's present action in the speaker's behalf and anticipates by faith God's action in the speaker's future.

In Psalm 13 the petition and the turn to praise can be readily followed:

> Turn and answer me...
>> Restore the sparkle to my eyes...
> Don't let my enemies gloat...
>> Don't let them rejoice at my downfall.
> But I trust in your unfailing love,
>> I will rejoice because you have rescued me.
> I will sing to the LORD
>> because he is good to me.   (Psalm 13: 3–6 NLT)

In Psalm 22, the petition reflects the psalmist's desperation:

> Do not stay so far from me,
>> for trouble is near,
>> and no one else can help me...
> O, LORD, do not stay far away!
>> You are my strength; come quickly to my aid!
> Save me...
>> spare my precious life.   (Psalm 22:11, 19, 20 NLT)

The turn to praise looks back and forward both to God's action and to His character.

> Yet you are holy.
>> enthroned on the praises of Israel.
> Our ancestors trusted in you,
>> and you rescued them.
> They cried out to you and were saved.

They trusted in you and were never disgraced...
I will praise you in the great assembly.
    I will fulfill my vows in the presence of those who
        worship you...
    Future generations will hear about the wonders
        of the Lord.
His righteous acts will be told to those not yet born.
    They will hear about everything he has done.
(Psalm 22:3–5, 25, 30b, 31 NLT)

Similarly in Psalm 31, the petition reflects fear and urgent danger:

O, Lord, I have come to you for protection;
    don't let me be disgraced.
    Save me, for you do what is right.
Turn your ear to listen to me;
    rescue me quickly...
Pull me from the trap my enemies set for me...
    Rescue me, Lord, for you are a faithful God.
Have mercy on me, Lord, for I am in distress.
Rescue me from those who hunt me down relentlessly...
    In your unfailing love, rescue me.
Don't let me be disgraced, O Lord,
    for I call out to you for help.
(Psalm 31:1–2a; 4a, 5b, 16b, 17a NLT)

Then the turn to praise:

How great is the goodness...
Praise the Lord,
    for he has shown me the wonders of his unfailing love.
    He kept me safe...

In panic I cried out,
　　"I am cut off from the LORD!"
But you heard my cry for mercy
　　and answered my call for help.
　　　　　　　　　　(Psalm 31:19a, 21a, 22 NLT)

The praise components of the lament psalms are precisely that—praise crafted in the midst of the struggle, praise when the struggle has momentarily eased, praise in anticipation of God's faithful intervention, and, at times, celebration and praise when the immediate struggle has been resolved. These praise components carry the overtones of danger, pain, and desperation even while they anticipate and celebrate rescue; they remember the conflict and sense of alienation even as they affirm the faithfulness of God in the covenant relationship. Praise in the lament psalms sings to God in the tradition of the prophet Habakkuk, whose lament was followed with his great "and yet" doxology:

> Even though the fig trees have no blossoms, and there are no grapes on the vines; even though the olive crop fails, and the fields lie empty and barren; even though the flocks die in the fields, and the cattle barns are empty, yet I will rejoice in the LORD! I will be joyful in the God of my salvation. The Sovereign LORD is my strength! He will make me as surefooted as a deer, able to tread upon the heights (Habakkuk 3:17–19 NLT).

Learning to Make Our Prayers of Lament

Praying the content and the pattern of the psalms of lament is a skill that we often delay learning until we have an urgent need for it. However, ironically, this can have some advantage.

The times when we are living at the uncertain edge of life provide a practical incentive for learning and openness to God. Learning to read ourselves into the text permits the text to shape our lives in times of disorientation and loss of control. And as we learn to carry our lament and protest directly to God, in some way the experience of the pain itself and its impact on our lives is changed.

Learning to pray the psalms is for most of us a lifelong process. However, we can begin to pray the psalms through three relatively easy steps. The first step is straightforward and self-evident: We begin by reading the text. What is a bit more complex, however, is choosing the way we read the text. It is important to come to the text openly, honestly, seeing the text as it is with mind and heart, *reading the text aloud*, and hearing it as the cry of a person in deep trouble. Reading aloud may initially feel awkward, but doing so proves surprisingly helpful once we get past our initial inhibitions. The book of Psalms consists of songs and poetry composed to be sung and said; the text comes alive most fully when we read it aloud. It is important as well to read from a modern language translation that uses words as close to our everyday speech as possible.

Step two is a second reading of the text, but in this step we re-read the text and then *say the meaning of the text in our own words, paraphrasing the text aloud*. An easy way to learn to read the text, then paraphrase, is to use materials available that do just that. For example, lay a copy of Psalm 13 in a modern language translation, like the *New International Version* or the *New Living Translation,* on a table or desk and then lay a copy of Psalm 13 from *The Message* on the desk beside it. In this way you can easily compare a good translation and a paraphrase by a master of the art. When the text and a paraphrase are placed together in this way, we can see in concrete terms what the process looks like: First, the translated text is read for its meaning, then that meaning is spoken in everyday language—the truth of the text spoken in the talk of the common life.[16] Parallel presentations of Psalm 13 appear thus:

> O LORD, how long will you forget me? Forever?
>> How long will you look the other way?
> How long must I struggle with anguish in my soul,
>> with sorrow in my heart every day?
> How long will my enemy have the upper hand?
>
>> (Psalm 13:1–2 NLT)

> Long enough, God—you've ignored me long enough.
> I've looked at the back of your head
>> long enough. Long enough
> I've carried this ton of trouble,
>> lived with a stomach full of pain.
> Long enough my arrogant enemies
>> have looked down their noses at me.
>
>> (Psalm 13:1–2 *The Message*)

It is important to emphasize that when we paraphrase the Scriptures, we are not free to revise God's Word to make it say whatever we want it to say. Paraphrase properly done provides faithful representation of the meaning of the text as translated but expresses that meaning in words and idioms of everyday usage. The process of paraphrase has risks, of course. But in today's biblically illiterate society, there is an ongoing cultural risk that is even greater: the risk of perceived biblical irrelevancy. In this culture it is all too easy to respect the Bible as a religious document but make no experiential connection between the Bible and our lives. We may associate Scripture with religion and church. We may even consider it to be a special book given to us by God. We can think this way yet from a functional point of usage regard the Scriptures as an ancient book full of archaic words that has no relevance at all to the pain with which we are struggling or life as we know it. Culturally we find ourselves in a place much like that of God's people when they returned from Babylon.

During the seventy years of exile God's people gradually lost their understanding and their living connection with Torah, the written law. When they returned to Jerusalem, Ezra, a priest and leader, assembled the people and stood to read the Law. Ezra quickly discovered that he faced a major problem, however. Ezra could read the text—that was not the problem. The problem was reading the Law in a *way that the people could understand it and apply it to their lives*. Ezra's solution was brilliant: He assembled around him a group of helpers and initiated a two-step presentation of Torah. Nehemiah described what happened: "The Levites [the priests selected to help Ezra] . . . instructed the people in the Law while everyone remained in their places. They read from the Book of the Law of God and clearly explained the meaning of what was being read, helping the people understand each passage" (Nehemiah 8:7b–8 NLT).

When the people heard God's Word in this way, they burst into tears. Nehemiah, Ezra, and the officials comforted the people and encouraged them to rejoice: "And the Levites, too, quieted the people, telling them, 'Hush! Don't weep! For this is a sacred day.' So the people went away to eat and drink at a festive meal, to share gifts of food, and to celebrate with great joy because they had *heard God's words and understood them* (Nehemiah 8:11–12, NLT, emphasis added).

I had read the paraphrase of Psalm 13 in *The Message* with a client, and then asked, "How would you say that?" She thought for a moment, reread the line about a stomach full of pain, and then said, "I'd say, 'I've carried this stuff so long my gut is twisted with pain.'" We sat, considering what she had said and the grim reality that her words carried (her doctor had referred her for counseling). Then she added, "You know, I've gone to church all my life, but I never thought about asking God to pay attention to pain that twists up my guts. I guess I never thought of God being real in that way." This woman had used the text and the paraphrase of *The Message* along with her own paraphrase to connect her life with God in a new way. This was Nehemiah's story in modern dress; she had, in Nehemiah's sense, read God's words and understood them. Today, as in the days of God's ancient people, when we read the Scriptures in faithful translation, then make the text alive in the words we use daily, God moves from religious possibility into a real player in the joy and tragedy of daily life.

Step three in praying the Psalms entails linking the text to the reality of our experience and expressing this connection in spoken prayer. This step involves using the text and the paraphrase of it as a guide to shape our expression of our experience directly to God.[17] George's first experience with step three permitted me to see the Scriptures function again as the living word in changing human experience. To help George deal with the anger that he felt toward his ex-wife and her boyfriend, I had proposed that George and I start first with working out an "I'm mad, God" prayer and do the "I want to get even, God" prayer later (first using portions of Psalm 13, then Psalm 109). George had agreed somewhat reluctantly, clearly registering his discomfort about the whole idea of talking to God out loud. "Religion's not my thing," he said brusquely.

"I understand that," I told him, "But this isn't about religion. It's about praying. And it's about you learning to talk to God about this mess as a part of your keeping your temper. I think keeping out of jail is worth risking some embarrassment. Come on—give it a try. If it doesn't help, I promise—no more praying out loud."

In a previous session, George had been quite taken by Peterson's paraphrase of Psalm 13 in *The Message* and had made his paraphrase somewhat similar, but short and to the point. George's paraphrase read: "Look, God, how long are you going to ignore this mess? I'm getting an ulcer." We re-read Peterson's paraphrase, reviewed George's paraphrase, and then I prompted George to begin step three by saying, "Now, take what we've got here and use it say to God in your words what you feel about Doug (Nancy's boyfriend) and Nancy and Sarah."

George paused. He had come to trust me but was uneasy about his awkwardness and lack of experience and was clearly dubious about the value of the process of praying aloud. I waited. Eventually George took a deep breath and said, "Look, God, how long are you going to ignore this mess with Sarah? How long are you going to *not* pay attention? Are you going to play around until I get an ulcer or I lose my temper and end up in jail?" George continued, his speech colored with profane adjectives describing Doug: "And God, how long are you going to let Doug act like he does with me when I pick up Sarah? You hadn't ought to let him get away with this." By the last two sentences, George's voice had changed somehow, and for a brief moment he was only tangentially aware of me. George had entered into serious audible conversation with God.

George was quiet for a long moment when he had finished, then said with a note of surprise in his voice, "Haven't said a prayer out loud since I was a kid." After a second long pause, he continued with more surprise. "You might be right. Maybe this God stuff will help. At least now God knows what I think."

George would have scandalized many proper religious folk with his profanity and his "rude" practice of talking to God with his eyes open. I doubted, however, that the God George was just beginning to know took serious offense. In a PBS interview with Bob Abernethy, Stanley Hauerwas, noted theologian and writer,[18] described his prayer life as talking to God from a place he describes as straight and sometimes angry. Hauerwas explained, "I don't try to assume a persona when I pray. I speak to God the way I am. And I never try to protect God. I figure God can take it."[19] So, intuitively, did George. And so do the psalms of lament and vengeance. That is why they are gathered carefully in the Bible for our use in life's most difficult times.

Jesus directed His followers to avoid public display when they prayed (Matthew 6:6). It is particularly important that during difficult times we find a private, relatively soundproof place in which we can talk aloud to God without interference or audience. A friend of mine does "praying the hard stuff" in his car; he often drives to the remote back corner of a park a few miles from his office. During a particularly difficult time in my life I was reminded that ensuring privacy for prayer is a good idea for reasons in addition to obedience to Jesus' teaching. Assuming I was alone in the house, I was sitting at my kitchen table one morning, paraphrasing the first two verses of Psalm 130 in what was a rather desperate prayer. As best I remember, I was saying something like, "Oh, God, *pay attention—please* pay attention. I'm calling for your help. I'm drowning in despair. I'm in a depression that no Prozac will cure. Only you can help." I was saying this aloud, repeating the "God, *pay attention,*" with tears and passionate intensity when a neighbor walked in through an unlocked porch door.

"Who are you talking to?" she asked, looking curiously at my tear-stained face. "You sure do look upset." It was not a day I'm fond of remembering.

If George demonstrates the place of beginning in praying the Psalms, Ann Weems, poet and author of *Psalms of Lament*,[20] shows us the place where, with practice and a committed heart, we may at length arrive. None of us are likely to achieve Ann's mastery of language and her poet's sense of phrase, but that is not the goal. What we can learn from her work is an honesty of presence before God and the wholeness with which pain can be expressed through protest, petition, and praise. Weems's son Todd had been brutally killed just hours after his twenty-first birthday; his death and her grief and loss form the context of the personal pain out of which Weems writes.

Lament Psalm Twelve

O, God, what am I going to do?
He's gone—and I'm left
with an empty pit in my life.
I can't think.
I can't work.
I can't eat.
I can't talk.
I can't see anyone.
I can't leave my house.
Nothing makes any sense.
Nothing seems worth doing.

How could you have allowed this to happen?
I thought you protected your own!

You are the power:
Why didn't you use it?
You are the glory,
but there was no glory in his death.
You are justice and mercy,
yet there was no justice, no mercy for him.
In his death there is no justice for me.

O God, what am I going to do?
I'm begging you to help me.
At least you could be merciful.
O God, I don't remember a time
when you were not my God.
Turn back to me;
you promised.

Be merciful to me;
you promised.
Heal me;
you promised.
My heart is broken.
My mind is broken.
My body is broken.
Nothing works anymore.
Unless you help me
nothing will ever work again.

O Holy One, I am confident
that you will save me.
You are the one
who heals the brokenhearted
and binds their wounds.

You are the power
and the glory;
You are justice
and mercy.
You are my God forever.

There is nothing censored about Weems's expression of grief and despair and her protest against the bitter circumstances of her life. There is nothing tactful about her charge against God, who failed to protect. There is nothing simple about the issues of God's power, justice, and mercy with which she confronts God directly. Her petition for healing recounts again her utter brokenness, then appeals directly to the promise of God, reminding God that only He can bring life again into this place of loss. Then, as the psalm moves through protest and petition, the turn to praise appears.

"You will save me," she sings in unflinching trust. Her trust, she teaches us, lies in her confidence in God's character and in her covenant with Him. "You are the one who heals the brokenhearted and binds their wounds… You are justice and mercy. You are my God forever."

Weems shows us what it is to pray in the pattern of the Psalms—to protest the devastation and disorientation, to speak in the words of our common life the raw grief and brokenness, the unanswered questions, voicing our desperate appeal for help, then, at the end, turning from despair to doxology, affirming God's character and confirming covenant. This is being in the moment of pain and reaching through the pain to hope, praying our psalms of lament into the suffering and uncertainty of life as we experience it. And as we do this, our pain is changed. So are we.

Choosing the Long View: Remembering
That God Has a Story Too

In the hard places, taking our pain and anger directly and honestly to God is fundamental to keeping the heartbeat of our relationship with Him steady and strong. Keeping our perspective clear in the hard places is equally important—we need both strong hearts and clear minds. Keeping our heads straight in times of disorientation and struggle is difficult, in part, because pain tends to keep us focused on the immediate present. It helps both our relationship with God and our sense of perspective if we can remember that loss and pain are only part of our story. And it helps if we can see that our story with its pain is part of another story. God has a story too.

For the most part, in telling our stories, we consistently assign ourselves the starring role, hero or villain, as we perceive the case to be, and limit the material in the story to our human experience. We make the story all about us. It is true that the story *is* about us, and it is important that we tell our story because it *is* our story. But ours is not the only story. God has a story too.

We understand that thinking about God's story might change the way we view our own. Nevertheless, we humans have a great capacity to focus on ourselves. We have a powerful deeply rooted impulse to place—and keep—ourselves center stage in the drama of life. Consequently, genuine interest in God's story emerges most often in those times when pain and disorientation push us up against the limits of our old ways of seeing ourselves and our world.

We considered earlier the book of Ecclesiastes, one of the oldest books in the Bible, in which the Teacher set out to investigate life and to understand human experience. He described a great mysterious cycle of opposites within which the human story is played out. There is a time to be born and a time to die, he wrote, and went on to describe other paradoxical parameters of life that he had identified (Ecclesiastes 3:1–8). However, there was much he could not understand about the stories he observed.

He described some of the things that puzzled him. A man may seek wisdom, pleasure, and wealth—indeed, he may attain them—but then death comes, and he is forced to leave all things behind. His wealth may go to the lazy and undeserving and his wisdom and good deeds be forgotten. In perplexing ways, in the human story the final end of the righteous and of the wicked appears often to be the same. And even more troublesome, there is the hard dilemma of the pattern of injustice in which bad things happen to good people and good things happen to those who are evil. Neither philosophy nor pleasure can provide ultimate meaning to the human story.

Life cannot be made predictable (Ecclesiastes 9:11–12), he concluded. And further, things that are wrong in the pattern apparently cannot be fixed (Ecclesiastes 1:14–15). However, while the Teacher found that he could not solve the riddle of life by anything he discovered or observed "under the sun," he did draw a conclusion about the human story. What he concluded, in effect, was this: I was unable to make sense out of what I observed, but I discovered how we should live (Ecclesiastes 12:13–14). And this prescription for living? Live out our human lives in the context of God's story. "Now all has been heard," the Teacher summarized briskly, and "here is the conclusion of the matter. Fear God, and keep His commandments, for this is the whole duty of man. For God will bring every deed into judgment, including every hidden thing, whether it is good or evil" (Ecclesiastes 12:13–14 NIV). Life will remain a puzzlement, the old teacher seems to say, until God, in *His* judgment at the conclusion of *His* story sorts it all out. So, he advised, live in view of this ending that you cannot see from the vantage point of this life.

Times of pain and disorientation bring us into living connection with the parts of the cycle of life that we like least and want most to be changed, including death, uprooting, and the tearing down of what we have built; weeping and mourning and the scattering of those things we have gathered together. There is loss of the warmth of embraces we have cherished; the tearing of the very fabric of life; the throwing away of what was once guarded and carefully kept. There is hatred where there was love. There is silence where there was laughter and song.

Intellectually we know that losing and weeping and death can in fact be windows of grace through which God reaches us and we connect with Him. But despite this understanding, we are not at all fond of incorporating these experiences into our story. Indeed, we do our best to convince God to arrange things so that we may avoid such experiences altogether. It is one thing to know that suffering, human sinfulness, and ignorance—all the bent dimensions of our broken world—can indeed be windows of grace. Unfortunately, it is also true that while we are in the experience, it doesn't feel like a window at all. It feels like what, in fact, it is—the experience of darkness and the abandonment of the pit. Like David, like Job, we cry out to God in the hurt, the alienation and suffering in life, and we want two things. We want God to come make sense of our experience. "Why is this happening?" we cry. "Why me?" And we want God to come into our story in such a way that the chaos, suffering, and darkness are taken away.

When we discover that God is unwilling to edit our story to accommodate our comfort index, when we learn through painful experience that God does not always restore our loss at our demand, we often experience a crisis of faith. And through this crisis of faith it is sometimes possible to grasp for the first time the full significance of the great truth that God has a story too.

When I was quite young, I worked for a time as a lay pastor in a small church in an isolated rural area of the South. It was a world of poverty and struggle, of disease and limited resources. Many adults had difficulty reading and writing. The soil was poor and depleted; the hopes of the people were depleted too.

Things were going well in our small church family until, without warning, tragedy struck. The infant son of one of the young couples died a few hours after a difficult birth. I attended the funeral, of course, and it was there that I first experienced the life-altering impact of knowing that God has a story too.

The hearse was parked at the edge of a narrow country road. The baby's body had been placed in a simple pine box. Uncles and cousins carried the tiny casket from the hearse across the grassy edge of a field to a family cemetery for burial.

I have no memory at all of the content of the sermon that the baby's uncle preached, for I was in the midst of a passionate dialogue with God. I had asked God to preserve the baby's life. My angry questions carried a clear challenge to God. From *my* place in *my* story, God had failed to keep covenant. I had cried out, but He had failed to come, to deliver that child from the enemy death. Inwardly, I was demanding of God: "Where are you? Where were you when we needed you? What is the sense of this loss? Why have you permitted this to happen?

I was young, but my rage was not limited by my lack of years. I raged and cried, but when at last the small casket was lowered into the ground, there came a great silence within me and within the small group gathered around the open grave. It was spring. The smell of the dogwood and the green young leaves was everywhere. But there in the midst of that April sunlight there was death and suffering and what seemed to be the absolute silence and inscrutable absence of God.

Then, softly, in that silence, Miss Lena's clear soprano laid out the line: "When I can read my title clear to mansions in the sky," she sang. Gradually, others joined in, and they sang, flinging their faith *in God's story* straight into the face of the loss and suffering with which we were faced. Although it is closer to fifty years than to yesterday, I can still remember as though it *were* yesterday, the rich, haunting harmony of that old gospel hymn:

When I can read my title clear to mansions in the sky,
I'll bid farewell to every fear and wipe my weeping eyes.
There shall I bathe my weary soul in seas of heavenly rest,
And not a wave of trouble roll across my peaceful breast.
When I can read my title clear to mansions in the sky,
I'll say farewell to every fear and wipe my weeping eyes.

There in the midst of *my* grief, *my* rage, and *my* disorientation of faith, I suddenly grasped a new and powerful truth. It *was* my story, *my* story with loss and uprooting of early simplistic beliefs, *my* mourning, *my* confrontation with death. It was *my* story with all the parts of my story that I wanted to be different. It was *my* story with pain that would not go away.

But it was not *just* my story. For the first time, I understood that if I looked at my story as part of God's story, the meaning was different indeed. In God's story, that small pine box being lowered into the ground was not the end of the matter.

When pain and loss push us up against the limits of our story and we find, like the Teacher in Ecclesiastes, that the human story taken alone makes no sense at all, then we are ready to consider seriously the fact that God has a story too.

Then we can see that we have stood the truth of God's presence in the universe on its philosophical head. With profound spiritual narcissism we have assumed that the ultimate meaning of our story lies in *our* presence in it. We have then assumed that God, being great and loving, is responsible to come into *our* story and make *our* story a good story in which there is no hard thing that *we* must endure. If He is a good God, we argue, He will come be in *our* story and make everything *there* all right.

It is part of the great good news of our Christian faith that God is passionately interested in making everything all right. But God has a plan for doing that, and that is a part of *His* story, not just of ours.

God—Father, Son, and Holy Spirit—decided in the limitless reaches of eternity to make a world. The world they made was beautiful and good. But a great and terrible tragedy occurred. God's creatures, made in His image, chose to disobey Him, and a terrible chasm was established between God and His own. But God had a plan. God the Son came down to us and was human with us—God's lost and fallen creatures—and in love He laid down His life for us. When He returned to heaven, He left an empty tomb, the promise of the Spirit, and, through John, a glimpse into the last chapter of God's story. In that last chapter, the bent and broken things are all made new, and evil is utterly destroyed. At the end *in God's story* there is no more pain, no more tears, and no darkness—there is only light—the indescribable undimmed timeless light of God's presence with us in a world in which the old and terrible things have passed away (Revelation 21:1–5).

God is not unreasonable nor is He uncaring. But He is unwilling to abandon His great story in order to function simply as a divine footnote in our own. Yet, at the same time, God is committed to our story too. When we become willing through relationship with Him to incorporate our story into His, God in turn enters into our story in a new way that empowers us to accept and to transcend the brokenness of ourselves and of our world. Our story takes on both personal meaning and eternal significance when we become part of God's story too.

There were two thieves crucified with Jesus, one on each side of His cross. But only one experienced that terrible agony as a window of grace. Luke tells the story of those two thieves: "Two others, both criminals, were led out to be executed with him... One of the criminals hanging beside him scoffed, 'So you're the Messiah, are you? Prove it by saving yourself—and us, too, while you're at it!'" (Luke 23:32, 39 NLT).

This is the angry cry of human anguish, "God, prove yourself! Come be in my story, and make it all right. Make the pain and suffering go away." But the second thief had a different request: "But the other criminal protested, 'Don't you fear God even when you have been sentenced to death? We deserve to die for our crimes, but this man hasn't done anything wrong.' Then he said, 'Jesus, remember me when you come into your Kingdom.' And Jesus replied, 'I assure you, today you will be with me in paradise'" (Luke 23:40–43). The second thief, we can see, had come to a profound realization. His story, with all its brokenness and waste and its sordid wretched suffering, would look different indeed if he could, through a connection with Jesus, make His story a part of God's story too.

And whatever the disorientation, the pain, the unanswered questions, we too have a choice about the perspective from which we view our story. As a part of God's story we may be confident that our story, however hard the journey, will someday come right in the end.

chapter 10

ENDING UP WHERE WE
INTENDED TO BE

Douglas Adams once said, "I may not have gone where I intended to go, but I think I have ended up where I intended to be." [1] When considering the journey through which pain takes us, many of us would echo Adams's comment. We certainly never intended to go to those places of pain and disorientation to which—without our permission or approval—life carried us. We cannot say that we enjoyed the journey nor the work required to manage pain productively. However, when we stop to consider the outcome of the journey, we discover that Adams was correct: We can go where we did not intend to go and still end up where we intended to be.

We wanted to become wiser and more mature through the journey, and that has happened, at least in part. But even at this point we are surprised—the wisdom and maturity with which we end up does not look at all like the kind we intended to develop. With the same sense of life's irony that amused Adams, however, we realize that it is a wisdom and maturity that permits us, by God's grace, to be more like the person we intended to be.

It's Not about Butterflies—Yet!

We begin redemptive management of pain by agreeing with God that the journey through pain can change us in ways that prosper our souls. We then choose in the journey to cooperate with God in this change process. As we work our way through the journey, however, many of us discover that the idea of transformation with which we began contained a rather odd mixture of truth and error. Metaphorically speaking, we confused people with butterflies, and pain with the experience of cocooning. Wishfully, we half expected that out of our experience of pain the caterpillar self would emerge as a glorious butterfly of breathtaking beauty. What we discover, however, is that pain does not make people into butterflies.

Rightly understood, it is resurrection, not pain, which makes possible that butterfly kind of transformation. The empty tomb makes clear and real the nature of God's promise to His people. We too shall break out of the dark cocoon of death; we too shall emerge with the essence of our being, the very DNA of our souls preserved and kept and transformed into glorious beings that in this life we cannot imagine. Death could not hold our Lord, and because of Him it will not—cannot—hold us either. Someday we shall be utterly transformed, and we will be like our risen Lord and see Him as He is. Our butterfly day is coming. God promised, and He keeps His word. But that is the triumphant end of the story. The continuing journey through pain points forward to that transformation and produces real and substantial change in the process. This change, however, does not reflect butterflies but rather the "already" but "not yet" of the Christian experience. Gordon Fee describes this "already" but "not yet" reality in the following way:

> God's final salvation of his people has already been accomplished by Christ. In a sort of divine time warp, the future condemnation that we all richly deserve has been

transferred from the future into the past, having been borne by Christ (Rom. 8:1–4). Thus we "have been saved" (Eph. 2:8). Since our final salvation has not yet been fully realized, he [Paul] can likewise speak of salvation as something presently in process ("we are being saved," 1 Cor. 1:18) and as yet to be completed ("we shall be saved," Rom. 5:9). "Redemption" is both "already" (Eph. 1:7) and "not yet" (Eph. 4:30), as is our "adoption" (Rom. 8:15 and 23) and "justification" (the gift of righteousness, Rom. 5:1 and Gal. 5:5).

Believers have tasted of the life to come; and the full and final realization of the future is so certain that God's new people become heavenly radicals as they live in the "already" but "not yet" of the present age.[2]

And it is in the "already" but "not yet" of the present world that we work out redemptive management of our pain. The "already" but "not yet" world requires us to understand our change in the context of the epiphany–pickle jar principle that was discussed in chapter 7, along with Paul's reminder to the Christians at Corinth: "We… *are being transformed* into his likeness (2 Corinthians 3:18 NIV, emphasis added). The writer to the Hebrews summarized the "already" but "not yet" of the transformation process: "Because by one sacrifice he [Christ] has made perfect forever those who *are being made holy* (Hebrews 10:14 NIV, emphasis added)." In joy or in sorrow, in plenty or in want, we remain God's people *in process.* The life journey that will culminate in our final glorious transformation is marked by change that, en route, occurs in small increments, change that emerges out of small steps followed by more small steps, the long obedience in the same direction.[3] It is change that, with rare exception, occurs with modest overt evidence and that, regrettably, retains a great deal of continuing distinctly unsaintlike behavior.

Pain leaves us what we were at the beginning—saints in process—but changed saints in process who in subtle but powerful ways have come to see life differently and to know ourselves more deeply. We have learned some truths we didn't want to know, lost some illusions, and gained some wisdom. We have learned the reality of paradox and the practical necessity of mystery. We have gained perspective and a sense of proportion. We are different yet the same. Pain as a part of our life journey has fostered change in us that is not finished but has given us, in the process, promise of that which is to come. While we learn and change, we will not fully understand ourselves or our journey until our final transformation takes place. T. S. Eliot described this continuing journey of lifelong learning in this way:

> We shall not cease from exploration
> And the end of all our exploring
> Will be to arrive where we started
> And know the place for the first time.[4]

Something We Didn't Want to Know

From the outset pain confronts us with a fact that evokes strong resistance and, at times, outright resentment in the human soul. We do not want to know that there are things in life that we simply cannot get our heads around. We like even less the accompanying reality that we are confronted with living through and managing what we cannot understand. We feel neither pleased nor blessed by our limitations or by the concurrent necessity to deal with life in a context that stretches us beyond our cognitive comfort zone.

We do not wish to consider even the possibility that life presents enigmas and mysteries that lie beyond our capacity to explain. The good life comes through knowing, we think; if knowing is not the key to heaven, it at least provides entry to the narthex. This seductive faith in the possibilities of knowing is as old as Eden. However, its arrogance came to full flower in the Enlightenment, with its unshakeable belief in reason and man's mastery over nature through reason. While we rarely mark our "why" tirade with God as a product of the Enlightenment, this attitude reflects, nevertheless, a man-in-the-street application of the Enlightenment idea that the universe is knowable and controllable through rational means. While there is unquestionable value in rational processes, the world and our journey through it have not turned out to fit the model those eighteenth-century thinkers developed, as postmodern writers regularly point out. Nevertheless, we continue to entertain the idea that as "rational human beings" we are entitled to a world that functions in ways we can rationally explain. We become angry at our pain and angry that we cannot fully explain our pain; we are angry as well that the pain that we cannot explain calls into serious question our chosen faith in a rational universe. Grief and loss and disorientation confront us with events and responses that at best we understand only in part, and at times appear to echo a blind, randomly driven universe that functions in utter indifference to our well-being and lies beyond our control.

At the same time we are challenged with the limitations of our knowing, we are confronted with managing what we cannot understand. Frederick Buechner described this reality in the context of Job's experience. Even if he had been granted full understanding of his children's deaths, Buechner points out, "Job would still have to face their empty chairs at breakfast every morning." We encounter pain and the disorientation of loss in the context of experience that in significant ways lies beyond linear logic and its language. But, understood or not, we must manage what appears to be irrational; we must live through what we cannot rationally explain. There is discomfort in this unknowing, but there is no way around it. Our best option, as Rilke pointed out to his student, lies in patient cohabitation with emotionally uncomfortable questions until, out of the process of living, wisdom emerges.[5] Initially, at least, we do not readily welcome this process.

Our overindulged affection for rational processes shapes our openness to God as well. If we face squarely our resistance to agreeing with God, we soon discover something quite unattractive about our mindset. We like the idea that God can (and will) bring something good out of chaos and loss, and we are quite relieved by God's promises not to leave us alone or to permit us to become lost on the journey. But we are not at all pleased when we learn that we may be required to live out the reality of His promise without sufficient evidence to satisfy our rational mind. If God is present, we reason, God—reasonably—ought to provide rational evidence of His presence.

In theory we affirm warmly the concept of walking by faith, but in practice we opt for walking by rationally perceivable evidence. Pain tempts us to pivot faith around the amount (or absence) of rationally accessible God-evidence we have been able to assemble. We know that God has promised—we understand that—but we want to *see* hard evidence of His promise-keeping activity. We strongly favor a plan in which God provides evidence of His presence by elimination of pain and restoration of lost things, particularly to *us*. We are both indignant and frightened when we begin to understand that on our journey through pain our much-loved rational evidences, particularly in these forms, may continue to be in short supply. And to our further discomfort, we begin to suspect that successful completion of the journey may require us to learn the peculiar logic and language of God's kingdom, rife as it is with paradox and mystery.

But once our faith in reason as the ultimate good is thoroughly shaken, we begin to sense the exhilarating possibilities of faith-based life in the Spirit, the fullness of life that extends beyond the limiting boundaries of rational thought and the linear logic of this world. Pain gifts us with troubling new awareness of God's refusal to function solely within the box of evidence-driven logic. Thankfully, pain also graces us with God's presence, those epiphanies *outside our box for God* that transcend linear logic but are utterly congruent with His power, His love, and His freedom to be God. In the words of Walter Brueggemann, we find ourselves saying to God, with awe and astonishment,

> Just when we imagine that we have you figured out
> You show up working the other side of the street
> In your frightening freedom.[6]

Then, as on the journey we slowly learn to think God's thoughts after Him using His logic, we find our stumbling prayers begin to reflect our awareness of God's different reality. One of Brueggemann's prayers reflects this change that begins to happen:

> We pray in the name of the utterly humble One
> whom you therefore exalted.
> Give us wisdom and freedom

that we may sense the ways in which we may best live
   in this world
where the last become first and the first become last.[7]

The journey through pain teaches us to be grateful for God's refusal to fit into our box for Him. We find ourselves stretched and blessed by the logic and the language of God's kingdom that is not our native tongue. We discover with gratitude that learning what we did not want to know has indeed changed us in ways we intended—and needed—to be changed.

A Lost Illusion and Some Found Wisdom

The journey through pain results in losing an illusion that at least initially we would like to keep, but in this loss we find some wisdom that is comforting. The discovery process plays out much like the story of the emperor who had no clothes. Like the boy in the story who points out the obvious reality that the emperor is wearing nothing, the journey through pain points out the reality of the nature of the world around us and gives us a clearer understanding of who we are stripped of the self-deception with which we have clothed ourselves.

Pain rather quickly confronts us with our illusion concerning the nature and reliability of the safety net we assume we have built into our lives. We say to ourselves, "Who would have believed that I could lose my health... my house... my marriage... my child... my job... my friend... my dream... my bank account"—or any of the many things we value? Pain and loss lead us to places where we did not expect to go, and we experience this undesired, unanticipated outcome as a failure of our safety net. This was not supposed to happen—at least to us.

There is no illusion about our human need for safety; that is hard-wired. The amount of safety and the ways in which we seek to ensure it vary widely, of course. However, we all organize our lives to meet our yearning for an orderly, predictable world in which we meet the familiar frequently and deal with the unfamiliar only as often as is convenient to prevent boredom and to make space for creativity. We seek to structure our lives so that injustice and inconsistency are kept under control, that we love and are loved, and belong in a community of others. We organize our work and play in ways that provide rich potential for expression of our gifts and our abilities. We begin each day expecting that whatever the risks we may face, we will be able to navigate through the day's dangers and challenges safely. Despite James's warning about the transitory nature of life (James 4:13–17), we live in the illusion that we can construct a safety net for our lives that will not be breached.

Then, inevitably, events from the dark side of the great cycle of life happen: there are uprooting and tearing down; there is the scattering of stones that we once gathered. There are violence and hatred. There are weeping and silence where there was once laughter and dancing; there are emptiness and cold where there was once the warmth of human touch and love. We are compelled to throw away that which we have treasured. Life becomes torn in ways that cannot be mended. Healing fails; death comes (Ecclesiastes 3:1–8).

We look in stunned astonishment at our vitamin bottles, our exercise routine, our insurance policies, our employment contracts, our families, our achievements, our investment folios, and our bank accounts, the love and relationships with which we have surrounded ourselves, our regular church attendance, the honesty with which we have paid our taxes, our volunteer hours at the shelter for the homeless, our neighborhood watch. Viewing the structure of our lives, we say, "How could this have happened to *me*?"

What has happened is, of course, that the safety net has broken, and we have dropped through our illusion into life as the Teacher in Ecclesiastes described it. Often we find that we have arrived at this place with the abruptness about which James cautioned us.

More often than not, God gets blamed for the broken safety net in a quite unfair fashion. It is not as though God has not made His point of view clear through the long history of His people. Israel's treaties with the nations that surrounded her never earned God's approval or ensured Israel's safety. Her religious pluralism and outright consorting with Baal and Molech did not ensure fertility of crops or people. The psalmist states the issue bluntly: God takes no pleasure in the strength of the horse, nor delight in the legs of man [our resources; our human strength; our tolerant, religiously acceptable compromises] (Psalm 147:10). It is God himself, the psalmist explains, who strengthens the bars of Jerusalem's gates, who grants peace to Zion's borders, and satisfies His people with the finest of wheat (Psalm 147:12–14). The psalmist goes on to be quite specific: God delights in those who, recognizing His protection and sustaining provision, put their hope in His unfailing love (Psalm147:11).

Jesus made a comparable point in His unforgettable story of the man who, blessed with a large harvest and huge grain reserves, tore down his barns to build bigger storage facilities, telling himself that his vast resources would permit him to enjoy "easy" living, to eat, drink, and be merry for years to come (Luke 12:16–21). In Jesus' story, God called the man a fool (not God's usual form of address, even to His admittedly foolish people) and promptly put an end to the man's plan by abruptly ushering him into eternity. This was no small mistake. Jesus said bluntly, "A man's life does not consist in the abundance of his possessions" (Luke 12:15 NIV). And neither does our safety—and that is the unwelcome point pain makes when our safety nets crash, as they inevitably do. Because Christians can sometimes behave in a rather silly fashion about sensible things, it is important to say clearly that common sense and prudent living are not antithetical to faith. The psalmist's point, and the point of Jesus' story, had nothing to do with God's dislike of horses or disapproval of either strong legs or reserves of grain. The issue is not a matter of having or not having an alarm system, a flood insurance policy, or scheduling oneself for annual flu shots.

The issue lies in the way in which we define the bottom line of our security. It is God who keeps us in the storm *and* in sunny weather, whatever the technological glories of our weather forecasting systems or our absent-minded human failure to bring an umbrella on a rainy day. Our ultimate safety lies in God's faithfulness, whatever the structures we build into our lives, whatever our skills, whatever the abundance or scarcity of our human resources. Out of wisdom, we may behave prudently and influence the degree of safety we experience, but it is God, not ourselves, who sustains us. We are kept in His care. At the Areopagus, Paul summarized the issue plainly for those questioning Greeks: "God...who made the world and everything in it... himself gives all men life and breath and everything else... For in him we live and move and have our being" (Acts 17:24a, 25b, 28 NIV).

When he saw the naked emperor parading down the street, the boy said aloud the truth the people were afraid to acknowledge: "The emperor has no clothes." Pain, similarly, says aloud a culturally unwelcome truth: humanly, we cannot construct a safety net that ensures uninterrupted merrymaking and years of trouble-free living. In our journey through pain we lose the illusion of the reliability of the safety nets we have constructed. But as we make our way through grief and loss and the shifting parameters of our changing world, we experience as well— sometimes in astonishing ways—the faithfulness of God and His provision. We lose an illusion and we find a paradoxical wisdom. It is true: We cannot, humanly speaking, insulate ourselves from pain and loss. There is no fail-safe safety net. And make no mistake—it is a gravely serious matter if—indeed, when—the safety net breaks. Nevertheless, God's people discover that for an eternally reliable reason, a broken safety net is not fatal. In him we live and move and have our being, and "underneath are the everlasting arms" (Deuteronomy 33:27 NIV).

Paradox and Mystery

Pain immerses us in a reality thick with paradox and mystery.[8] If we are still struggling with our addiction to linear logic, we do not welcome this experience. However, pain frequently compels us to function beyond our preferences and habits. That is one of its great gifts.

The paradox that *little is big* is embedded in the mastery skills discussed in chapter 5, for example. Particularly in the early stages of loss and disorientation, we are often working with very small things when we choose to do what we can with what is available. My client's initial effort at mastery involved sorting the silverware drawer. Our initial resistance to doing the small things that we can do grows in part from a rooted resistance to the paradox that the little thing often brings big results. A smile when talking is too much effort, a step when walking is too hard, an e-mail when meeting for lunch requires social skills held dormant by pain—such small things may lead to surprisingly significant outcomes. In Scripture, both mustard seeds and yeast (Matthew 17:20; 1 Corinthians 5:6) are used to illustrate the large consequences (for good or ill) that grow out of small things. Part of the wisdom we gain in our journey through pain is a new understanding of the sometimes astonishing outcomes that follow when we do what we can with what is available.

The paradox that *doing nothing is doing something* is even less popular in our culture. We resist Sabbath and we remain chronically sleep deprived and endlessly enamored of our multi-tasking capability. We are fiercely impatient with any circumstance that requires us to wait. We are unrepentant action addicts whose idea of waiting on the LORD (Psalm 27:4; Psalm 130:5) is breathing a high-speed prayer while waiting for the light to turn green. However, in times of pain and grief, in loss and disorientation, we find ourselves immobilized in ways that challenge these lifelong habits of hyper-thought and hyperactivity. In the words of the old adage, at these times life itself orders us, "Don't just do something—stand there!" Until circumstances compel us to modify our hectic pattern of living, we are slow to question our presupposition that a reliable safety net requires frantic commitment to endless activity.

The necessity for waiting—doing nothing—comes unavoidably somewhere along our journey through pain and loss. Psalm 88 shows us one example of this waiting and, for all the darkness of this psalm, can encourage us when we see that the waiting experience is not foreign to the journey of God's people through pain. Our inexperience with inactivity along with our bewilderment and our resistance to waiting make Psalm 88 an enigma to us, however. In truth, we are afraid of this psalm—its utter despair, the darkness, the helpless immersion in grief and loneliness, the inscrutable silence of God, His hiddenness, His failure to rescue. This psalm does not recount the memory of God's history with His people; there is no turn toward praise. When we face straightforwardly the terrible reality of this psalm, the closing refrain becomes nearly unbearable—"You have taken my companions and loved ones from me; the darkness is my closest friend" (Psalm 88:18 NIV).

At this point our response is not simply to flinch from the pain or to wish desperately that things would get better. We want something to happen—for the psalmist to *do something*, for God to *do something*. We are frightened by this terrible psalm not only by its pain but by its ending where there is darkness and loss and no apparent option for action anywhere. What can be done? Psalm 88 confronts us at the end with the wordless answer we least wish to hear—there is nothing to be done. Nothing—but wait.

The paradox is, of course, that at times doing nothing *is* doing something—indeed, at the moment we confront this paradox doing nothing may be the only thing that it is possible to do. Learning about waiting is one of the gifts of our journey through pain. Waiting enables us to be present in the moment—to be focused here, now—and to begin to detach ourselves from the agendas, the responsibilities, the expectations, and driven goal-directed activity with which we make our souls frantic and by which we seek to deliver ourselves from our difficulties. At times only despair has the power to unleash us from our addiction to action and to usher us into the space that the present moment provides, that quiet space where hope can open fragile wings. David, despite his natural bent toward hard-driving, impetuous action, knew this. In the midst of great trouble, surrounded by enemies on every side, David sang:

> I am still confident of this:
>> I will see the goodness of the LORD
>> in the land of the living.
> Wait for the LORD;
>> be strong and take heart
>> and wait for the LORD. (Psalm 27:13–14 NIV)

No one suggests that David dispersed his armies while he waited, and the psalm makes it clear that David did not spend his waiting time in despairing anticipation of defeat. David understood that waiting took strength and courage—standing is far from effortless. And David, resisting passive resignation, waited, holding a space for hope—standing, looking to see the goodness of the LORD in the land of the living. In times of trouble, when we simply stand, waiting to see God come, doing nothing can be both simultaneously and paradoxically the best and only thing that we can do.

Loss for Gain—Gain for Loss

Perhaps the hardest paradox to embrace is the one of gain and loss.[9] God's Word explains that pain teaches us that to lose can be to gain, and, standing the paradox on its head, to gain can be to lose. We do not like this paradox, but we are not the first to have trouble with it. The disciples, having identified Jesus as the Messiah, must have been more than slightly disconcerted when Jesus then immediately explained to them that following Him as the Messiah (eternal gain) entailed little glory and lots of difficulty, things like picking up crosses on a daily basis and saving their lives by losing them (enduring real loss in the present world) (Luke 10:23–25; cf. Matthew 10:39).

We are not overly fond of truth in paradox form, and, like the disciples, we are even less open to the idea that vitally important things can be gained only by losing. Having is better than not having, we think. More is better than less; less cannot be more. Big is better than little; little cannot be big. Satisfaction requires new acquisitions; contentment cannot coexist with present resources. Enough cannot be what I have; enough is what I must acquire. The litany goes on—more, bigger, better, different. We do not wish to live gracefully and gratefully with a half cup; we want to find a way to get the cup filled, not just to the brim, but running over. And the paradox of loss as gain in the context of pain takes dead aim at this passionate desire of our hearts.

But in order to understand rightly the paradox of gain and loss, we must distinguish the issue of gain/loss from our chronic half-cup complaints. In the first place, we need to reconsider the "problem" of the half-full cup. If I am dying of thirst, the half-full cup of water represents a life-sustaining gift. It is only in the context of our single-minded pursuit of *more* that the half-cup comes to symbolize the discontent of unmet expectations. Nor, viewed from God's intent for us, is there anything inherently problematic in our desire for a full cup. David used the image of the full-to-the-brim, running-over cup as a picture of God's provision and extravagant generosity (Psalm 23:5). Jesus said that He came so that we might have life abundantly (John 10:10), although the abundance He had in mind did not center on possessions (Luke 12:15). God does indeed have an opinion about what are desirable contents for our cups, but full measure, pressed down and running over is an image of both His love and grace. In the paradox of loss and gain, the problem does not lie in the measure—half cup or full cup—but rather what happens to us when the cup we have been holding is broken, and we are faced with the possibility of no cup at all.

Recently I was having lunch with a friend, and we were talking about paradox as a paradigm for truth. Noting that we had finished eating, the waiter, with unobtrusive professional skill, began clearing our table. He reached for my cup, half full of what was by then thoroughly cold coffee, a fact that had not escaped his watchful eye.

"No," I said, immersed in conversation and oblivious of the waiter's intent, "I'll keep my cup."

"If madam will permit me," the waiter said with impeccable politeness and a hint of British accent, "I will bring you fresh hot coffee."

After the waiter carried my cup away, my friend smiled and shook her head. "Hanging on to that half cup of cold coffee when you could have a full cup of hot coffee. Hmm... hanging on to what we have doesn't make sense sometimes."

What was clear in the restaurant about cold coffee is not always so clear in life. To give up what I did not value highly—cold coffee—in certain exchange for what I did indeed value—a cup of hot coffee, fresh from the pot—was no problem once I became aware of my options. But even with cold coffee, the exchange would not have been so simple had I believed that the cup of cold coffee was the last coffee that I would ever have opportunity to taste. Cold coffee or no coffee—ever again? Not necessarily an easy choice for a coffee addict like myself. However, understanding the lose/gain paradox is not about deciding whether to exchange cold coffee for hot; it is deciding about managing the loss of the cup itself. The lose/gain paradox faces us with real loss, not an exchange program in which we relinquish something in order to negotiate a better option. And it is at the point when we grasp that we are dealing with real loss, not simple exchange, that our struggle with the gain/loss paradox becomes plain.

This is a quite different matter from our first contract with God. The Gospels outline an exchange program in which the benefit lies all to our advantage. Writing to the Christians at Corinth, Paul described the foundation of the exchange this way: "For God made Christ, who never sinned, to be the offering for our sin, so that we could be made right with God through Christ (2 Corinthians 5:21 NLT)." At the point of actual exchange the terms are absurdly one-sided: I give God my sinful self and behaviors, and He gives me, in exchange, Christ's righteousness and unqualified eternal life. When we clearly understand these options, it is difficult to see why anyone would resist such an eternally advantageous bargain. But what then follows this gain in the "already" but "not yet" world of our journey through pain is nothing simple or easy. The story of God's people leaving Egypt makes this clear.

The departure from Egypt, leaving the brutality of slavery, following God triumphantly through the sea on dry ground—that part of the story was absolutely marvelous. What a great exchange—slavery traded for freedom and the promise of a new land, with Pharaoh's horses and chariots destroyed at the bottom of the Red Sea. But what followed the gain of freedom was a long trip through the desert—the sand, the wind, and the dreadful daily sameness of that bland, tasteless manna. In the desert, the reality of the loss emerged. "Oh, for the leeks and cucumbers and garlic, the food of Egypt, those things we had in the world that we have lost," God's people cried. Looking in on the story from our vantage point in history, we view their protest as faithless and absurd. "Those people!" we think indignantly. "Imagine—

fussing about leeks and cucumbers and garlic when they were safely out of slavery and on their way to the Promised Land, where there was milk and honey. What is the matter with these folk?"

The matter with these folk is, of course, the same thing that is the matter with us all. James Sanders, distinguished Bible scholar, once remarked that when we celebrate ourselves as "good guys" in a biblical narrative, it is often because we have failed to grasp God's point in the story. Egypt—whips, guards, and murdered babies—was gone, blessedly. However, in the desert, God's ancient people discovered that the gain of freedom from Egypt was linked with the irretrievable loss of the life they had known: the leeks, garlic, cucumbers, the familiar things, the things they had cherished, the things that—despite their slavery—had value to them. Looking out over the endless miles of sand—sand in their sandals, sand in their hair, sand in their mouths (and in the manna)—they must have remembered with longing the waters of the Nile spreading over the land in flood season; the green gardens that produced the leeks, the garlic, the cucumbers, the melons (Numbers 11:4–6); the cooling squish of mud between their toes. They remembered too the fish and pots of meat cooking over evening fires.[10] In gaining freedom they had lost forever some things they loved. Now there was only the terrible desert, armed enemies, this terrifying God who led them by fire and cloud and who fed them with this miserable everlastingly boring manna while they walked and waited for the milk and honey yet to come.

We do ourselves no favor if we set ourselves up as superior to God's ancient people. In the wilderness of pain, faced with the disorientation that loss brings, we too have a strong inclination to cry for what we have lost, having little faith in what lies ahead and even less patience to wait for it. The issue in the loss/gain paradox lies in the necessity it poses for us *both* to embrace the reality of loss *and* to see it as the prerequisite to God's production of His new thing in our lives. As we enter our own wilderness journey, most of us find ourselves to be true descendants of those who cried for the leeks and garlic of the Egypt now behind them. It is difficult to live through a sandstorm anticipating a land of milk and honey that lies ahead, still unseen. The fruit of the new land was a gain that followed the real loss of the old. God did not have in mind some casual replacement of cold coffee with hot, some replication of Egypt replete with leeks and cucumbers and retooled with a properly reformed Pharaoh. God had in mind a desperately difficult, dangerous journey through the desert wilderness into a new land that—not incidentally—held dangers and challenges of its own.

It is not extraneous detail when, in the biblical narrative, the spies returning from their initial exploration of the new land list specifically the food available there: milk and honey, grapes, figs, and pomegranates. This food was evidence of the rich and fertile place to which God had faithfully brought His people. Nevertheless, the list did not include leeks, garlic, cucumbers, melon, and fish. The loss of Egypt, its pain *and* its pleasures, remained. The new land held enormous promise, but it did not provide a replication of that which lay behind or restoration of that which was truly lost.

There are many ways in which loss can be gain and gain can be loss. But in the journey through pain, at the core of our losses lies the potential gain through that loss of God's new thing in our lives. But make no mistake. While metaphorical, the desert experience remains as real now as then in the story of God's ancient people. Reaching the gain of God's promised new land requires living through the wilderness journey into a new place.

Loss can become gain in God's economy—full measure, pressed down, running over—paradox though it may be. But entering into that gain requires us to travel the desert with endurance and faith, valuing God's plan for our future more than the fish and leeks and garlic we have forever left behind.

Unintended Positive Consequences

The human mind has difficulty recognizing things that occur gradually in small increments. While we are clear that our journey into and through pain is unintended, it is easy to miss some of the positive consequences of the journey simply because they come gradually, in small increments, over the long space of the journey.

Pain reduces our confidence in our ability to explain life, but our journey through pain increases our ability to identify the things in life that matter. People who have learned to manage pain and loss successfully rarely consider themselves to be the great gurus of the universe. We read Job with new eyes and, like Job, are content to leave some questions about life unanswered. But we have a new understanding about the things that ultimately matter in the end.

Pain teaches us to rethink the biblical virtue of hospitality, delivering us from the superficiality of appearances and the prescribed boundaries of social systems. We discover that the process of sharing does odd things to the distinctions we once made between stranger and friend and giving and receiving. We learn gratitude for those who, fully aware in their own journey, give freely—a smile, a practical helping hand with the unglamorous tasks of daily living, a word of encouragement, careful listening—and are glad for our receiving, knowing it to be a gift in turn. We both give and receive as the natural rhythm of life. This giving and receiving does not arise from reciprocal trade agreements or from social obligation, however. This uncalculated exchange grows out of recognition of our mutual human brokenness and the generosity of God's provision for us all in the risks and the resting places of the long journey home.

We think differently about time. We know that the sky that brings winter's snow will, in the long, slow turn of the seasons, bring harvest's sun, the honeyed gold of Indian summer, and then, once again, returning snow. We know that in the great cycle of life time brings change that lies beyond our control. Nevertheless, we learn to fix markers in time's passing: that was then, this is now; this is today, not tomorrow; yesterday is not tomorrow; today is enough. We learn to use these markers to hold old pain and trauma at bay. We gain skill in choosing the use of our time. Pain teaches us the value of remaining in the moment and redeeming the gift of the day, whatever the season of life or stage of our journey home.

Pain teaches us a radical disconnect from the culture if we permit this gift. We learn to distinguish between the gift of shelter and the value of the square-foot measure of a house. We learn to recognize God's gift of daily bread made present in simple food, however plain. We discover that the courage to walk one step at a frightened time brings life, even when we cannot explain the darkness or still the fear. We learn to accept that life comes to us through mystery and paradox; we recognize that we both receive love we do not merit and loss we do not deserve. We become better able to distinguish the gift from the package in which it appears. We find joy in the shape of life outside the safe boxes in which we once packaged our lives and acknowledge loss as the gift that can open up sacred space where new life can come. We learn the value of scraps and the worth of once discarded things and the sheer fun of making more from less. We discover that truth is embedded in experience, not separate from it, and that as we live our questions with integrity, we live our way into truth.

Pain teaches us humility. We develop new gratitude for things we once took for granted—the healing gift of sleep, the patterns of spring rain on windows, money enough to buy six apples at the farmer's market, the public library card that grants access to the great book collections of the world. We learn new humility about our limitations. We find that avoiding mistakes and failures is not possible and the pursuit of perfection a waste of time. We learn the value of embracing failure through honest assessment and investing our effort in the task of beginning again. We experience new energy that emerges with restarting and using what lies at hand to rebuild. We learn to distrust the theatrical and to trust the power of the practical. We learn to rethink resources and to rejoice in God's great gifts of baling wire and duct tape. We discover that finding our way in the difficult places can be as simple as doing the next right thing and carrying life's responsibilities in small packages, taking small steps. We know that slow movement brings progress, one step at a time—left foot, right foot, left foot—but then we must stop to *breathe.*

We learn, if we choose to do so, to think about people and ourselves in ways that are quite different from our former point of view. We learn both to be cautious and to say *no* firmly; not everyone has our best interests at heart; not everyone understands what is good for us; living for the approval of others is dangerous and distorts our journey. We learn that what is essential in helping us toward our goal is not always important or impressive to those around us. But, on the other hand, we learn too that others have been this way before us; others have gifts and a generous unconditional willingness to help; not all people we encounter are exploitative or willing to betray. We learn too an odd new trust in ourselves. We learn that while we cannot insure our lives against loss, pain, and chaos that our plain, ordinary essential self can survive total destruction of the safety net we had constructed for ourselves. We learn that aloneness is not the same as loneliness and that to be alone is not to be unloved. We learn, often to our astonishment, that we always have a choice and then another choice—then still another; that we always have something to give, no matter how small; that we can always find something at which to laugh, something to bring to the table, some way to help enable the dreams of someone else. We gain perspective; we are not the only person on the stage; the story is not just about us. We learn if we will relinquish the illusion of control we can gain the power of influence and the joy of cooperative interaction with others. We learn that pain can strengthen faith. We come to understand that, as Paul Claudel once wrote, "Jesus did not come to explain away suffering or remove it. He came to fill it with his presence."[11] Graced by His presence, we learn that each day can be lived with strength and purpose. We learn that while we are always less than perfect, who we are, by God's enabling grace, can be enough.

Community matters. We learn to prize the gifts of community: a friend who will sit with us while we grieve; a listener who will hear our story and help us hear the truth we cannot see; a companion who challenges us with the expectation that loss does not eliminate our capacity—or responsibility—to give. In the context of community we are enabled better to keep our perspective on both ourselves and the world through which we are making our way. Community provides companionship in the grief of saying goodbye to what has been lost, in the long spaces of waiting, and in the celebration of new life, new skills, and new beginnings. And community is the place where pain teaches us new connection that permits us to honor our brokenness in the fellowship of others. Howard Clinebell has expressed this potential gift in his prayer:

> For my pain, Oh God—which I did not choose,
> and do not like, and would let go of if I could—
> Give me the wisdom to treat it as a bridge
> A crossing to another's pain—to that person's private hell.
> Grant me the courage not to live alone
> behind my shell of hiding.
> My make-believe side which tries to always seem "on top,"
> in control, adequate for any crunch,
> not really needing others.
> Let me own my inner pain so that it will open me
> to those I meet,
> to their pain and caring—
> that in our shared humanity,
> we may know that we are one—in you.[12]

Last Chapters, Last Words

Last chapters play a critically important role in book making. The last chapter is so crucial, in fact, that it is one of the first things a writer considers. At the outset, I knew that I wanted to talk with my readers about practical ways to manage pain. I wanted to examine with them patterns of thinking and choices that would lead through pain to growth and godliness rather than to bitterness and cynicism. Once I established a satisfactory beginning place for this dialogue, I then considered the infamous last chapter. I asked myself, "What do you want the last chapter to say about pain?"

Much of my difficulty stemmed from the desire to have too many last words with my readers. I made progress, however, when I rephrased my question: "What is the most important thing to say?" The most important thing to say is this: Redemptive management of pain is measured by the persons we become in the process of living into and through our pain. While by necessity we manage our pain in the "already" but "not yet" of the present world, we live with the assurance that life in this world is not the only life that we shall enjoy. And in this life, the most important thing is not the pain or the joy or the ways in which we manage either. The most important thing is the person we become in progress through the long journey home.

In the end, we discover that one answer to the "why" question is a "who"—the person we can become.

Life, including both our joy and our journey through pain, provides the living space in which we may become family with whom God will be happy to spend eternity (Revelation 21:3–4). We can make vital connection with God through our joy, but the journey through pain provides a grimly splendid option. Uniquely there, we can come to know Christ, the power of His resurrection, and the fellowship of His suffering, and, in this knowing, become like Him (Philippians 3:10–11). It is a prospect to strengthen the weariest pilgrim, worn with the worst of pain.

I think at times about my own journey through pain in this way. It was not—and is not—where I would have wished to go. Nevertheless, this unwelcome journey provides for me the option of becoming who I intend to be. By God's grace I shall arrive home at last. When I join that huge joyous family crowding around our first-born brother, Jesus (Romans 8:29), I intend that everyone present can know simply by looking that I belong to the family *because I look so much like Him* (1 John 3:2–3). There I will be glad for His forgiving grace and for every part of the journey—for the joy, and for the pain and darkness too. I shall be glad there for everything that changed me so that I could carry forever His family likeness in my face.

ENDNOTES

Chapter 1: Does God Promise a Happy Ending?

1. Barbara Brown Taylor, "The Suffering of God," in *God in Pain: Teaching Sermons on Suffering,* ed. Ronald J. Allen (Nashville, TN: Abingdon Press, 1998), 121.

2. This is a paraphrase of the title of one of Lewis Smedes's early books on theodicy. See Lewis B. Smedes, *How Can It Be All Right When Everything Is All Wrong?* (San Francisco: Harper and Row, 1982).

3. "That I may know *Him*," Paul sang, "and the power of His resurrection, and the fellowship of His sufferings… that I may attain to the resurrection from the dead" (Philippians 3:10–11 NASB, emphasis added). Paul wasn't looking forward to mastering a set of rules. He was anticipating, *in the context of suffering,* an intimate relationship with the risen Christ.

4. See chapter 6.

5. See chapter 7.

6. Chapter 9 deals specifically with the psalms of lament and vengeance and ways of learning to pray our pain.

7. See chapter 9 for a discussion of the strong provision for protest found in the Psalms.

8. Eugene Peterson quotes Friedrich Nietzsche and explains, "The essential thing 'in heaven and earth' is… that there should be long obedience in the same direction; there thereby results, and has always resulted in the long run, something which has made life worth living." Eugene Peterson, *A Long Obedience in the Same Direction,* 2nd ed. (Downers Grove, IL: Intervarsity Press, 2000), 17.

9. Frederick Buechner, *Wishful Thinking: A Seeker's ABC* (New York: HarperCollins Publishers, 1973), 56– 57.

10. Author's paraphrase of Job 42:5.

Chapter 2: Whose Fault Is This Anyway?

1. Barbara Brown Taylor, "The Suffering of God," ed. Ronald J. Allen in *God in Pain: Teaching Sermons on Suffering* (Nashville, TN: Abingdon Press, 1998), 121.

2. C. S. Lewis, *God in the Dock*: *Essays in Theology and Ethics,* ed. Walter Hooper (Grand Rapids, MI: Wm. B. Eerdmans, 1970).

3. 2 Corinthians 11:14–15

4. See chapter 6.

5. Barbara Brown Taylor, "A Cure for Despair," ed. Ronald J. Allen, *God in Pain: Teaching Sermons on Suffering* (Nashville, TN: Abingdon Press, 1998), 25.

6. Ibid.

7. From *Psalms of Lament* by Ann Weems. ©1995 Ann Weems. Used with permission from Westminster John Knox Press. "Lament Psalm Thirty-Five," 69.

8. See Jesus' story of the rich man in Luke 12. In this text, Luke reports that Jesus told the crowds bluntly that life does not consist in the abundance of what we possess (12:15). However, it is important to note as well that the Gospel texts do not present Jesus as placing high value on poverty as such. The important thing, Jesus taught, is not what you have or do not have materially; the eternally significant thing is membership in the kingdom of God.

Chapter 3: How Can I Discover Where I Am?

1. T. S. Eliot, "Little Gidding," in *The Complete Poems and Plays, 1909–1950* (New York: Harcourt, Brace and World, 1971), 126.

2. Joan Didion, *The Year of Magical Thinking* (New York: Alfred A. Knopf, 2005).

3. From *Psalms of Lament* by Ann Weems. ©1995 Ann Weems. Used with permission from Westminster John Knox Press, xvi–xvii.

Chapter 4: How Can I Think Sensibly about Pain?

1. Rainer Maria Rilke, *Letters to a Young Poet* (New York: Vintage Books, 1986), 34–35.

2. What choosing life looks like in terms of everyday living is dealt with at length in chapter 5.

3. Dealing productively with loss is a part of mastery (see chapter 6) and a part of living with paradox (see chapter 9).

4. Issues of domestic abuse and violence remain a deeply troublesome reality in the Christian community. For any reader who is caught in the cycle of violence, changing the situation includes teaching yourself about this painful issue and working out a biblically relevant guideline for a plan of action. The author strongly recommends materials available online from RBC Ministries at www.rbc.org and through mail at RBC Ministries, P.O. Box 2222, Grand Rapids, MI 49501, telephone 616-974-2210. PASCH (Peace and Safety in the Christian Home) is a network addressing domestic abuse from a Christian point of view. Prayer support, biblical and practical resources, literature, and referrals are available through www.peaceandsafety.com and through PASCH, 1095 Stony Brook Road, Brewster, MA 02631, telephone 508-896-3518.

5. Brian Quinn has produced a reader-friendly book for understanding depression and its treatment, including medications commonly prescribed. See Brian P. Quinn, *The Depression Sourcebook,* 2nd ed. (Los Angeles: Lowell House, 2000).

6. See chapter 7.

7. See chapter 9.

Chapter 6: How Do I Evaluate Self-Care?

1. MEDDSS—mastery, exercise, diet, drugs, spirituality, sleep—is an acronym commonly used in the treatment program known as Dialectic Behavior Therapy. See Cathy Moonshine, *Dialectical Behavior Therapy* (Eau Claire, WI: PESI, LLC., 2006), 43.

2. Lilian Calles Barger, *Eve's Revenge: Women and a Spirituality of the Body* (Grand Rapids, MI: Brazos Press, 2003).

3. American Academy of Sleep Medicine, "Sleep Disorders." *SleepEducation.com.* www.sleepeducation.com/Disorders.aspx. Accessed July 22, 2009.

4. Vickie Contie, "Lack of Sleep Disrupts Brain's Emotional Controls." *National Institutes of Health Research Matters,* November 5, 2007.

National Institutes of Health. http://www.nih.gov/news/research_ matters/november2007/11052007sleep.htm. This study, directed by Dr. Matthew Walker and colleagues at the University of California, Berkeley, and Harvard Medical School, was published in the October 22, 2007, issue of *Current Biology.* The study was funded by NIH's National Institute of Neurological Disorders and Stroke (NINDS), National Institute of Mental Health, and National Center for Research Resources in conjunction with the American Academy of Sleep Medicine.

5. Ibid.

6. *Book of Common Prayer (*New York: Oxford University Press, 1990)*, 127, 133, 134, 135.

7. Contie.

8. The lament psalms, with their burden of grief and pain, can certainly be a part of nighttime praying. However, as we will see in chapter 9, these prayers are truly the God-patterned work of pain management, and in times of intense trauma when sleep is difficult, trauma praying is more effective when entered into as a part of spiritual work expressed in serious daytime conversation with God.

9. Abraham Heschel*, The Sabbath: Its Meaning for Modern Man* (New York: Farrar, Straus and Giroux, 1951, 1979), 30.

10. *Book of Common Prayer*, 133.

11. Marjorie Thompson, *Soul Feast: An Invitation to the Christian Spiritual Life* (Louisville, KY: Westminster John Knox Press, 1995). Thompson has organized a series of suggestions for practice of some of the basic disciplines of the Christian spiritual life (worship, prayer, self-examination, hospitality, and others) that are helpful in enriching and deepening spiritual growth. The guide can be used individually or as a group and can be adapted easily for use in times of great pain and loss.

12. Lewis, C. S. *A Grief Observed* (New York: Seabury, 1961). Philip Yancey, *Disappointment with God: Three Questions No One Asks* (Grand Rapids, MI: Zondervan, 1988).

Chapter 7: What Shall I Do with Failure?

1. See chapter 4.

2. See chapter 2. Deeply rooted patterns of self-blame practiced over a long period of time are particularly destructive in the ways in which they corrupt honest, non-judgmental sorting of the failure event.

Chapter 8: What Difference Does Community Make?

1. Ann Barr Weems, *Searching for Shalom: Resources for Creative Worship* (Philadelphia: Westminster John Knox Press), 1991.

Chapter 9: How Can I Pray in This Pain?

1. In 1979 James Sanders completed a book of sermons which he titled *God Has a Story, Too.* While credit for this phrase belongs to James Sanders, the use of the phrase and the ideas as developed here are wholly my own, for which Sanders is in no way accountable. This book has been reissued. See James A. Sanders, *God Has a Story, Too* (Eugene, OR: Wipf and Stock, 2000).

2. Walter Brueggemann, *The Psalms and the Life of Faith*, edited by Patrick D. Miller (Minneapolis, MN: Augsburg Fortress Press, 1995), 117.

3. Walter Brueggemann, *The Message of the Psalms* (Minneapolis, MN: Augsburg Publishing House, 1984). Brueggemann notes in his introduction to this early influential study of the Psalms that lament psalms have nearly dropped out of usage in the worshiping community (23). See also his more extensive essay, "The Costly Loss of Lament," in Brueggemann, *The Psalms and the Life of Faith*, 98–111.

4. Brueggemann, *The Message of the Psalms*, 10.

5. Psalm 50 is an example of the important exceptions to this general rule. In Psalm 50 God speaks to His covenant partner regarding the charges of covenant breaking that Israel has lodged against Him and asserts His "Godness" as profound sovereignty and otherness. While Israel does indeed need Yahweh, God's connection with Israel is one of love and choice, not necessity. Psalm 81 follows a parallel course. See Brueggemann's exposition of both Psalm 50 and Psalm 81 in "Psalms of Disorientation," *The Message of the Psalms*, 89–94.

6. See Brueggemann's insightful discussion, "Letting Experience Touch the Psalter," in *Praying the Psalms* (Winona, MN: Christian Brothers Publications, 1986), 15–25.

7. Brueggemann, *The Psalms and the Life of Faith*, 58.

8. Ibid.

9. A simple and highly useful description of the pattern followed in the psalms of lament is included in Walter Brueggemann's foreword to Ann Weems, *Psalms of Lament* (Louisville, KY: Westminster John Knox Press, l995), ix–xiv. Brueggemann's more extensive exposition of the form and function of the psalms of lament is included in "Psalms of Disorientation," *The Message of the Psalms*, 51–121; and in "Psalms and the Life of Faith: A Suggested Typology of Function," in *The Psalms and the Life of Faith*, 3–33.

10. The passages cited below are representative only and obviously do not exhaust the expressions of pain throughout the Psalms. Other psalms you may wish to reference that similarly express pain include: 31:9–10; 55:1–2, 4–6; 77:1, 3–9; 88:1–3, 5b; and 130:1–2. The following psalms specifically express pain linked to God's apparent abandonment and seeming unreasonable absence: 77:10; 88:6–8, 15b–18; and 88:13–14.

11. Brueggemann, "Psalms and the Life of Faith: A Suggested Typology of Function," in *The Psalms and the Life of Faith*, 19.

12. Walter Brueggemann, *Praying the Psalms* (Winona, MN: St. Mary's Press, Christian Brothers Publications, 1982), 79.

13. Walter Brueggemann, "Praise and the Psalms: A Politics of Glad Abandonment," in *The Psalms and the Life of Faith,* 115–116.

14. Brueggemann, *The Psalms and the Life of Faith,* 116.

15. Brueggemann, *The Psalms and the Life of Faith,* 117.

16. I continue to find this procedure helpful in my own private prayer life as a way to bring my experience, joys and sorrows, to the text, as Brueggemann would phrase it.

17. Eugene Petersen, *Eat This Book: A Conversation in the Art of Spiritual Reading* (Grand Rapids, MI: William B. Eerdmans Publishing Co., 2006).

18. Stanley Hauerwas, a committed practicing Christian, theologian, and fierce critic of the secular culture, is a gifted teacher and writer

as well. At the time of the PBS interview with Abernethy, he was on the faculty of Duke University.

19. Stanley Hauerwas, *The Life of Meaning: Reflections on Faith, Doubt, and Repairing the World*, interviews with contributors to PBS's *Religion and Ethic News Weekly,* Robert Abernethy and William Bole, editors (New York: Seven Stories Press, 2007), 135.

20. Ann Weems, From *Psalms of Lament* by Ann Weems. ©1995 Ann Weems. Used with permission from Westminster John Knox Press, 20–21.

Chapter 10: Ending Up Where We Intended to Be

1. Douglas Adams (1952-2001), author and actor, is perhaps best known for his trilogy, *Hitchhiker's Guide to the Galaxy.*

2. Gordon Fee, *Paul, the Spirit, and the People of God* (Peabody, MA: Hendrickson Publishers, 1996), 52.

3. As previously noted, the phrase "a long obedience in the same direction," first used by F. Nietzsche, has been used by Eugene Peterson as the title of his book, *A Long Obedience in the Same Direction* (Downers Grove, IL: Intervarsity Press, 2000). The quotation in full and Peterson's discussion of it can be found on page 17.

4. T. S. Eliot, "Little Gidding," in *The Complete Poems and Plays*, 1909–1950 (New York: Harcourt, Brace and World, 1971), 145.

5. Rainer Maria Rilke, *Letters to a Young Poet*, translated by M. D. Herter Norton (New York: Norton, 1934), 35.

6. Walter Brueggemann, "The Other Side of the Street," *Awed to Heaven, Rooted in Earth: Prayers of Walter Brueggemann.* Edwin Searcy, ed. (Minneapolis: Fortress Press), 13.

7. Ibid.

8. Karen Mason has produced a very effective reader friendly book dealing with paradox in the life of faith. See *When the Pieces Don't Fit: Making Sense of Life's Puzzles* (Grand Rapids, MI: Discovery House Publishers, 2008).

9. See Mason, *When the Pieces Don't Fit.*

10. See Mason, *When the Pieces Don't Fit.*

11. Paul Claudel as quoted in *Journeying through Grief* (St. Mark Presbyterian Church Health Ministries, 2100 Mar Vista, Newport Beach, CA 92660, 2002), 12.

12. Howard Clinebell as quoted in *Journeying through Grief* (St. Mark Presbyterian Church Health Ministries, 2100 Mar Vista, Newport Beach, CA 92660, 2002), 8.

NOTE TO THE READER

The publisher invites you to share your response to the message of this book by writing Discovery House Publishers, P.O. Box 3566, Grand Rapids, MI 49501, U.S.A. For information about other Discovery House books, music, videos, or DVDs, contact us at the same address or call 1-800-653-8333. Find us on the Internet at http://www.dhp.org/ or send e-mail to books@dhp.org.

Epiphany.

malfeasance   p. 18.

pg. 23   redeeming our pain.

p 33.   God & Job.   God doesn't explain 'why' to
        Job.   But Job remains faithful in spite of his
        pain.

theodicy — the study of why God allows pain &
          suffering.